Reintroducing Chuck Mosley
Life On and Off the Road

Douglas Esper

Reintroducing Chuck Mosley
Life On and Off the Road
By Douglas Esper

Front Cover Photo: John Patrick Gatta
Front Cover Design: Jim Brown
Back Cover Drawing: Brian Walsby
Chapter Title Design: Amy Hunter
Editor: Brian Paone
Interior Formatting: Kari Holloway

Published by Scout Media
Copyright 2019
ISBN: 978-1-7330740-7-0

www.ScoutMediaBooksMusic.com

One hundred sixty shows, two rushed recording sessions, a reunion with an old band, and a Hail Mary shot at a comeback represent the tip of the iceberg of my twenty-year journey with Chuck Mosley.

Chuck (Faith No More, Bad Brains, Cement) toured the globe as a vocalist, appeared on magazine covers, rubbed elbows with idols, and, through it all, he remained 100% convinced he didn't deserve your praise. Yet, he desired acceptance more than almost anything else.

A self-proclaimed "junkie and a liar," Chuck shot himself in the foot over and over by shooting up elsewhere on his body. Meanwhile, I stumbled and fumbled and pushed and pulled and scraped and cried and begged and borrowed to earn him extra chances to prove himself. We loaded a van with a guitar, a conga, and an unfinished legacy hoping to reintroduce the world to Chuck Mosley.

About Chuck:
Jonathan Davis of Korn: "I was blown away by his voice. So original. Chuck has a great style that you can tell it's him as soon as he starts singing. I'm a big fan and I was honored when he asked me to appear on his new stuff."

DMC of RUN-DMC: "Some of Chuck's and Faith No More's songs sound like we all come from the same family! He tore shit up!!!!"

Matt Wallace, Producer (Faith No More, Maroon Five, The Replacements): "I was always a fan of his ... He wore his heart on his sleeve ... I thought he was pretty fearless to sing about some of the things he sang about."

For my friend, bandmate, idol, and road wife, Chuck Mosley. I miss you.

This book is dedicated to my wife, Michele Esper. Without her support and guidance, neither the Reintroduce Yourself Tour or Chuck's solo album would've happened.

And also to Pip, Erica, and Sophie. You were Chuck's true loves, his family. I am so sorry for all you endured and for your loss. If I learned anything through this it's that life is short, so I hope you find peace and acceptance and love within each other to move on as a family.

Thanks to everyone who booked, promoted, played, and attended our shows and to those who hosted us in your homes or fed us along the way. Special thanks to Donn Wobser, Matt Wallace, Thom Hazaert, and Anne D'Agnillo.

*Portions of an interview with Chuck Mosley by Justin Vellucci first appeared on PopDose.com. Used with permission.

*Portions of press release by Faith No More distributed by Speakeasy PR

"I'm a junkie and a thief and a liar.
You'll just have to deal with it."
~ Chuck Mosley

CHAPTER ONE

Are you sitting down?

Chuck is dead.

I'm surrounded by photos, CDs, videos, show posters, guitar picks, set lists, and endless memories of my time with Chuck. Each bit of the past represents a puzzle piece that, if joined, would tell the tale of my friend's life. The problem with that is I can't make sense of what he left behind, no matter how many songs I listen to or photos I examine. Some pieces have jagged edges, while others are outlined in smooth curves, and none of them look like corner pieces. I thought he would stick around longer for me to understand. And why should his puzzle fall into place? Chuck didn't do anything the easy way.

For years, he and I pushed and pulled at each other to get his autobiography written. One of the main sticking points in Chuck's hesitation was that he wanted a proper ending—a climax that showed how much he had accomplished. He wanted a positive comeback story full of success so he'd feel more comfortable talking about the dark times, the drug use, and the opportunities he squandered via his complicated process of excuses and self-sabotage.

He told Justin Vellucci of Popdose, "The book's gonna be a tell-all, but we don't have the exact ending yet. I'll either end up in prison or happily whistling down the road, playing shows. Hopefully, God forbid, it shouldn't end with my death."

I'm not going to let his death end this book or conclude his life's story, but unfortunately, it's where we must start. Although this isn't the tell-all bio book we had envisioned, I think it's an important look into the life of a true, unique artist who touched everyone he met in some form or fashion and the army of support staff that tried to help him return to the world. By the end of this novel, you won't understand his inner workings—after twenty years of friendship, I'm still searching to gain that insight—but you'll certainly get as good a glimpse as I can provide from my point of view.

Chuck was complicated. He hid behind layer upon layer of safe guards, rules of conversation, self-doubt, a disarming charm, and a never-ending drive to ensure everyone loved him. The flipside of that coin, however, was Chuck had no hesitation to tell any stranger he met on the street intimate details of his struggles with addiction or of maintaining his sanity day in and day out.

That's part of the fascination, for me anyway. I played over 150 shows with Chuck during the course of two years and had countless adventures with him over the last two decades, and to watch him operate was mesmerizing, frustrating, and humbling all at once.

Chuck's fear of failure was only eclipsed by his fear of success.

Greg Gould, who knew Chuck at an early age, put it this way: "Chuck seemed very much like Basquiat to me. Having gotten into art, I had spent many summers reading bios of various artists, and it kind of struck me, in afterthought, about Chuck. Some people just aren't born with that normal ability to create the calluses needed to grow up and be an adult in this world. As a result, you get a very genuine, somewhat childlike adult. I'm just saying that in my impression, Basquiat was very much the same—very fragile and gentle, not really thinking through some situations, highly spontaneous—but, to protect, Chuck often took drugs, and the side effects of that meant missing practice, not performing when it really counted, etc. He could be absolutely frustrating in those ways, but he was not an asshole, so, hard to hold onto a grudge for too long."

That comment hit home with me as I had thought Jeffrey Wright could totally nail Chuck if they ever made a movie about him, due largely to his portrayal of Basquiat in a movie about the artist. I also see a lot of similarities in his behavior to the stories I've heard of Jim Morrison of The Doors.

I think if Chuck had been given the option when he had turned fifteen to not age any further, he would've jumped at the chance. Surfing, skating, sneaking into punk shows, chasing girls on the beach, and making music was all he ever wanted. He desired an endless party that everyone was invited to attend. And no one had to work the next day. And no one got sick. And David Bowie played a free show every night.

A lot of people want this, sure. It sounds great—no bigotry, no sexism, no racism, no unpaid bills. The difference is, Chuck believed it would happen. His devotion to that idea never wavered, causing a lot of problems. Small obstacles often became massive roadblocks to him. He got distracted by tiny details and unrelated issues so that it became hard to make any progress on his art, his career, or his family life.

Hell, the guy had a hard time operating a phone, let alone a computer, to return emails and work on his brand. Getting him to mention completed projects or ones we had in progress in interviews, onstage, or in conversation was like pulling teeth.

Doug: "Hey, Chuck, the new Indoria got released by Infinitehive Records. Can you mention it on that podcast interview today?"

Chuck: "I don't know, man. You know more about it than I do."

Doug: "Hey, those new shirts arrived today at great cost and sacrifice to all involved because you took too long to confirm the design. Can you make sure to direct people to the merch booth, so we can sell some to start recouping money?"

Chuck: "It feels like begging."

Record-store owner: "This show is being recorded. The plan is to release a seven-inch single for Record Store Day, so let's get the audience excited."

Chuck: "Don't want to tell the crowd, otherwise their reactions might not be genuine."

And yet …

Interviewer dude: "What's next for you?"

Chuck: "The new VUA will be out in the next three months."

Forget the fact VUA hadn't written or recorded any songs; heck, they hadn't practiced or even been in the same room since the band quit mid-tour three years earlier. It's not to say they would never have gotten an album done, but to say "Look for a new VUA record within three months" was absurd.

Fan at show: "Chuck, why do you live in Cleveland?"

Chuck: "Doesn't matter. I'm moving to the UK in the spring."

Again, his daughters, Erica and Sophie, were leaving the nest to build a life of their own, he had several unpaid debts, he battled addiction and depression, he would need to secure a work visa and jump through hoops to be allowed to stay in the UK, along with a dozen other issues. Plus, he was facing a trip to court and possible jail time … more on that later.

If I had a nickel for every time Chuck mentioned the book we were "working on," when, in reality, no progress had been made in months, I'd be a rich man. He was great at hyping what was coming up when there was no substance to it. All I could do was shake my head.

There were nights Chuck sounded brilliant, spot on; typically, when we had a small crowd. When people showed or the press made their presence known, Chuck wilted. He'd blame his ADHD, his depression, his severe self-doubt, the soundman, a guitar tuner, bad breakfast, a sudden cold and sore throat, or any number of other issues.

Now, this book could quickly turn into chapter after chapter of, "look how crazy, stubborn, and airheaded Chuck was while I kept an even-keeled attitude based in logic and reality to make everything run smoothly," and to some degree, I can rest knowing you already know this (Ha!). But, I don't want to lose the other aspects of him, like his endless curiosity, his sharp mind, and his kind soul.

His former bandmate in Haircuts That Kill, Louise Bialik, described him as, "…quietly and privately shy and sensitive. Most people don't know that. And you know what else? Highly educated. He turned me on to Sylvia Plath and *The Bell Jar* and pointed me to push on with going after a poetry degree at UCLA."

In a press release following his death, Faith No More via Roddy Bottum said Chuck was a "reckless and caterwauling force of energy."

Not being as sophisticated as his former bandmates, I'd say Chuck was a handful. He was also one of the funniest people I've ever met. It might be more accurate if I told you Chuck and his alter egos were some of the funniest people on the planet.

Anne D'Agnillo, a longtime friend of Chuck's, told me this story about one of his characters: "Chuck calls me and says, 'Come meet me in Philly. We're opening for the [Red Hot] Chili Peppers.' I had just seen the Chili Peppers three days earlier with Thelonius Monster opening. So, I go backstage, and I see Flea, and he gives me this look like, 'What the heck are you doing here? Who are you?' Y'know, not in a bad way, just 'cause I keep showing up. And then I see Chuck with this waist-length blond wig and glasses. These fans are talking to him, asking if he knows where the Chili Peppers are hanging out. Chuck goes, 'Hey, it's me, it's me, Sy Greenburg. I book these shows. I know who everybody is. Who do you want to meet? Anthony? The Chili Peppers? Faith No More?' The fans were all confused, like 'Who is this?'"

Chuck could make you laugh, yell, cry, think, and rethink all in one quick conversation. And he had a mischievous grin that got him and others into and sometimes out of a lot of trouble.

Throughout this book, I hope to give you an accurate peek into our lives over the last few years and let you see just how a genius operates. How a man in constant pain, both physical and mental, struggled through each day to make a positive impact on so many lives and create stellar new music in the process.

So, who am I, and why do I matter enough to spin this tale? For the last twenty years, I've been Chuck's bandmate, babysitter, tour manager, booking agent, conga player, chauffeur, unknowing drug mule, co-author, enabler, AA meeting plus-one, voice of reason, sparring partner, fake lawyer, confidant, and friend.

In one interview, Chuck got asked about who was guiding him in his comeback.

Chuck started saying, "Doug is my—"

"Don't call me your manager," I interrupted. "'Cause maybe a real manager is listening, interested in taking you on. I don't want to scare them off."

Chuck continued his interview. "He's my … Doug."

But above all else, and way more important, the reason I needed to write this book is that I am you. I'm a Chuck fan, a fanatic. I know what you want to know, hear, see, smell, and understand about this whole circus, because I do too. Even though I became a part of the story, I still want to step back and just observe, enjoy, cry, giggle, shake my head, kick, and scream … and *kick!*

That being said, many people knew Chuck before me—longer than me—and there are those who had different relationship dynamics with him than I did. To some, Chuck is a legend; to others, he was simply a junkie; and to a few, he was a friend, a lover, a dad, a grandfather, a bandmate; and anyone lucky enough to taste his cooking knew him as one hell of a culinary expert. All I can do is relate what I observed first hand.

This story is also about my journey. I didn't realize that until after I had finished writing the book. Reading about me isn't as fun, but you've gone this far, so let's keep on, yeah?

Chuck and I are two dudes with totally different life experiences and attitudes. We got together in a faux marriage his lifelong partner, Pip, lovingly dubbed "the Bickersons," and we tried like hell to give Chuck back to the world.

Think of all the foul, dastardly, nasty, underhanded things people do every day just to sniff a chance to break into the entertainment industry, and yet, when he faced worldwide success and a career as a cover boy in all the music magazines, Chuck's response was basically, "Eh, yeah, that might be cool, but only if it happens on my terms." The attention, the glamour, and the power are addicting—make no mistake, Chuck wanted it all—but to his credit/detriment, he pushed away from the table to forge his own path.

As a young, mixed-race, adopted boy, Chuck felt like an outsider, even when hanging with other outsiders. He related with David Bowie's appearance and lyrics. They both somehow had no place in the world, while informing and influencing so many different factions of it. He often talked about singing Bowie in the shower—a hairbrush as his microphone, his afro waiting to be washed.

This guy surfed, hung out with cults, snuck off to punk concerts he had been forbidden to attend, delivered flowers to celebrities, peed next to Jack Nicolson, helped shut down the UCLA campus during a tent protest against apartheid, was an extra in several movies, snuck onto movie lots and stole props, recorded demos at Dana Plato from *Diff'rent Strokes*' house, and that was all in a typical weekend. On the other hand, I grew up in the Midwest in a stereotypical, vanilla household. A wonderful, loving one, but I never rubbed elbows with anyone cool in the bathroom.

Chuck told people he and I were, "The Odd Couple, through and through."

I hit my stride—a play-it-safe Felix as Chuck developed a comfortable relationship with a sloppier Oscar-type existence. His behavior got more erratic as he developed an impenetrable cocoon to protect his psyche as he moved from one band to the next.

In 1979, the year I was born, Chuck joined his first band, The Animated, as a keyboardist. He didn't sing, didn't even consider singing, but he quickly established his character and contributed to the songwriting.

Darryl Wims told me, "My first experience [with Chuck] was when I was ten years old. He was part of a band that my older brother and Billy Gould were in called The Animated, from 1978-1982. They used to practice in my living room in LA, and then eventually, when my mom had had enough, they got banished to the garage.

"The Animated was a post-punk, new-wave, power-punk type band that was weird enough on its own, without being in a predominately black neighborhood in the late 70s. I mean, nobody was feeling what was blasting from the garage, but they certainly made a statement. Most people I knew were listening to Top 40—Earth, Wind & Fire, Sister Sledge, Commodores, etc. I used to sit in the garage as a ten- or eleven-year-old and just listen and hang out. They were all odd to me because they were into different things, playing music I didn't hear on the radio and talked about it like it was so serious. I mean, the record exchange they did was awesome, and I would benefit by listening to these cool records from Sparks, Roxy Music, XTC, and Joy Division. I would come to realize later that this time saved me musically at a very young age.

"The King of the Strange was Chuck. I mean, as a kid, I thought he was from Mars. He would dye his hair, wear all these cool buttons on his clothes, smoked cigarettes, and drank Old English during the day. He was fascinating to me. He played keyboards for The Animated—no singing whatsoever but wrote some really great songs. He would totally give me time in the garage when he probably could have ignored me. He was nineteen or twenty, and I was eleven or twelve. He would joke with me and talk to me like I was a real person, not the punk kid that I was. He would even let me ride his moped around while they rehearsed—just kind of a reckless friendliness.

"Chuck made it cool to be weird. I wasn't weird at all, really, and had already unknowingly formed some narrowminded opinions living in a typical suburban and mainstream black neighborhood in the late 1970s. Chuck was responsible for me meeting openly gay/lesbian and bisexual people for the first time before I even knew what the fuck that even meant. He normalized non-mainstream society for me, and I know for sure that opened my mind and changed how I thought socially and politically at a very early age."

The Animated recorded an EP and made the rounds at various Los Angeles clubs but started to splinter when their bassist, Bill Gould, left to attend college at Berkley.

Mark "Stew" Stewart, the band's vocalist, went on to form The Negro Problem before delving into writing books and theatrical plays, including the well-received *Passing Strange*—a semi-autobiographical story Chuck was convinced he had a hand in helping create via his time with Stew. Also, and fittingly random for this book, Stew wrote and recorded the song, "Gary's Song," featured in the television show, *Spongebob Squarepants*.

Chuck joined Haircuts That Kill, an art-punk band with a liquid line up. He took over vocals duties only when they couldn't find someone else to do it. They recorded and played rambunctious shows, often renting a hall or club themselves rather than deal with promoters. Chuck described their drummer, Troy, as "a black Keith Moon."

I asked Louise Bialik about the Haircuts That Kill tune, "Indian Song," and she said, "I would sing the vocal with him as a duet. It was fucking cool, like [the band] X. We would shift off and complement one another, plus give each other breaks to keep belting it. That was the trick for power-cord vocals. No one can stay constantly on *and* loud, so we would alternate. We were good together that way."

The band recorded during several sessions, but many of the songs remain unreleased. The controlled chaos of the group coupled with anti-apartheid protests on UCLA's campus, afternoons spent "fishing" for grunions under the docks at the beach with members of Fishbone, and the cracks in Chuck's self-esteem all combined to make those years a wild ride.

Louise again provided some perspective: "[Chuck] had like an ADHD poet's ennui depressive mood disorder that was calmed by thrill busking. Drugs were the artificial substitute and immediate fix, but mostly, it was producing good quality music and work. Chuck was highly organized when sober."

While sharing bills with the likes of The Minutemen at the Anti-Club on Melrose, Haircuts That Kill often found themselves in the crosshairs of the police. Louise said, "We got arrested several times—well, not arrested, but cops would barge in on our sessions to break up our band practice even before we were plugged in! The LAPD were lying in wait to pounce on us, and they deliberately roughed up Troy [the band's drummer] and Chuck because of color. Barry and me, they put aside but harassed Cindy more, and I would pull out my police ID card for Burbank Police Department—I had gone through bootcamp and graduated as a rookie but left the force due to sexual harassment, yet I held onto my ID as it bailed me out of punk-rock busts. I would show my ID and say I was undercover in a sting op, and cops would let me go because I could speak Cop. And with the busts they did on Haircuts That Kill, it would prevent the bad cops from hauling away the whole band."

Chuck got a call from Bill Gould, asking him to fill in some dates on vocals with his new band, Faith No More. That band was also prone to mixing in and out guitarists and vocalists show to show. Eventually, he joined them as lead vocalist and almost immediately started demoing songs for their debut album, *We Care a Lot*.

They toured heavily in the states, with bands like Metallica and Red Hot Chili Peppers, and also headlined a couple tours of the UK and Europe as their second album, *Introduce Yourself*, found a wider audience on MTV and college radio. Chuck got his first taste of success, recognition, and the business side that comes with it. While the band committed to raising their game and acting more professional, Chuck doubled down on his bratty, punk, Devil-may-care ways, causing immense friction and stress for all involved.

Bill Gould told me, "Chuck liked to give the impression that he didn't take it all that seriously."

When they fired him in 1988, Chuck found himself doubting his talents, instincts, and his sobriety. He described these as dark days.

The itch to learn further detail into Chuck's time with Faith No More can be scratched by picking up Adrian Harte's stellar, *Small Victories: The True Story of Faith No More* (Jawbone Press 2018), and you can find tons of audio and video floating about that convey those times better than I can here.

In 1991, Chuck and Pip relocated to Woodstock, New York when Chuck became the singer for Bad Brains. He told me, "It was like rock n' roll bootcamp. They worked me hard, challenged me, and made me a much better singer."

They toured the US and did some shows overseas. He got down on himself—the same self-doubt returned—but he did have a moment in the band that meant a lot.

Chuck told me, "I was listening to a recording of one of our concerts. Doc [Dr. Know of Bad Brains] came in the room, pointed at the speakers, and said something like, 'You hear that? When you can do that, you'll be on the right track.' Doc thought it was an old recording with HR [their original vocalist] singing. We listened through the rest of the song. When he heard my voice talking in-between songs, Doc realized his mistake."

They wrote and recorded a batch of songs, but before it got released, Bad Brains received a massive offer to reunite with HR. Chuck took the news in stride, moved back to Los Angeles, and gathered some friends together to form Cement.

The band actually had legs before Chuck came on board. Senon told me, "Chuck's girlfriend Diana was my older sister Della's best friend. It was 1979 or '80. I was ten or eleven at the time. I started to tag along to shows and house parties a couple years later. He became like a big brother. In '91, when I moved back to LA from New York, I started playing with Sean Maytum, a childhood friend. We made home recordings and played a couple gigs as O.G. Crunch. Chuck would jam with us and asked us to back him up for a demo. We wrote a few songs together, including 'Shout.' Soon after, we started playing shows as Cement and got a little record deal. We slid into being a band, naturally. Doug [Duffy] came into it after a few drummers but was there on the first album."

Chuck said, "[Senon's] my bro, and I love him. I gave him his first mohawk when he was ten."

The recording for their self-titled debut was quick. Chuck recalled a long night of recording vocals, telling me, "I finished all the vocals in one session, but there was a problem with how it got recorded, so I had to stay and redo the entire album."

He said his voice was toast by the time the sun came up.

Cement hit the road, hard. The band often found the crowds clamoring for more at the end of their sets, so they started to jam unpolished riffs, which helped them quickly write new songs.

They recorded their second album, *The Man with the Action Hair*, and with the help of Kirk Hammett of Metallica and the album's producer, Bill Metoyer, they signed record deals in the United States (Dutch East India Trading) and in Europe (Rough Trade).

Senon recalled one of his favorite moments during those sessions: "I was having trouble when we recorded ['Crying']. I hated the bass line I tracked. I told Bill [Metoyer], the producer, I was going to replace my bass the next day. I went home and wrote a whole new bass line and remembered the satisfaction of Chuck when I laid it down and added a whole new dimension to the song. I always loved playing it live after we recorded it."

Cement began what would've been a yearlong tour to promote their new album, but while driving west of Tallahassee, Florida, the van crashed.

Douglas Duffy told me, "It was fucking terrifying. Chuck was in the way back on a futon on top of all the gear. I was lying in the back seat. Senon, Sean [Maytum, guitarist], and the soundman were up front. I woke up to screaming, and we were rolling over. A truck driver helped pull us out. All but Chuck. We stood next to the freeway and saw our stuff getting run over by trucks. We couldn't get Chuck out."

Chuck spent months in the hospital.

During his rehab, he got hooked on pain pills. When his prescription ran out, he discovered, like many others have, that heroin could dull his aching back for much cheaper, and he didn't need a doctor's note to get it. His addictions got so bad,

Chuck wanted to move from Los Angeles to someplace where he didn't know anyone who could sell him drugs.

He told me, "Pip and I closed our eyes and spun a globe. We each touched it. My finger was on Hamburg, Germany, and hers was on Cleveland, Ohio. I always wanted to live in Europe, but we couldn't drive our car there, so we picked Cleveland."

Also, and probably more practical, was the fact their close friend, Mary Jo, had relocated to Cleveland and had a house they could rent.

I heard rumors in 1996 that Mosley had moved to my hometown. I kept my eyes peeled at every show I attended, in hopes he'd be there.

I read somewhere—a local zine probably, or maybe heard it on college radio—he had formed a new band with various members of other bands from the area. The band called themselves, The Chuck Mosley Theory, or The Chuck Mosley Experience, or a dozen other names that I heard, all of which were wrong. They were VUA. In the summer of 1997, I auditioned for a band at the same warehouse where VUA practiced. I roamed the halls hoping to run into Chuck, with no luck.

Taken from my liner notes inside VUA's *Demos for Sale*:

> *Then, on Tuesday, September 23, 1997, standing by himself, just beyond the security guards patting me down at the Cleveland Agora, I saw Chuck. With no time to plan something cool or witty to say, I walked up, shook his hand, and yes, I introduced myself. Chuck was welcoming, funny, and tolerant of an eighteen-year-old kid with stars in his eyes.*

The liner notes referenced the night I saw Faith No More on their *Album of the Year* tour, and I asked Chuck, "You gonna get up and sing something tonight?"

He stared, focused on something fascinating on the ground, shaking his head.

I pressed, "It would be a dream come true to see you do 'As the Worm Turns' with the guys."

"I would be way too nervous."

I laughed. It was such an out-of-leftfield statement that I couldn't even process it. Chuck Mosley nervous? This guy had been performing for years, all over the world, and had found success not just with Faith No More but with other projects as well. As we got to know each other, I discovered how brutally honest and haunting his words were.

At that point, someone walked up to him and muttered something. Chuck handed the guy a ticket. A few moments later, the same guy walked up, and Chuck handed him another one.

I asked, "What are those?"

Chuck said, "Eh, backstage passes."

My heart flipped. "Can I have one?"

He shrugged. "That was my last one."

Damn.

After that show, our path's crossed enough that Chuck and I developed a comfort level with each other to just be friends, not that he needs any courting before friendship starts—I did. Chuck loves everyone he meets right off the bat, and it's only when someone lies to him or hurts him in some way that he pulls back. I had a hard time wrapping my head around the fact that he would even waste time with me, so I always wanted to make our conversations important. Every time we talked, I focused on some aspect of his career and tried to push it forward, even if in a tiny way. If I didn't have new info or ideas or contacts, I didn't call him. But then he started calling me, checking in. I felt guilty during those calls and tried to spin them into something positive, but Chuck's reason for calling didn't revolve around progress. He just wanted someone to talk to.

One year, I invited him over for an impromptu Labor Day party at my place, and he brought his family. His young daughters, Erica and Sophie, ended up writing, directing, and performing a play with my brother, Craig, based around a Pepsi commercial for the partygoers.

Chuck had a way of getting everyone around him to take risks, to not only step out of their comfort zone, but to race away from it with reckless abandon. When I interviewed him for an internet radio station, where I had a midnight to 6 a.m. program, he arrived wearing his "Failed Artist" t-shirt and holding a plastic cup full of beer. I let it ride. Sometimes you gamble your low paying gig for the rock guy.

I started DomainCleveland.com with two friends. We focused on promoting and booking concerts, reviewing shows and CDs, and interviewing bands. VUA jumped on a couple of bills and performed for way cheaper than they should've accepted. Chuck showed up to one show in a suit, a curly blond wig, and thick-framed glasses. He walked around introducing himself to people with a fake name and voice. Sy Greenburg had been reborn; only, at the time, I didn't know his long and storied history as a famous rock-concert promoter.

Since I had a car and a few bucks, I helped Chuck run errands and make stops at the pawn shop, the dollar store, the grocery store, etc. You can say it was a friendship of pure convenience for him, and I'm comfortable with that. Each time we met, he was usually trying to pay the bills while I tried to get him out of his shell. I wanted to see him playing live more often, writing new songs, or simply back in the public eye. He wanted his phone turned back on.

Chuck and Pip ran a well-respected restaurant in town, until Chuck slipped during a shift and ended up with a double hernia. He ended up back on pills. He ended up broke again. He ended up back in the cycle.

In 2006, VUA stalled when Chuck ran out of money to finish their record. Aside from occasionally playing solo at coffee shops, he had resorted to being a hermit.

I told him I'd fund a session at my friend's studio to cut a few stripped-down, acoustic songs focusing on his vocals and lyrics.

Without considering it, he said, "That's a really bad idea."

Unsure why he felt that way, I tried to explain myself. "You have songs like 'Chip Away' and 'Sophie' that are so powerful and simple and really allow your voice to drive the emotion home. If you put out an EP of tunes like that, I think people would latch on to it."

"My acoustic guitar playing is awful. I mean, I'm not much better on an electric, but at least I can use effects and distortion to cover up my mistakes. Tim [Parnin from VUA] and I are on the same page. He knows just how to mask my lack of abilities and make me sound a lot better than I am."

"I've seen you live and heard enough show recordings to know you could pull it off. Your voice is what drives your songs. Your lyrics—"

"I mean, I'd consider it, if …"

CHAPTER TWO
Will Rap Over Hard Rock for Studio Time

The 'if' was simple. He wanted to meet with the owner of the studio VUA had recorded at to work out a deal to finish their songs.

Later that day, we pulled into Ante Up Studios on the near eastside of Cleveland. Chuck introduced me as his business partner/associate, as he often did.

We were guided into the studio and bombarded with gold records and other plaques by Regina Spektor and Gerald Levert. This was a legit studio with a history of success far beyond where I was used to throwing down my music. The engineer/owner, Michael Siefert, has worked, in some capacity, for Tori Amos, Dave Matthews Band, Bone Thugs-n-Harmony, Too Short, J. Mascis (Dinosaur Jr.), and a huge list of others, including one of my favorite Cleveland-area bands, Mr. Gnome.

Going into the meeting, I guesstimated there stood as good of a chance that we left with everyone cussing each other out than there was Chuck negotiating a path toward a finished record. Turns out, though, Michael had a proposal of his own.

He was launching a record label, and he wanted to release the VUA album on it. He walked Chuck through the specifics and how they would split the money, then he detailed a few promotional ideas. Chuck took in the info and then asked for a few moments to speak with me alone.

Chuck stared me down. "So, what do you think I should do?"

I had no idea. "Well, you want to get this record done. He's offering a chance for that to happen."

"Well, what about your thing that you want to do?"

"What I'm proposing is small scale, tiny budget, start from scratch and put out a disc to help remind people who you are and what you're capable of. This guy has national distribution, a top-notch studio, and he's compiling a team to help promote worldwide."

Chuck said nothing, apparently expecting more from me.

I nodded at Michael's office. "You've worked with him before. Can you trust him?"

Chuck nodded. "It was the other guy that took my money."

"There's no reason you couldn't do both."

But I could see the money signs in his eyes. He knew one path could lead to an easy payday and possibly get him back in the game. My option was to spend the winter in the basement, pounding out songs and releasing an album with zero buzz built. Chuck loved to remind people he was a "blue-collar musician," but he lacked the grind-it-out workman part. He typically took the path of least resistance, often creating his own resistance in the process.

Michael was thrust into the responsible, babysitting role many of us who are friends with Chuck have assumed at one point or another.

Babysitting Chuck is a job and a half, and it was especially tough for someone in Michael's role, trying to mix VUA the best way he saw fit for commercial success while Chuck made his opinion clear: "The album should be raw, punk, noisy, *and* psychedelic."

I remember getting calls that Chuck had been thrown out of the studio a few different times. Knowing Chuck's temper, attitude, and unwavering ear for his music, I found it hard to vilify Michael but still felt awful that Chuck found himself in this situation in the first place.

Mind you, at this point, I'm still woefully, blissfully unaware Chuck had fallen back into the horrible habits that exaggerated all the issues in and outside of the studio. Once again, Chuck was broke and borrowing money from anywhere he could get it. And then promptly buying drugs to avoid life's pressure rather than paying bills to alleviate the stresses.

Chuck had a vision of what the album should sound and look like that conflicted with the general desire to gain radio airplay, have mass appeal, and to sound current. Chuck had no concept of how radio play worked or what rock stations were currently looking for. He thought, *Write good tunes and the radio will play them.* That attitude certainly didn't help Michael and Chuck mix the record together, resulting in a lot of stress and fighting.

Michael told me he didn't recall Chuck speaking up much at all, so it hurt extra when he started hearing Chuck talk ill of the record after it had come out.

I felt a bit of pride as I entered the Beachland Ballroom on the night of the CD release party in 2009, knowing—though my role was small—I had helped to see that the record finally got done. For better or worse, it was out in the world.

Unfortunately, the label fell apart, the band never toured, and Chuck's dream of a comeback faltered and then failed spectacularly.

Chuck allowed the negativity and inaction to consume him. He withdrew further into his addictions. His car broke and, I think, got repossessed. He wasn't working in any kitchens, he wasn't writing songs, and he didn't even have any of the VUA stuff to sell or have the knowledge of social media to promote on his own or, hell, to keep in touch with the world.

I would try to pull him away from his *Band of Brothers* DVDs and out and about with little success. Chuck was convinced the VUA album was a hit; if it had been promoted full tilt and if a tour would've been booked, the path to success was open.

I'm not saying I didn't think the album was awesome, but the reality of commercial radio made heavy rotation for any of these songs highly unlikely. The songs are great and the recording is polished, but in the fifteen or so years it took to see the songs from start to release, the industry had changed two or three times in major ways. Napster and downloading weren't issues in the mid-90s when Chuck first demoed the song, "Sophie." By the way, in typical Chuck form, he forgot to bring his acoustic guitar to the studio, so the first version got recorded on electric and certainly has a different, spacier vibe.

The VUA album became many CDs and vinyl and t-shirts and stickers rotting away in a closet. Chuck and Michael had conversations about Chuck buying the masters and all the merch from him, but Chuck couldn't afford to keep his rent less than three months behind due. Any amount was unattainable.

I woke up one day in April of 2010 to texts from friends asking if I was there with him. Having no idea what they meant, I said no.

Turns out, Chuck's old band, Faith No More, had invited him to sing a few songs at a show in San Francisco. Though Chuck was terrible at keeping secrets, he hadn't even told me. I was crushed. Having been too young to see him with Faith No More, Bad Brains, or Cement, I thought I would never have the chance to see any of that old material live.

Watching the videos online is funny, as he strolls on stage wearing Pip's red robe and sunglasses. You can see and hear the nerves he fought during that appearance. It had been over twenty years since the last time he had shared a stage with Faith No More and so much had changed since their paths had forked.

After he got back, Chuck and I worked on his autobiography, but he had these hang ups that made any significant progress nearly impossible. Here's how it worked:

Chuck would call. "Hey, man, you want to get some work done?"

I'd say, "Of course."

"Come grab me when you're done with work. How do you want to do this?"

"I'll start by asking you questions about a specific time and then branch off from there. Then I'll go home and transcribe what you say and flush it out into more of a story."

"What time?"

"I'll be there around six."

"No, what time are we going to talk about?"

"Oh. Well, agents are going to want to read two sample chapters. They'll want the most interesting bits, the stuff that'll really help sell the book. Maybe we could talk about a specific show with Faith No More or the path leading up to you joining the band?"

"Eh, I don't really remember those days. Maybe we can talk about cooking or about Haircuts That Kill?"

"We'll cover all of that in the book, but for these first two—"

"Hold on. I'm getting a call."

He clicks over as I wait a couple of minutes.

"You still there?"

"Ayup. I was thinking about the Haircuts stuff. If we—"

"Totally, got it. Just come over when you're ready. Would be cool if we could get the book out for the holidays."

"Well, it's November, so …"

"Yeah."

"Okay, see you soon."

I'd get to his house and he'd be walking the dog or on the phone or he hadn't gotten dressed yet. So, I'd sit and wait and wait and wait.

Finally, he stumbles to the car, bitching about the cold, and gets in. "Hey, man, we can get started, but like, in a minute. Can we stop at Dairy Mart?"

"Sure."

"'Cause, like, well, I need my AriZona mango iced teas."

"That's fine. Let's just go now and get it done so we don't get interrupted."

After entering, he stomps around the store, talking to the owner, and comes out with two bottles. He looks pissed.

"Damnit. I told him to hold me a case for Tuesday. They were half off until Tuesday. This is all he had left."

He stops outside my car to have a smoke. We stand in the cold and talk about the book and his various ideas on how to proceed.

"Well, let's get star—"

"So, um, can we check at Rite Aid? They typically don't have these teas, but they have my Big Cups."

I roll my eyes. "Dude, Rite Aid's parking lot is such a pain to get in and out of."

"Not this time of day."

"It's the end of rush hour ... Fine, whatever, let's go and get this done."

We reach the counter at the store, empty of tea.

Chuck is now sourer. "Can I get three packs of blacks?"

The clerk nods and goes to grab them.

Chuck asks her, "So, how did everything work out?"

She returns with a quizzical expression on her face. "How did what turn out?"

Chuck stares at the three packs she places on the counter. "No, can you grab the buy-two-get-a-dollar-off three pack?"

"We're out of them."

He shakes his head. "No. This morning I spoke to Zach, the shift manager, and he said the next order was due between two and four today."

She glances around. "Must not've gotten here. I know the roads are bad."

"Can you check by the photo lab? He said when they came in he would set a few aside for me."

She goes and finds them. "Oh, you were right. Do you want all three?"

"No. I just have enough for one. Can you stash those other two somewhere, and I'll get them as soon as I can?"

"Sure."

"Where?"

"Huh?"

"Where're you going to leave them?"

She glances around.

"I just want to know in case you're not here when I come back. Try over by the return bin, maybe?"

She nods and stuffs them in there.

"So, did you pass that test?"

The clerk's cheeks blush. "Oh, that's what you were talking about. Yeah, I got there on time after all, but I didn't pass."

"That sucks. Are you guys getting AriZona mangos in anytime soon?"

"Not sure. Want me to check?"

His phone rings. He nods to her as he answers. She returns with Jim the manager in tow to explain something about iced tea, but Chuck is pacing and yelling on the phone about his cable bill. They wait patiently for a bit, but eventually, Jim heads back to his office.

Meanwhile, as all of this is happening, I'm tapping my feet, rolling my eyes, and watching our limited time slip away. In the end, he buys the cigarettes, and we leave, presumably to begin work on the book, but Pip needs nine-volt batteries and he forgot, so we head to another store. We arrive and there's no parking, so I tell Chuck to jump out and I'll circle around. I go a few blocks and double back, thinking he'll be done, but there he is, in the parking lot smoking and talking to some people. I do the loop again, and this time he's ready. Or so I think.

He crouches to talk through the window I roll down. He spins a tale about how he was talking to Jonsie just now and how the dude needed to get on the bus, so Chuck gave him two bucks—or at least he thought it was because he had a ten and two ones but now he just has a one left—and he needs to get those batteries.

I give him a few bucks and do the loop again ... and again because Chuck needs a smoke when he comes out.

This is life with Chuck; it's so different than how I do things it infuriates me. The errands might not be a big deal, and it's not like I'm mad, but I am annoyed we made no progress.

I take a calming breath as he reenters the car.

He smiles. "Jackpot. They had my Big Cups buy three get one free. See? You would've paid full price back at the first place."

"And been done and home an hour ago, yeah. The fifty cents you saved just cost me twelve bucks in gas."

"Twelve bucks? Whatever. You exaggerate everything."

This is true. Later on, Chuck started calling me Captain Xaggerate, pronounced *Zaggerate*, and I can't deny my penchant for doing it around him a lot. It made my wife laugh every time Chuck pulled out that nickname.

We chuckle and bust each other's chops a bit. I point the car back to his house as his phone rings again. I pull into his driveway as he ends the call and gives me a look—half grin, half trepidation in his eyes and all mischief everywhere else. "So, um …"

Whenever he gives me the dreaded "So, um"—or worse, the "Well, like, uh"—I know he's about to say something I don't want to hear.

"So, um, this guy owes me twenty bucks, and I need to grab it 'cause they're going to shut off our cable if we don't pay tonight."

"How long is it— You know what? Never mind. Tell me where he lives."

And just like that, we're onto the next leg of adventure … after another smoke.

As we drive, Chuck is telling me old war stories from his time in Los Angeles. At one point, he worked as a flower-delivery person. One day, he got an order of flowers for Rhea Pearlman from her husband, Danny DeVito. Chuck had taken some drugs and was coming off a long bender. He blacked out and drove around for a few hours and never delivered the bouquet.

There are more details he told me, but again, this was as I was driving through the snow, after work, and frustrated by all these errands, so it wasn't recorded officially. After another hour of driving around chasing a few bucks, I head home, late for dinner and with zero progress made.

Chuck had hundreds of cool/funny/sad/frustrating/mind-blowing stories, but as soon as we were sitting down and the recorder was running, he— I won't say clammed up, but— he held back.

Chuck called once to tell me he had been sitting on his porch and a car had stopped in front of his house. "A guy gets out and says, 'Chuck?' I recognize him, but I don't know who it is. He tells me how we met years ago and recounts some things we did, which I sort of remember, but now he's directing commercials for Nike. He's out and about, scouting the area, and needs a porch to shoot a scene with an elderly guy talking. I think Lebron is involved somehow. Anyway, he's going to pay me to use my porch for the commercial."

Does this kind of stuff happen to other people?

It wasn't until later that I realized if he did get any money it should probably have gone to his landlord at the time, right?

Chuck's life at that point was a daily grind where nothing progressed, but on the positive side, nothing really negative had happened to set things back.

… And then Chuck did what Chuck does—and got arrested.

The arrest and subsequent court dealings led to him being assigned/forced into rehab.

He first spent time at a place on the eastside of Cleveland, which I got to know well as almost every day he called asking if I could bring cigarettes, CDs, or simply to talk. A couple times, he had me bring him notebooks to work on his autobiography, but during his stay, nothing panned out.

Chuck was miserable at that facility and transferred to a place in Youngstown, Ohio, about an hour east of Cleveland. He spent a month there in isolation and did, in fact, get started on the book. I've included what he wrote in a later chapter.

The first paragraph of his writing was:

> *April 20th 2012. I think I'm in fucking heaven. Last October I was arrested for felony possession of heroin. This outcome comes as no surprise to anyone. I've been a mess most of my life. So where did it all go wrong?*

A long time ago, actually, on a beach far, far away ...

Even facing jail time and rehab and the wrath of his family and more and more unpaid bills, the guy still managed to write with his humor intact. When he got home, Chuck seemed focused and excited to get to work. It made me happy to see him not only becoming proactive but interested in restarting his career.

I saw positive reviews of *Will Rap Over Hard Rock for Food* and frustration from fans that it wasn't available, so I convinced Chuck to sit face to face with Michael and hash out their differences. By meeting's end, we had an agreement to sell the albums online independently to try to raise money and keep the VUA name out there.

Being a new dad, working a busy job, pretending to be an author and a musician and, owning an aging home needing updates, I told Chuck getting the merch up for sale and promoting and monitoring sales would be up to me but shipping fell on him as I couldn't get to post office often enough.

The immediate response felt good. We sold some CDs, vinyl, and t-shirts to folks around the world. After the initial wave, things tapered off to an order here and there. About a month into the sales, I sent Michael his cut. After a few weeks later, I was surprised I hadn't heard from Michael, who had been positive and hands on with us.

Turns out, I had made an error with his email address when I used PayPal. He had never received the funds, so he thought we were dropping the ball or, worse, not following through on our agreement. I got it straightened out, but I felt like an arse for putting the shaky agreement in jeopardy.

Of course, Chuck was already working on his own ways to goof up things. He had only shipped a small portion of the packages. He was paying others to pack and ship them, meaning he had already spent the shipping/handling money for every order that we had received on the first batch—or at least that's the story I got.

I also take the blame for part of this, as we didn't charge enough for overseas shipping, and a vast majority of orders came from Europe and South America. Upset emails started to flow in as people waited on their packages. I ended up fronting the money, as usual, to get us caught up, but it took time, and many people waited too long to receive their stuff. It became enough of a hassle that I pulled down the merch, offering it only in digital downloads.

During all of this, we were working on a second VUA project, *Demos for Sale*. It serves as another great example of why Chuck and I are friends.

Aside from tolerating his endless scams and adventures to the pawn shop, throwing him a few bucks here and there, making him laugh when it was the last thing he wanted to do, booking his band, and helping him with all things social media, Chuck kept me around because I owned a computer that could burn CDs. His computer, on the other hand, had, if my memory proves correct, been built from cardboard in 1929. Powered by two hamsters and featuring an 8-track player, his computer was only useful for holding papers to his desk, even in windy conditions.

Typically, when we would get together, Chuck would ask me to burn him songs from CD-R discs he had gotten from the studio so he could listen to what he had done during a recent session and finalize guitar riffs or lyrics. I often found myself burning the same songs over and over as he would lose the disc I had given him.

I've talked to several other people who provided the same service to him through the years, so he lost even more copies than I had realized. I worry about the future of Western Union, Reese's Big Cups, AriZona mango iced tea, and anyone who manufacture's blank CD-Rs, as without Chuck's steady support, things might crumble.

In the end, I had several versions of songs that ended up on the VUA disc. One I enjoyed heads-and-tails more in demo form than on the album was "Bob Forest." The album track was a six-minute mess of heavy riffs and effected drums, while the demo spanned around eleven minutes and had this massive psychedelic vibe of echoed vocal lines—some melodic, some yelled—mixed over hypnotic, sludgy music. I would play that song and zone out, over and over.

"Exactly," Chuck would say when we discussed the demo version. "It starts out like a straightforward folk song and then just catapults off into space. We talked about extending it even longer when we recorded."

I nodded. "I could listen to that for hours on end."

"See?" He would say; apparently, my word was enough that the album version fell flat of his vision.

"The album version sounds dated and incomplete," I told him. "They tried to make a modern rock song out of a sprawling psychedelic epic."

As I collected a pile of discs, each with a song or two, all unlabeled as to when/where/who/how it was recorded, we started to reengage with the demos. On the album, the track "Enabler" features guest vocals by Jonathan Davis of Korn and guitar by John 5 of Rob Zombie's band. The track starts *Will Rap Over Hard Rock for Food* with a jolt. It's a nu-metal-esque tune that, had Chuck released it ten years earlier, might've really garnered some attention for him. Even today, eight or so years after they'd released the album, it stands the test of time, but it's not the vision Chuck had for the song when he had written it. It sounds more like someone covering a Chuck Mosley song with him singing on it. It's polished and aggressive and flashy and, damn, Chuck and Jonathan sound great together, right?

But you play the demo and hear the buildup, the tension, the movement, and the freedom for Chuck's vocal line to slip and slide without strict barriers, and it has a charm. The track has dynamics while still slapping you in the face with its drive and energy.

Michael Siefert even got involved with the release when I dropped by the studio to pick up a hard drive of video, photos, and promo materials he had left over from the label. We spoke about the song "Tractor," which I always heard rock radio potential in, barring a few changes.

Chuck was dead set against a radio edit, feeling assured that if the song was good enough it would get picked up and played. Having briefly worked in radio and then a longer stint on internet radio, I disagreed.

A few elements held "Tractor" and a few other Mosley songs from even getting considered for spins. Runtime, dead air, and inappropriate language are a few obvious ones. For "Tractor," I thought the song ran too long and that the middle bridge section brought the vibe to a crashing halt. It's the same with "Killing an Angel," one of Chuck's finest songs. He had a habit—I call it a habit; he called it a preference—for moments like these. His latest solo album has several more. I pictured my time board opping for Pat "The Producer" Johnson, who ruled Cleveland's airwaves for years, as he, in his role as music director, skimmed through new songs. He would have several stacks of discs amounting to a hundred or more singles to preview to decide if the music belonged on the air or not. He would give the tunes fifteen to twenty seconds to hook him and then another minute or so if it caught his attention. Within minutes of starting this process, the garbage can in the studio would be overflowing. I hated to think of this happening to Chuck's music.

So, even though Chuck wasn't truly on board, I sat with Michael, as he sliced a radio edit of "Tractor." Now, we were limited in what we could do without the multi tracks, only having a two-track master of the song to work with, but in about an hour, he had cobbled together what I thought represented a shortened yet still true-to-the-original take of the song. We included it on *Demos for Sale* as the last track to give us a polished song to promote the album if we found a label interested in pursuing such a push.

We kept the booklet design for the CD super minimal, using photos my buddy, Matt Glad, had taken of VUA in the past. Most or maybe all the photos were from their *Will Rap Over Hard Rock for Food* CD release show back in 2009. We enlisted the help of a graphic designer and a Chuck Mosley fan from Chile, Cristian Sepulveda. He and I discussed ideas, art direction, sizing, deadlines, budget, and proper use of the templates the disc manufacturer we typically used had provided.

In the end, the design made for a throwback/tribute/echo of the *Will Rap Over Hard Rock for Food* CD that, I think, showed how similar and related the two releases were while maintaining each also stood on its own.

To promote the release, we had no money or connections or time to build a buzz, so Chuck wrote a quick statement about the album. Here it is unedited:

Hey everyone, Chuck Mosley here, i'm gonna try and make this as short as possible.

In 1998 VUA started working on recording the LP Will Rap Over Hard Rock For Food. I paid about 8000 dollars out of my pocket to get this project done. Money that should have gone to my family.

But we had no representation, we just had a good band and we were ready to hit the road.

The project stalled when the engineer decided he was finished. What we had was an unfinished, unmixed, half of a record. The producer of the project felt responsible, seeing as, he was the one who put us in touch with this, so called engineer, and vowed to make things right by finishing the LP.

Unfortunately it took 10 years for that to happen, and the label that producer started and talked us into signing with closed down less than a year after releasing our LP. And sadly, we did not see eye to eye about how this LP should sound. I don't hate the production of w.r.o.h.r.f.f., lets just say my tastes run a little more to the left of mainstream. Kind of like the way it was sounding half way through, before it was over-thought, i think. We here at Vanduls Incorperated would like to share that with you, our fans, if any, can decide for yourselves.

I want to apologize for being gone for so long and then putting out an album and not

> *touring. We are in the process of trying to fix all of that crap and getting the fuck on the road. i get emails everyday from around the world, so much to the point that i feel guilty. So we our releasing this EP of demos, songs that were at that point of nirvana, just before they became too polished, in our opinion, so that we can share with you what we had in mind to release when we started, and, to raise money to record some of the plethora of new music that we have been waiting to get to....we hope you like it and I welcome any questions, comments, and/or straight up put downs, any animosity being haboured towards me. Not my band, just me. my band is perfect, they have no faults, i'm the messed up one. ask me anything, i'll tell you everything. I love you all, thank you for your time, and i hope you agree!*
> *Chuck*

Initially, in May 2013, we released it as a digital download only. This concept was a tough one for Chuck to grasp and agree to, but we had no money to print any physical copies, and I sure as shit didn't want to revisit the shipping-to-Europe nonsense again. The hope was we'd generate some interest and sell enough to catch the attention of a label or management or distributor or someone in the media to help champion the cause.

Our immediate hopes fell as sales came in far short of our goals. And those goals were pathetic to begin with. It didn't help that VUA was once again inactive.

We struggled to get offers for VUA to play dive bars in town, and yet investors from Chile reached out to bring Chuck and his band down there. As the promoter, Michel Lefranc and I pounded out details while Chuck flipped burgers to keep a roof over his family's heads.

VUA had suffered many lineup changes over the years, and in 2013, they had been dormant for some time, so even "getting the band back together" was proving difficult. In April 2013, three months before two shows in Chile, Chuck still hadn't confirmed who would be the other guys traveling with him. The promoters were panicking as tickets had already begun selling, but no promotions had started. They also were in a race to complete the work visas, buy airline tickets, etc. I spoke to them and Chuck daily to get things moving.

As time expired though, things worked out, and the band flew down. Chuck called me from the airport in Chile having left without writing down anyone's contact info, and he had no idea what the next step was. This started the phrase, "You don't want to get mosleyed out here in the middle of nowhere."

Steve Rauckhorst, VUA's bass player, told me, "With us, it was like a three-piece rock band playing at the same time as a one-man noise project. It was always an experience keeping the train on the tracks."

The shows in Chile were a team up with The Talking Book, featuring Jared Blum and Bill Gould, both known for many other projects over the years. They had released their debut a year prior.

Each night, VUA added some Faith No More material into the set and brought Bill onstage to play with them. The first night, Bill added electronic atmosphere via computer to the song, "Why Do You Bother?" And on the second night, he played bass on "Death March."

The reunion meant a lot to Chuck as his relationship with Bill stretched back to when they used to attend punk shows around Los Angeles before either of them were in bands.

Upon coming home, Chuck did a couple interviews, and we sold a few downloads, but without more things to promote, the buzz of VUA's return fizzled.

Later that year, VUA played a fundraiser in Toledo, Ohio for a young boy named Connor Requena, who was battling leukemia. It was freezing cold that night, which hurt the draw at the Mainstreet Bar and Grill, but we still got to meet some of Chuck's fans who had driven from Columbus, like Christopher Juhl and locals like Donn Wobser. After years of seeing Chuck with the same handful of people in town, it was great to interact with fresh faces and witness their excitement at meeting Chuck—not to mention having interacted online with these guys for years prior to the show.

VUA's drummer, Steven Melhman, couldn't make it, so Chuck had enlisted Jason Isom to play. He had been in a band with Steve Rauckhorst, so a comfort level existed bringing in someone on short notice. Not that Chuck was nervous. I was.

Yeah, I wasn't even playing, and I had more jitters than Chuck. He was so comfortable jumping onto the stage with whoever was around and making it work. I had seen VUA with three or four different drummers and probably the same number of bassists through the years, and they always played loud and sloppy and helped reel in Chuck whenever possible and let him fly into space when he couldn't be contained. Jason didn't hesitate to refuse the money when they tried to pay him, insisting it went to Connor.

The local news came out to cover the story, even interviewing Chuck, but they didn't stick around to tape VUA; instead, they used footage from the opening band in their story.

Around the time of that show, Chuck contacted a promoter interested in helping VUA get on the road. Within a month or two, VUA was booked for a string of dates with Detroit funk-rock band, Downtown Brown, and Drugs Delaney, who I think are from Illinois. I know, I know ... Funk rock. I hate labels just like you guys, and maybe that's not the perfect one for Downtown Brown. Sorry, Neil, if my lazy, uninformed classification disturbs you, but hey, I'm no rock critic, okay?

The run included long trips with too many off days in between. The band expressed concern to Chuck before the tour started, but he had given his word to perform, so he didn't want to cancel.

Per Chuck, the tour quickly spiraled out of control when Steven Mehlman quit during one of the shows. I spoke with Steven about the whole episode, but he asked to not go on record about it.

Steven is a madman behind the kit, like Animal from the Muppets, long hair flying in every direction at once. I thought his style really fit what VUA was about, but he also had steady work with other bands, like Pere Ubu, and had certain, reasonable expectations on how things should get handled on the road. Apparently, to save money, VUA was sharing some equipment with another band, and the kit they were using wasn't handling Steven's hard style of play. The hi-hat stand and snare drum stand kept dropping, causing Steven to either have to readjust them mid-song or alter what he wanted to play. After neither option worked well enough, Steven stood up and kicked over part of the kit and walked off stage in front of an energetic crowd.

Chuck was angry and confused. After several years of bad luck, here he was, with a captive audience, and now this happens. The band returned home after the first few dates, having lost money without proper merch to recoup typical tour costs. Chuck found himself alone with no band and several more dates to play.

Not wanting to cancel any shows, thus giving everyone more ammo to say he was unprofessional or a failure, Chuck decided to go it alone. He took his guitar and rode greyhound buses to several gigs. He enlisted the help of Downtown Brown to join him onstage for "Bob Forest" each night they shared the bill, so his set still had some rock to it. From most accounts, the shows were less than stellar, leaving the audience more confused than appeased.

Would it have been better for him to cancel and regroup? The argument can certainly be made, but performing solo on those dates gave Chuck a new perspective on the idea I had pushed back in 2006 about him doing a set focused on his more mellow, singer/songwriter side. It was possible. He could get onstage without a wall of noise and still hold an audience's attention. As down and out as he felt and knowing VUA might be done—or at least forced into an extended hibernation—Chuck had stuck to his guns and put himself out there.

The financial repercussions, however, weren't disappearing. He had left a part-time cooking job and fronted money for the van and other expenses, and all of that was gone plus much more. To make matters worse, both of his daughters had unexpected health issues, which buried them further into debt. Chuck didn't see a way out.

On December 3, 2014, Chuck sent me this email to look over before he posted it to his Facebook page:

> *hey doug. anyway, something like "hey friends and other peoples, i am really dreading this, i have fought myself over this*

for more than a couple months, i seem to have no other choice than to lose my pride due to the lacking ability to provide a sense of security for my family. the shocking truth is that i'm not rich. we struggle everyday, just like most everybody, more, right now, worse than ever, in a long time. our landlord wants to sell the house we've lived in for ten years, and yes, we are behind in our rent, so he's using that as leverage, to get us out so he can fix up and sell, right away, technically, we're supposed to be out tomorroow, dec 3rd, but he's deciding whether to give us another week. so here i am, for my family, on my knees, asking for help. I'm ashamed for being in this condition, that i have to burden others, who look to me, only to be my friend, and for me to be theirs, and i am abusing that relationship, and i apologise, but for my family, i'll do anything..................leagle. and that's the reality, i could go into a dissertation, about how and why, but the bottom line is we are broker than we've been in a good good long time, and can't bail out, so here i am asking that anybody who could afford to send a few dollars to my/our paypal acct., and for any substantial donations, we will offer up my better half's portrait of my dog, Fredo, and me, real scarface meets........................ me. she's an awesome artist, her name is pip logan, and there's a few more pieces of her work, she's willing to part with, for a few of

> *the more generous donations . just throwin that out there....our band, VUA, has had to put off trying to tour or play any shows, we're starting to record new stuff, but even that is suffering at the hands of my family's financial situation, so, please, if you can, help, we will be eternally greatful and i will be eternally self loathing for having to be at this level......i'm sorry for asking, if i could do anything for you, please ask, and i swear i will do everything in my power to serve you, any way i can. thank you.*

He was stressed, humbled, frustrated, and unsure what else to do. I had wanted him to try offering the VUA merch and maybe some rarer higher-end items that collectors might pay bigger bucks for, but he didn't have time to wait.

He posted, and the world responded. I know because his email forwards to my account as well. For a solid week, my phone didn't stop buzzing with alerts. A buck here, five there, and the occasional fifty-spot put Chuck a-pocket-of-change south of three thousand dollars within a few weeks. He paid bits and pieces of the bills and avoided eviction. The family, already without a car, also cut down to one cellphone to split between the three adults in the house.

Their landlord kept his decision to put his house on the market, so Chuck, Pip, and Sophie moved a few minutes away into a much smaller upstairs of a duplex located in a less-desired neighborhood.

Chuck found employment working for a friend of a friend who operated several restaurants and a catering business in Cleveland. He would call on break when he was staying up all night preparing five thousand of some appetizer or another. He got along with the staff, and though he had to bus or bike downtown, he enjoyed some aspects of the job.

Chuck caught wind that Ante Up Studios had moved out of the building it had occupied for years, possibly leaving the VUA merch behind. I swung over to pick him up, and we paid a visit to the landlord. At the time, I was working as a salesman, so I was dressed in a decent shirt and tie, had my hair freshly shaven and my beard trimmed. I won't go as far as to say I looked professional or neat but close enough that I could pass for an attorney or manager to some degree.

Chuck wearing pajamas and slippers with his dreads and earrings and wristbands et al. and me in my big boy business attire were a pair to see.

I enjoyed the confused expression on the landlord's face as we entered his office. "Can I help you gentleman?"

Chuck, typically a man who avoids conflict to a fault, took the lead. "Yeah, I don't know if you remember me, but I recorded in the studio over there, and I still have a bunch of my stuff in it."

The landlord said nothing, his expression now befitting a poker tournament.

Chuck continued. "I heard Michael was no longer in there, but I want to get my stuff before it's too late. It's my stuff. I can show you contracts and proof if you need to verify who I am. We came by recently, but the doors were locked, and no one answered."

The guy's gaze flicked to me and then back to Chuck.

Chuck continued to talk, mostly repeating his story until the man held up his hands in an open-palmed hold-on/surrender gesture. He told us he had no issues with us getting our stuff, but the lights had been turned off, and he didn't know how safe it was in there. Apparently, a lot of junk had been thrown about, and he didn't want us tripping or bumping our heads or anything. We assured him we were fine with taking the risk. We just wanted to grab the stuff and go.

He led us in with a flashlight, and thank goodness he did. It was torn up and pitch black. I still managed to bump my head and run into some metal machinery that left me limping all afternoon.

Not only was the studio trashed, but someone had made holes in the ceiling, so rainwater had been dripping in for a few months. This hurt the most when we opened the closet and found a lot of the merch had been water damaged. I'm not only talking about VUA stuff either. The label had signed several bands and housed their merch in the same space. T-shirts, vinyl, CDs, press packets, stickers, and all other manner of stuff was rotting away as the rain came down.

We dug through the piles and found a few boxes of vinyl and maybe five cases of CDs that appeared unscathed, along with many more beyond use. We loaded them into my car—the landlord being accommodating enough to lead us in and out each trip—and left.

We tried to reopen the merch thing, but the European and South American orders quickly bankrupted us, even after raising the shipping fee. USA orders fizzled out, and we were back to selling digital copies only of both VUA releases. I say "we," but again, I wasn't a part of the band or getting paid. My goal was to see Chuck doing what he was born to do.

In spring of 2014, Chuck got asked to record vocals on a cover song for a compilation on Cleopatra Records. He was hesitant to do it, very hesitant, but Chuck found himself still broke and needed the few dollars promised for lending his vocals.

I arranged an afternoon to record at my buddy Adam Probert's studio. We worked on the track, and while hanging out, Adam played a few demos he and I were cooking up for our next release.

Since 1999, Adam and I have had a music project called Indoria. Through the years, we've recorded songs in many different sounds/genres and had a liquid lineup of people culled from whoever was around and interested in working with us.

A week or so later, I picked up Chuck for one reason or another, and he was humming a tune. He said it had been stuck in his head and he couldn't figure out what it was. He hummed it a few more times, and it clicked. He had an Indoria song stuck in his head. Specifically, it was a vocal line I had sung on an Indoria demo.

I asked if he'd be interested in singing my part on the song. He agreed, and we got him back in the vocal booth. After a few rough takes, he found his voice and range, and Adam and I kept glancing at each other, excited by how good it sounded.

Typically, for a part of a song like this, Adam would play only that section and have me record it, but Chuck kept asking him to play the whole song so he could get the vibe and get more familiar with it. As he got comfortable, we heard him mumbling to other parts of the song.

I asked Adam to open a channel so I could talk to Chuck in the booth. "Chuck, what you're doing on the chorus, singing with Michele [my wife who sang lead on the song], sounds super cool. Wanna give it a try?"

"Sure. Just keep going through."

He did take after take—experimenting, adding, changing, second-guessing, third-guessing—and after a few hours, we had a bunch of useable stuff. He became an integral part of the song, even changing how it ended, and we realized how good Michele and Chuck sounded together.

We're more of an indie pop-rock type band, so it felt good to give Chuck a chance to use his vocals differently than he does in VUA. We started working on a new project that would feature Chuck on lead vocals. The initial idea was a throwback to my 2006 acoustic Chuck disc. We would write an EP of simple, catchy tunes and give him something new to offer fans and maybe something to tour on.

Through 2015, we plugged away on new songs. One of the first tunes we worked on was written around a clip of Chuck talking into a microphone during a previous session. The expectation was always that we'd replace the clip with something new from Chuck during the hook, but eventually, we decided it fit too well to cut. That was one of the fun things about working with Chuck; you never knew where content would come from or what direction things could take.

Chuck and Adam have polar opposite strategies for working on music. While Adam likes to keep a quick pace and a constant flow of progress, Chuck prefers to live in the vocal booth, rambling take after take, layering ideas on top of and around each other.

It didn't help matters that Chuck wasn't at his most focused this time. I never saw him doing drugs, but signs pointed to him arriving less than sober. During one session, Chuck didn't want to try anything in the booth, instead focusing on Adam's keyboard. We sat for a few hours as Chuck noodled along to whatever was in his head, which certainly didn't seem to coincide with what we were playing for him.

Again, Chuck always operated this way—a long warmup period, rambling and apparently directionless, smoke breaks, beers, shots—and mixed in are these moments of brilliance that leave you in disbelief. One moment he could record a track that sounded like he had channeled a Paul McCartney melody and then follow it up with off-key grunts and nonsensical rants. It's hard not to think he's messing with you. Maybe he was; it certainly fit his sense of humor.

Adam and I spoke many times about using what we had and filling in the rest with me and Michele, but whenever we reached that point, Chuck would pull something out and insist he wanted to see the project through.

By winter of 2015, we realized it had morphed into more of another Indoria disc than a Chuck solo record, mostly because I had written the lyrics and vocal patterns over Adam's music rather than Chuck offering input.

Around that point, Thom Hazaert proposed rereleasing *Demos for Sale* on his new label after the two did an interview together for a podcast.

Thom had recently partnered with David Ellefson, the bassist of Megadeth, on a new label project under the name The EMP Label Group. With solid distribution, realistic expectations, and a fan in Thom heading the charge, it felt like a good fit. I encouraged Chuck to take the plunge even though he was weary of rushing into another situation like he had experienced with VUA's previous label.

I really wanted the album to help Chuck move past *Will Rap Over Hard Rock for Food* and *Demos for Sale* so he could focus on more new music. That collection of songs had taken up most of his late thirties, all his forties, and into his fifties. Chuck was a different person than the one who had written most of those songs.

Thom, Chuck, and I kicked around ideas on how Chuck could make steady money in music. Thom felt confident that

Chuck could do better or at least make a similar amount of money on the road than he could in the kitchen.

The issue was that VUA wasn't a viable option, nor was affording a whole band to go on tour. Chuck needed to be making money for himself. He needed to have the focus on his name and his music. He needed to do the damn solo acoustic thing I had suggested to him ten years earlier. It made sense on so many levels. Jeez, maybe I am as stubborn as they say.

Chuck and I talked constantly on the phone for weeks as he hemmed and hawed about it. "My guitar playing isn't good enough to stand on its own."

"Chuck, no one coming to these shows is buying a ticket to hear you play guitar."

"What do you mean?"

"They want to hear your voice. They want to understand the lyrics. Any guitar or bass or whatever else you add is extra layers, but the main selling point is your voice."

He made some *mmm*-type sound. Typically, he does this when he doesn't buy what I'm selling.

"Chuck, if you get on stage and play 'Chip Away', 'Sophie,' 'Nameless,' your cover of 'Life's a Gas', throw in a few Faith No More tunes, maybe a Bad Brains song, and jam on some new stuff, people will love it."

"You think?"

"It's what I pictured you doing when I first brought this up. Take away the fuzzy guitars and punk drums and just let your voice carry the set."

At that point, I fully expected Chuck to take the concept and run with it. Though I never expected him to drag me along.

CHAPTER FOUR
02/2016 - 05/2016:
Quitter was Full

While a dream of mine, I never intended or expected to tour with Chuck. I'm not a drummer. I'm not a percussionist. Aside from a limited vocal range and a burning desire to perform in front of crowds, I'm not really even a musician.

In February of 2016, I traveled to the UK with my wife. She went there for work and used some miles to bring me along. During the trip, I had taken a train from London to Edinburgh, Scotland to meet with Robert Anderson, a guy I knew online as a fellow Faith No More fan. He ran a place called the Black Bull Tavern a few paces from the train station—which you can see in the movie *Avengers: Infinity War*.

I sat at the bar next to a local who had logged some serious hours on the same stool he now occupied. Within minutes, the subject of Faith No More arose, and we discussed a show that had happened in town about thirty years prior. The guy remembered things Chuck had said onstage and had followed Chuck to a bar after the show.

Robert took me to a nearby concert club called Bannerman's, with a stage in an arched stone room. That night, they hosted karaoke. I thought about signing up, as even if I sounded terrible, I'd never see those people again. The place was full of character and history, and I wanted to say I had "played" there—karaoke or not. I chickened out, but Chuck and I would play that stage seven months later.

Chuck called me the following day as I waited to catch the train back to London. He asked me to jump on as tour manager if the tour did happen, but I declined. I had a family, decent job, two mortgages (thanks housing market crash of 2008), and I'm not what you'd call a *risk taker*. Not to mention, I had only limited experience to bring to the table.

When I returned to London, I told my wife, who then encouraged me to not jump to the conclusion that we couldn't make it work. I told her there's no money in music, and touring can often end as a losing proposition even when everything goes as planned, and this was Chuck we were talking about. I love the guy, but reliable, trustworthy, hardworking, and 'see things through' aren't the first words and phrases that came to mind when describing him.

I told her, "Chuck is the king of shooting himself in the foot."

"Then you'll have to be the responsible one to keep the ship afloat."

"I hesitate to say *me* and *responsible* in the same sentence."

She didn't argue.

Upon our return to the States, I helped Chuck assemble a list of musicians who could go with him, and I formulated an uneducated budget based on assumed numbers.

Chuck's first and most-obvious touring member choice was Tim Parnin. They had a steady twenty-year working relationship in VUA. Tim had touring experience with other bands as well. The two of them already knew most, if not all, of the songs that would most likely comprise the set, and Tim knew how to keep Chuck on track or cover up his mistakes. Unfortunately, between running his custom guitar and amp shop and touring and recording with other bands, Tim had too many conflicts.

Steve Rauckhorst's flexible, humorous attitude and comfort with the material, coupled with his road experience, made him another strong candidate, but he also had too much going on to commit. A cover band making decent money, a serious relationship (now a happy marriage), and a studio he ran all stood in the way.

We continued down the list. Leah Lou, the female vocalist who guested on a VUA song would fit great, as she could sing and play guitar. She had fallen off the radar though, and we didn't know how to reach her in a timely fashion.

A longtime keyboard player for Mushroomhead, Shmotz, had recently left the band, and Chuck had known him for a while. We figured guitar, keys, and vocals would be a cool mix, and the band would have more freedom in song selection. They got together a few times to jam.

Shmotz said, "Man, it was always a great time for me hangin' with Chuck. He was a total sweetheart. Very humble too. As much of an icon that he was, he still never had that asshole *rock star* gene. He wasn't afraid to be honest nor was he afraid to ask for assistance putting together a band or a tour. He was smooth and cool as a cucumber. I loved that dude for being that way. He was a trip. I miss him dearly. The world needs guys like Chuck to keep the younger generations of musicians believing in themselves and reaching for their dreams. He always inspired me to do those things."

Shmotz had a new steady job and didn't want to get back on the road, so, after a while, he removed his name from the running. He let Chuck borrow his keyboard for a month or two to work on music and helped Chuck learn a few songs on it that Chuck wanted to play. One of them, a cover of The Zombies' "The Way I Feel Inside," had been on the soundtrack to *Life Aquatic with Steve Zissou*.

Things at work were falling apart for me, so I wondered if passing on the tour offer had been a mistake. My employer had been family-run for decades, but changes to the industry had forced them to sell to a larger corporation that shared few morals or ethics that the family did. My boss's boss spent a lot of the winter sabotaging my department's progress and worse, my pay.

In April, they fell more than three months behind on issuing our commissions and reimbursing our business expenses. The company also laid off people, restructuring salaries, cutting bonuses, and updating general day-to-day job operations to make things tougher to succeed.

I spoke with Chuck and said if he could make sure I met a few numbers, I would take the plunge to get him going. I was never the permanent fix or even a good solution, but the first shows were a couple weeks away, and I was what I was.

He asked, "Can you play anything?"

"No, but I can keep a steady beat."

"On what?"

"Conga?"

"Do you have one?"

"Nope."

"That should work."

I found a conga on Craigslist. I met the guy in a Walmart parking lot. When he asked what I planned on using it for, I told him I was going on a world tour.

At that point, all Thom had booked were three Midwest area shows in May, and I had added a free Cleveland appearance at a coffee shop to serve as practice, but it still felt good to say *world tour*.

Chuck and I constructed our rider:

1 hotel/motel room (reserved under Douglas Esper or Charles Mosley)

1 case bottled water

6-12 beers (local if possible)

6 dry/clean towels

6 juice/tea/fruit tea (mango, peach, whatever—AriZona is fine)

Assortment of fresh fruit/vegetables, dips

Chips/snacks

*1 pint of whiskey (Jameson or Jack Daniels preferred)

*Optional but appreciated

Dinner for 2 or $20 buyout x2

I ordered three kazoos from Amazon or eBay and bought a mini xylophone at a drug store nearby, and Adam let me borrow a banana-shaped shaker before the first practice.

Chuck had a six-string and a twelve-string guitar, but both were in the pawn shop. We retrieved the six-string and put a few bucks on his other items while there. Chuck dug around his attic and found his pedals and some cables. We spent an afternoon figuring out what still worked, and I quickly realized what a mess we were already.

Chuck rummaged through his bag. "Man, I swear I have more stuff somewhere. And picks."

I bought a small speaker so he had something to plug into, as his amp was missing/broken/imaginary—I can't remember. I brought a microphone, mic stand, and a vocal-effects pedal I had purchased thinking Indoria might someday get back onstage.

I asked, "What do you want to start with?"

"What were you thinking?"

"'Chip Away?'"

He played a few notes and sang a line or two but couldn't remember what came next. Hearing him play it sent butterflies through me. Here I stood, a part of the project, and my favorite song would be a staple of our set.

He stopped. "Yeah, that could work. What else?"

"'Sophie.'"

"Definitely, but I'd like to work on some delay for my vocals at certain parts."

I pointed at the effects pedal. "That should do it, but I gotta figure out how it works. We're going to Adam's house to record practice, and he knows a lot more about pedals than I do."

Chuck played "Sophie," and it sounded fantastic, if a little rough around the edges.

"Next?"

"Well, we should get a few Faith No More songs into the set."

He shrugged. "Eh, I don't know if any would work."

"Obviously, we'd have to change them up a bit, but I think 'Anne's Song'—"

Chuck shook his head. "Nope. Not gonna happen."

"I think it'd be cool with just drums and guitar and vocals. We don't really need to do the solo, and it's one of the songs that keys don't lead the way. We could fade out the end."

Chuck continued to shake his head. "And don't ask about 'We Care a Lot' either."

I agreed. "I don't see how we'd pull that off with this setup. Well, you're calling it the Reintroduce Yourself Tour, so 'Introduce Yourself' makes sense."

"No, I don't see it."

"'As the Worm Turns' would be sweet, if we could get keys."

"But we don't have them."

"Maybe Shmotz or you could program them into a keyboard, and I could trigger them live?"

"*Mm.* One of my favorites is 'Why Do You Bother?' We did that with Billy in Chile, but it wouldn't work with this."

Pip was in the kitchen, half listening. "I don't think people want to hear the Faith No More stuff anyway."

I rolled my eyes, frustrated I didn't have any support. "Well, we certainly don't want a full set of it, but people will expect some sprinkled in. Especially with the tour name."

Chuck wasn't sure. I could tell. He wanted to say more, but he moved us onto other songs. "What else?"

We discussed several songs from his various bands. For each one, Chuck had a reason not to play it.

"What if we did 'Wisdom Comes?'"

"What's that?"

"One of the songs you did with Bad Brains. It's got some of your catchiest vocals."

He couldn't remember what song I meant, so we plugged his laptop into the TV and pulled it up on YouTube.

"Oh, 'Wisdom Dub.' Yeah, no."

"Why not?"

"Because those guys are master musicians, untouchable."

"We wouldn't be doing it in their style, man. Take your vocals and we work around them."

He grabbed his guitar and noodled while the video played. He had me start and stop it a few times as he listened to the lyrics too.

He said, "Let it play, and we'll play along."

We tried it a few times. Again, I was buzzing just from hearing him singing to a song I had fallen in love with, only having that one live video as a guide. Chuck recorded several songs with Bad Brains. Aside from some live songs and a live cover of The Damned they released on a live split with Danzig, nothing he did with the band has seen the light of day. I thought covering one of these tunes would be a treat for his fans.

Chuck offered feedback and advice on my drum pattern, and we tried it again.

He raised an eyebrow and said something to the effect of, "Well, it's not as bad as I thought."

As far as compliments go from Chuck, that was high praise.

"I have this newer song I played at Bella Dubby's a couple times."

He played, and I loved it right from the get-go. I played along, unsure if what I drummed fit. He sang a verse and a chorus and then repeated the guitar part a few times. When he didn't sing again, I assumed I was distracting him with my beat, so I stopped.

He glanced over. "No, keep going. I like that."

We grooved a bit, and eventually he started singing the song again.

When finished, he said, "I only have the one verse and the other part, so I usually just doubled it when I played it. I can either come up with a second verse or maybe we'll just play half of it."

"I'd lean toward a second verse."

"It is the exact same though, so I don't want it to get boring live."

As far as I can remember, aside from him writing the second verse, nothing else changed about the song at all, which we played at all but one or two shows. He did eventually retitle it "Bella Donna." It was the first percussion part I wrote that ever became the *official* part. A big deal? Probably not. However, it helped me feel like I could hold my own and contribute more than just my pretty face to the tour.

I floated the idea of "Death March," and we tried that. Chuck knew the words and had a pretty good idea about the guitar, so we added it to the set without much fuss. I then remember he had mentioned doing a Faith No More medley. The intro for "Crab Song" made a lot of sense and sounded great, but Chuck couldn't figure out what sounded off about the guitar riff leading to his first vocal lines.

"The guys played your era songs a lot after you split. I think hearing a Patton-era track in your voice would sound cool."

"I had thought about that."

"Two in particular I think fit your range and what you're doing."

Chuck leaned back on his couch, wincing. He had been sitting on the arm of the couch, and his back had flared up again. "Which ones?"

"'Take This Bottle' and 'Last Cup of Sorrow.'"

His eyes grew distant. "I think I know one of those but not the other. Can you play them?"

I played "Take This Bottle" on my phone. He glanced off, nodding and listening.

The song reached the two-minute mark before he said, "I dunno. It doesn't really go anywhere, but the progression is simple enough. Play it again."

He noodled along, and we tried it a few times. Though he didn't commit, I thought it sounded cool. It felt weird hearing him sing a song that basically consists of an addict freeing his family and admitting his wrongdoing. To me, it fit the vibe and his real life, but I don't know if he ever took the lyrics to heart or saw what I did.

When I suggested "Faster Disco," I took the angle that his vocals lead that song forward, and everything else reacts to his patterns. I know what I play has little relation to what Mike Bordin created on the original tune, but it was so fun to perform.

During two or three more practices, we learned songs from Cement, like "Sleep" and "King Arthur." "Sleep" sounded great, but Chuck had a hard time with one of the guitar parts and a few lines of lyrics, so we kept postponing adding it to the set. We tried almost every song from the *Will Rap Over Hard Rock for Food* album by VUA, aside from "The Enabler."

"Come Around" presented a challenge, as the middle of the song features a long guitar solo before exploding into a noisy end. I told Chuck to keep the rhythm, and I'd play the guitar solo via kazoo.

Now, to help you picture this thing, it wasn't a regular kazoo. The company who made it had added this enlarged horn that protruded from top to help the sound carry and get directed at a microphone.

We tried the song a few times with limited success, having a good laugh in the process. The bit lasted until our first show but never saw the stage. I brought the kazoo on our first couple runs, just in case.

Chuck told me "Come Around" was actually two songs meshed together. The mash-up happened during his time with Bad Brains. He told me Doc had provided a bass line that tied the two songs together, and he thinks somewhere exists a recorded version with Doc playing bass on it. I haven't found that, but I did hear a demo version of the song before the second section had gotten integrated.

"Punk Rock Movie" has a great energy, but Chuck's hang-up was that the song originally ran only thirty or forty seconds, and he preferred it short, so sometimes he'd start it and play the first bit and then stop and tell a story and then we'd play some more and then he'd stop again. I always felt our set was too choppy, and that added to it, but some nights it worked great for laughs.

"Tractor" sounds massive no matter how few people played it. So, though he initially wrote it off as *impossible*, I fought for it. As crowds responded or called for it live, it became a staple. When we first went out, Chuck didn't have a distortion pedal, so it had a much different vibe than later in our tour.

"Bob Forest" is a juggernaut of a song. It starts as a jangly folk tune before launching into psychedelic waves of noise and chaos. If I had to bet what Chuck's inner thoughts sounded like at all times, the second half of "Bob Forest" is what I would lay my money on. The song is named after musician Bob Forrest who Chuck had had many adventures with in LA. I'm not sure if the song's title missing an "r" was intentional or an oversight.

With a single guitar, echo on Chuck's voice, and me hitting my conga as hard as I could, I think we managed to give that song, and its misspelled namesake, a proper showing. When it worked live, it left people's jaws hanging. When it didn't, we simply plowed through and let the chaos take over. Either way, it proved one hell of a set ender.

Chuck called me one day as I pulled in his driveway. He wanted to postpone practice for an hour. In the two weeks leading up to our first show, he had delayed practice a few times and had canceled once or twice all together. Couple in all his extra errands and breaks and phone calls, I felt the pressure of our first gig breathing down my neck.

We had only agreed on five or six songs, and he hadn't confirmed anything by Faith No More. He had ignored the Bad Brains song. And, as he did interviews, he sold the concert as an anthology of his whole career, when, in reality, we had three VUA songs, two Cement songs, a cover of a T. Rex tune he had performed live before, and one new song with unfinished lyrics. Two songs were less than a minute long. We had vague notions of covering The Zombies, if he could figure out a couple of notes and write down the lyrics. He also had wanted to fit "Bizarre Love Triangle" by New Order into our set, but again, he didn't know the notes, and that song has a ton of lyrics.

I drove around until he texted for me to stop by. We played, but Chuck had no energy. He was cranky. He started to shoot down all the songs again.

And then he passed out midsong.

I said to myself, this dude nodded off. I quit my job to try and help revive his career, and he's using something strong enough to have this effect. I collected my equipment and took it downstairs to my car. He never stirred. He slumped over with his head drooping and his guitar balanced in his lap.

I called my wife from my car in front of his house and told her I was quitting and going back to work.

She asked, "Why?"

"Because I think Chuck used, and I'm not ready to risk the tour imploding because of his inability to stay sober."

My family counted on me to help pay bills, and the way this was coming together, it could fall apart real fast.

"Just take a deep breath, and go back up there."

I did a doubletake at my phone. "Aren't you supposed to be angry that I quit my job, and Chuck isn't taking it seriously, and I might waste this year on the road with him?"

"He just started taking blood pressure meds. For all you know, this is a side effect from that. You know he doesn't take care of himself. Maybe he was up all night."

"Maybe he is using."

"Maybe, but quitting now doesn't make any sense. Give him a chance. Help him. Make the tour work and make the most of the opportunity."

I glanced over and saw Chuck stumbling toward my car.

"Alright." I hung up and rolled down the window.

He squinted in the sun. "What are you doing out here, man?"

"You tell me. You nodded off and—"

"I didn't nod off. I just fell asleep. I haven't been able to eat in two days, and I couldn't sleep last night."

He gave me the usual spiel about the dogs going nuts and the downstairs renters fighting all night and the cops slamming their neighbor's door. He told me to come back up, even carrying some of the gear. We played, and I relaxed a little. He was on-point, positive, and sounded great.

We organized a practice at Adam's studio. We wanted to record ourselves to hear what was what, get his input, and time how long our set could be. We dicked around with the vocal-effects pedal, but Chuck had already lost the instruction booklet, so, aside from basic operations, we never did much else. I made three different presets, titled *Bob Forest*, *Mosley*, and *Sophie*, to use throughout the set. In the end, I don't think we used the Mosley one ever, as, for some reason, it really killed the signal, making volume control tough, especially switching mid-song.

Adam is a bit OCD, so seeing our unorganized set up boiled his blood enough that he offered to lend a hand. He lent Chuck a pedal board and some shiny new cables and set it all up for him. I warned Adam that we'd be on the road, and I couldn't guarantee everything would come back in great condition, if at all.

We played our first show on May 15, 2016, at the Root Café in Lakewood. They didn't own a sound system, so I cobbled together stuff from Adam's house and my collection of junk.

I've spent time in front of crowds as a DJ, a Rock and Roll Hall of Fame battle-of-the-bands host, the vocalist for a few bands, and an author at speaking/reading engagements. I don't often find myself nervous, but I had a stomach full of butterflies as I paced around the coffee shop frantically trying to piece together the sound system. Oh, and for the first time as an adult, I wore pajamas. Why? Because Chuck always wore pajamas. Always. Of course, he arrived donning Dickies and a button-up shirt, so I looked more foolish than normal.

Aside from my wife, kids, parents, in-laws, regular patrons of the café, and Tim Parnin from VUA, a few Chuck Mosley fans came to see what this new acoustic project was all about.

They didn't get to talk to Chuck much before the set, because Chuck had disappeared with Donn Wobser, who told me, "Chuck looked a little panicked and asked me what I was doing. My statement was, 'Whatever you want. I came here for you.' He asked me to drive him home because he had forgotten his 'lucky' nail polish."

Yeah, you read that right. Chuck wouldn't perform without his nails painted with sparkles. I'm not saying it wasn't a fashion statement, but man ... come on.

We limped through the set. I say that with respect for what we accomplished and for what little practice we had. But I'm willing to call a spade a spade. Chuck played random riffs and added new effects to his guitar. Lyrically, he was all over the map. I remember playing "Death March," a song he had nailed at practice, and it felt like I was playing with a complete stranger who had only heard the song on an elevator. We did, however, start to understand what worked and what didn't. One of the things that felt natural was how we interacted onstage. We had a good push and pull. We made each other laugh, and we could handle some ball-busting. We fed off the crowd and managed not to chase away many people.

Rob Capiccioni gave me his input after watching our first show. "Chuck came across as very friendly and approachable, like we had been friends for a long time. His performance was heartfelt, and I enjoyed his sense of humor, as he'd sprinkle various funny anecdotes between songs."

The depth of Chuck's stage fright is hard to describe without underselling it. Somehow this gentle, fun-loving guy gets mortified every time he steps onstage. He felt like someone would call him out for being a fraud, for not deserving to get up there and do what he loved. He often linked it to some of the abandonment issues he had from being put up for adoption.

A highlight of the set was when we brought up my wife to sing a duet with Chuck on the VUA song, "Nameless." There had been no practice or soundcheck, it just happened—and it sounded good.

Donn Wobser provided me with a setlist from that night:
Chip Away
Sophie
Nameless
Come Around
Bella Donna
Death March

King Arthur
Punk Rock movie
The Crab Song (intro)
Take This bottle (Snippet)
Life's A Gas
Bob Forest

After the set, I tore down the equipment as the intimate crowd dispersed. I had survived the first show with limited mistakes, and though Chuck didn't have a legitimate worry about not being good enough, I, as a first-time conga player, certainly did. It felt good though, like we were on to something. I thought that if we worked out the bugs and got on a roll, we could make it work.

As we got closer to leaving for tour, I had taken on many other roles: flier creator, tour manager, booking agent, graphic design, merch guy, and PR. I enjoyed some of the work, despised other parts, and felt out of my league at times.

A few days later, we left for a three-night run. The plan had been to shove off early in the afternoon, as we had a ten-hour drive to Eau Claire, Wisconsin, and I wanted to get going. The show wasn't until the following night, so, if we got tired, we could stop somewhere or stay in the car. Chuck, of course, had other plans. All day he kept delaying and delaying and delaying.

I contacted Thom Hazaert, who lived in Green Bay, and told him we had gotten a super-late start.

Thom, his gravelly voice upbeat, said, "Just come crash at my place. I arranged for Chuck to get an ESP guitar, and it should be here in the morning."

We left after dinner, fueling up at a truck stop outside of Gary, Indiana. I remember Chuck's excitement, as that's where the Jacksons hailed from. I grew up listening to my parents' record of *Thriller* and hearing Michael on the radio but had limited knowledge of the Jackson Five outside of a song or two. I asked him a throwaway question about watching the Jacksons' rise to superstardom to pass the time, but Chuck took the question to heart. He loved him some Jacksons, so it turned into a surprisingly good conversation in which I learned a few things and gained insight into the music industry back then.

After nonstop orange barrels on Rt 80 through Indiana, we still managed to catch traffic in Chicago construction around 1 a.m. Chuck did an interview or two along the way, but mostly he slept.

He awoke as I pulled off the highway for gas. I warned him that we were in Manitowoc, Wisconsin, but he hadn't yet seen the show, *The Making of a Murderer*, which my wife and I had recently finished. I have no clue if Steven Avery is guilty or innocent, but I know the mustached DA made for the most unlikeable, creepiest villain ever, and it's scary that he's a real dude.

We got to Green Bay around 4 a.m., and I was fried. I crashed out for a couple hours before waking to a commotion. Apparently, the FedEx truck had passed us by. Thom and I jumped in my car and gave chase. When we tracked it down, the driver located the guitar. We gave him a CD of *Will Rap Over Hard Rock for Food* as a thank-you.

After lunch at a diner across from Lambeau Field, Chuck and I shoved off toward Eau Claire, a straight shot across the state on Rt 29. Here I was on day two of my first tour. It was real now, right? I mean, we hadn't played a show on the road yet, but we didn't sleep at home. Boom, this was *a tour*.

We pulled into town, excited and ready to play. No one was out and about on the streets. I mean, ghost-town levels.

The Eau Claire show served as a snapshot into how the majority of our tour played out, we just didn't know it at the time. In our minds, this was Chuck's first legitimate tour in almost twenty years and the first one that had even the slightest bit of planning. To top it off, we had a well-respected promoter, Tom Hooks, locally pumping the show. We certainly weren't looking to sell out big rock clubs, but playing in front of an excited, half-filled bar could be a ton of fun.

We discovered that that night happened to be the local college's Commencement Ceremony. So, not only did most people in town have something important to attend, but also almost every hotel had been booked.

Our concert didn't start until after a comedy showcase. I walked around the town, street after street of almost no foot traffic, and my gut turned inside out. I passed a couple other bars and saw a lot of empty seats. No one was coming, man. Fuck, no one was coming.

As the comedians ended, the crowd dispersed. The opening band's first song echoed around the empty club, and my stomach tightened. By the time we played, after midnight, the lack of turnout had drained any and all excitement. The club didn't have a soundman, so a member of one of the openers helped us set up and get started. Chuck straddled the line between playful nervousness and stumbling around drunk.

The club started cleaning and putting away chairs before we said, "Thanks and goodnight."

We retreated to a hotel south of town; Chuck found a World War II documentary to pass out to at full volume, and I grumbled that we had waited too long to book our stay to get any online deals. One show in the books, budget busted, and our dreams of crowds flocking to shows felt severely stunted.

Most people, when they sleep, get disturbed by noise. Chuck is the opposite. He gets thrown off by silence ... or even moderate loudness. Everything must be screaming at once for him to sleep—the TV, the radio, his phone going off, and whatever else noisy he finds around him.

So, the dude is snoring away, and I'm thinking, *Well, as much as I want to learn about the battle of Midway, maybe I'll just turn it down a bit.*

Within moments, his eyes pop open. "What happened?"

"To what?"

"Turn the TV back up."

I raise the volume, and he's snoring again.

I pull a pillow over my ears and finally get myself to sleep.

BAM!

He decided it was time for a smoke, and he let the door slam.

I drift back to sleep.

Before his return-door-slam can wake me again, I hear the loudest boots in the business clomping down the hall.

The following day, we encountered more of the same at our show in Madison, Wisconsin. The only difference was their commencement parties were even bigger. Chuck was in a bad mood and sleepy.

He told me, "Listen, when we play, don't ever tell people to move up or to sing along. I hate when bands do that shit."

"It seemed like people wanted to sing, but they weren't sure how you'd react."

Chuck sucked down the Pabst drafts they had offered us. The bands all shared a huge plate of nachos, which was probably the only thing any of us had eaten that day.

Kurt Baron, a fan of Chuck's, had been fired that day from his job as a radio DJ. He cheered up Chuck and then put a lot of things into perspective for me. Here was a guy who should've had us buying him shots and consoling, but he felt more concerned with helping us instead.

Chuck didn't get any more pleasant on the way toward West Chicago the following morning; in fact, I felt happier when he slept. When we reached the club, I paced around the parking lot, knowing something was wrong with my bandmate. No one could possibly sleep this much.

Chuck awoke and discovered we had over five hours to kill before doors were set to open. He asked to borrow the car to find coffee.

He left.

I called Pip. "Chuck doesn't seem right. He's been sleeping for three days, sweating a lot, and he's cranky as hell."

She sighed. "Yeah, you should probably know, we found needles after you guys left. He's using again."

I thought of Chuck driving the rental car while on heroin. I headed to the gas station and coffee place he had mentioned wanting to stop at. To no one's surprise, no Chuck in sight. He also didn't answer his phone.

I walked around for about thirty minutes, before I saw my rental van swerving down the road, going about fifty-five. He flew right by.

I hustled to the club and got right in his face. "Dude, did you just go buy drugs?"

"What?" A scowl replaced his smile. "No! Why the fuck would you think that?"

"Because you've been gone for an hour, and I know you didn't go to get coffee or gas. You've been asleep and cranky and sweaty for three days. What the fuck is going on?"

"Um, no. They didn't have espresso and—"

"Chuck, don't fucking lie to me. I'm tempted to get in the car and drive home right now."

"Dude, calm down." He winced as if battling a hangover. "Okay, I went to go look for drugs, but I didn't find any.

I used right before we left, and I'm all out. I'm just trying to find something to get me right until we get home. We're not canceling this show."

"Can you even play?"

"Yeah. I just need a few drinks. When does this place open?"

"We'll play tonight, but you know I have to quit, right?"

He said nothing.

"You know I can't afford to get pulled over and you have drugs in the car or have you drive while messed up and crash. I can't ask my wife to work her ass off, watch the kids, and take care of the house while I'm out getting messed up in this shit."

"I know. I just got nervous about playing, and, when I get nervous, I do the dumbest thing possible. I won't do it anymore. I can't."

I loaded in while Chuck fell asleep in the club. I spoke to one of the opening bands. Their singer/drummer, a cool dude named Dug Smith, had long hair and an easy smile. He could tell I was upset, so he spent some time with me, which I appreciated.

The promoter couldn't attend, and the owner didn't arrive until late. He shorted us on our money—something I got used to real quick. The free food and drinks we had been promised didn't happen, and dammit, the Chicago area is expensive. How do you people afford to live there?

Chuck eventually rejoined the living, and fans surrounded him—not that I wanted to talk to the dude.

Before we played, he came onstage and eyed me with suspicion. He could tell I was still fuming.

He plugged in his guitar. "I love you, Doug. You know that, right?"

I nodded, and we played what I assumed constituted my last show with him.

Midsong, I glanced at the ceiling and saw thousands of red splotches, like they had held a mass sacrifice at the club. I scanned the stage and saw red everywhere. When I asked the crowd about it, I was told an industrial band had played the night before, and they had put fake blood in their long hair and headbanged, sending the blood flying.

After our set, the owner—who had now arrived—told Chuck he wanted to party with him.

I didn't argue. "I'm hungry. I'll stay here and get a burger. Call me when you're ready, but don't make it too late. We've got a seven-hour drive home."

I sat at the bar. "Can I get a—"

"Kitchen's closed."

I ordered a beer and sulked.

About an hour later, Chuck called me. "Hey, we went to this other place on the southside. I'll get you the address."

Half an hour goes by, nothing.

I call him back, nothing.

Finally, he calls. "Hey, where you at?"

"You never texted."

"Oh, shit. We left there anyway. Just come down by the corner of …"

Mapquest informed me I had a forty-mile drive to get to him, mostly back roads.

I stopped to get gas, and I bought a Cinnabon. Go ahead and judge, but I was pissed, and I wanted to take my anger out one sweet bite after another. It was stale.

Around 3:30 a.m., I found myself rolling down some shady-looking area.

Chuck texted me. *Hey, they recommended a hotel we could crash at.*

I punched in the address and realized the place was right next to me. It resembled every *Unsolved Mystery* episode all rolled into one. I looked up the hotel, and the reviews were scary. In one, they had found multiple splatters of blood, and in another, cops had gotten involved. Those were the best of the bunch.

I caught a glimpse of Chuck stumbling down the middle of the street through a cloud of fog toward me.

He asked, "Did you get that hotel info?"

I pointed. "Yeah. That's the place. They charge by the hour, and it's extra if you don't want to get stabbed. There's no way I'm staying there."

I drove us home, having been up about twenty-four hours straight and pissed-off for at least twenty-two of them. Our first run sucked, and I hated myself for agreeing to get involved. I assumed I was done, but my wife encouraged me when I got home. She reminded me that we knew it wasn't going to be easy and that he wasn't capable of doing it on his own.

After Chuck passed, Pip told me, "I found him laying in the bathroom after you guys got home. He had OD'd. I didn't grab the Narcan. I didn't even think to. I grabbed my camera and snapped a few photos of him lying there, and then I kicked him, hard. Probably saved his life with the kick. He jolted awake, obviously confused. When he had a chance to reorient, he asked me what happened. I showed him the pictures I took, and I offered to delete them, but he told me not to. He lied again and said it was a one-time thing—a reward for making it through the first run. I told him I knew he was lying. I couldn't prove it, but I knew, and the truth always comes out eventually."

Pip painted a canvas based on one of the photos she took of Chuck nodded-out in the bathroom.

I called Chuck a day or two later and told him I'd stay on, but he had to stay clean.

I said, "No drugs."

"I know."

"Be honest with me. You know I'll go to bat for you over anything, but I can't risk that. Don't lie to me."

But, as Chuck told Greg Prato for an interview on SongFacts, "This is who I am. An obnoxious loud-mouthed idiot. Don't care about shit, and don't take no shit."

CHAPTER FIVE

06/2016 - 07/2016: Two Oceans, Neither of Them Named Billy

As the Cleveland Cavaliers fought deep into the playoffs, Chuck and I left town for one of the worst-booked runs you can imagine. We had only eight shows in over two weeks, and we had to go completely across the country and back.

A hodge-podge collection of promoters, contacts, and fans without any logical oversight had organized the shows. Well-intentioned, but ultimately harmful, morale-killing, and bad enough that the tour almost ended…again.

We drove through the night, through nonstop rain, as Chuck completed some phone interviews, finally arriving in Dubuque, Iowa. The city sits right on the Mississippi, and it marked the first time I had ever driven west of the river. The only previous time I had crossed the Mississippi was on a family vacation to California twenty years earlier, but we had flown. I had picked up my first copy of *We Care a Lot* on CD in a bargain bin and saw House of Discipline, featuring Mike Patton, in concert on that trip.

Dubuque's temperature sat right at 100 degrees, and we had nowhere to hide.

Chuck asked that I drop him off at a city park so he could lay under a tree to sleep. I visited the baseball diamond and farm featured in the movie, *Field of Dreams*. I parked and 'Mosleyed' around town, listening to the birds chattering. Then I heard another familiar noise—amplified guitar.

I followed the sound to a fairground and saw a poster for the free show that night featuring three established 80's bands. I don't remember exactly who played, but I want to say Cheap Trick, Styx, and like, Foreigner, or someone similar.

We had an in-store appearance at a record shop that afternoon, but no one knew about it. I talked to the clerk at the store, and he had no idea Chuck had a show. That's never a good sign. In my travels around the city, I saw no posters, fliers, or any evidence of our concert. When we got to the club, they didn't even have us listed on their door. Eventually, they put up a dry-erase board to mention Chuck had a concert, though they spelled his name wrong.

We stood outside watching as the traffic completely backed up toward the fair. Sucks too because we played in the basement of an old building, and it felt about forty degrees cooler down there than outside.

The small crowd supported us with applause and cheered on Chuck when he admitted how nervous he felt. A few people had driven several hours from Kansas City. The club, cleverly named The Venue, was in an old wagon sales room. It had several dungeonlike chambers—a unique setting that, if packed, is probably a killer atmosphere.

After our set, we loaded the gear and took off, as our tour had us playing 950 miles away in Colorado Springs the next night. We drove eighteen hours straight, including a two-hour accident delay on Rt 25 between Denver and our destination, arriving in time for load-in. Okay, it wasn't straight through. We pulled over to sleep for a bit, and Chuck made sure we stopped at a weed dispensary after we had entered Colorado. Within minutes, I had a headache listening to people discuss fifty different strains of marijuana. Chuck, however, was a kid in a candy store. A dank candy store.

Jennifer, a high school buddy of Chuck's, attended the show that night. Since Chuck had never matured passed a fifteen-year-old level, it probably felt like no time had passed at all.

When I asked about her memories of Chuck, she said, "It was the time of sex, drugs, and The Animated!"

Doug Duffy from Cement and his wife Sasha showed up too! They go way back with Chuck. The first ten years of Chuck and me talking on the phone always started the same way:

Chuck: "Hello?"

Me: "Hey, it's Doug."

Chuck: "Duffy?"

Me: "No. Cleveland Doug."

This guy played drums on some of my favorite songs and toured the globe with one of my favorite bands. Now I was trying to use a single conga to convey what he did on his kit.

I asked Doug recently about that show. "When we walked into the club and saw Chuck, I knew he was hurting. We talked a lot about it. Sasha and I were so happy to see him. We always stayed in touch, and sometimes a year or two would go by, but every time we spoke, it would be like we never stopped. He and I told each other the truth. We were buds forever. I miss my friend."

Chuck asked him to come up and play. He took over conga duties on "Tractor," while I played some hand percussion I had borrowed from another band on the bill.

Doug said, "I had a blast sitting in on a song, even though I hate playing congas."

I asked Doug what he loved about his time in Cement, and he told me, "Chuck always liked to go into new territory with music, like a Patsy Cline cover to hardcore punk to reggae to metal. We always tried new stuff live, ready or not, and sometimes it ended up being a beautiful train wreck!"

The following morning, Chuck woke up early and got on the phone. He had decided to try and get info about his birth mother while we drove out west. Over the next week, he spent a lot of time calling various adoption agencies, only to be told they had closed and that he needed to call someone else. He spent hours on hold, only to hear bad news.

Chuck has four modes of life: asleep, onstage, cooking, or on hold.

As soon as his eyes would open, he'd start dialing the phone.

He'd cough. "Gotta call the electric company and see if they'll delay turning off our power until tomorrow."

I'd say, "Damn, can't believe they're so quick on the trigger."

"Right? I'm only late a month."

I'd shake my head.

Then, he'd explain, "Well, like, I haven't paid the bill in four months, but last month she told me if I put something down within a few days I'd be square. I didn't have anything to give, so I told her I'd call her back. We've been on the road though."

Yes, for three whole days.

Non-stop, Chuck jumped from issue to issue. Electric company, gas, rent, water, ASCAP loans, other loans, and he even had to borrow my phone at times because, you guessed it, they disconnected his phone as well.

When his phone wasn't shut off, he would borrow my charger because he lost his … even though he wore it as a necklace. We bought chargers every couple of days.

I felt crazy listening to his chaos—and you can go ahead and blame addictions and drugs but talk to anyone who knew him as a kid, and they'll tell you it's how Chuck has always operated. He spent so much time chasing after his messes that he never had time or energy to get caught up, let alone ahead.

We accepted Chris Kniker's invitation for lunch in Denver. He treated us to an all-you-can-eat seafood buffet.

I hate seafood. I get sick from just smelling it. I also weigh 300 pounds, and I didn't want to be rude. I attacked the buffet, no holds barred. I shoveled down so many things I had never tried before, and I did it with a smile. To top off the meal, Chris and I ate the place fresh out of beignets.

Chuck calculated his every bite. "Well, the gumbo looks more like a soup. When I make it …"

His commentary could've taught me a lot, but my entire body felt too full to do anything but hate itself.

On our way to the club, a couple cars collided in front of us. Before I brought the car to a complete stop, Chuck had hopped out, lit a smoke, and headed to inspect the accident. One of the cars looked crushed, but everyone apparently escaped without serious injury.

My stomach gurgled.

By the time the ambulance arrived and the police took reports, I had my own emergency. The only thing crappier than my stomach that day was the turnout. The promoter went above and beyond, getting us food and a room at this crazy fancy hotel right across from the club. After our show, Chuck and I went to a death-metal concert and saw a band from one of the Dakotas.

We woke up the following day, Monday, and our next show wasn't until Thursday.

Days off on the road are killers. No incoming money means everything you do is bleeding you dry, and the next gig was over 1200 miles away.

Chuck took the wheel, driving a couple crazy long stretches, including our time through the Rockies. I stared at the passing scenery, my first time seeing the monstrous mountains up close. I was even enthralled enough by the views that I almost didn't register the dozens of close calls Chuck got us into and out of as we twisted and swerved through Colorado.

When I took over and drove us into Utah, I was stunned by the massive and stark landscape. It's like nothing I've ever seen.

Chuck peered ahead. "Hey, what is that?"

Going the 80-mph speed limit (and not one mile over, Steve Kalogiros), I shook my head.

Chuck said, "Looks like a bald eagle."

As if on cue, the bird rose off the street, revealing a huge carcass beneath it. The bird flapped, trying to lift the entire chunk of meat as we sped closer. Finally, it lifted off the ground, meat and all, as we cruised under it.

Around 5 a.m. the following morning, we stopped for gas and saw a casino next door.

Chuck asked, "Wanna take a break and gamble a bit?"

I shrugged. "I don't have any money, but I'll watch. I'd love to get out of the car."

Chuck sat at a blackjack table while I people-watched. He played for several hands, I think up by forty or fifty bucks. Eventually, he came back down to earth and lost the money.

We pulled into Tacoma after driving for hours in the rain. Chuck had done a huge stretch, including some bad traffic jams. We stayed with Chuck's wife's high-school friend's older sister and her family—so basically, complete strangers. The Glassmans couldn't have treated us better.

Chuck, exhausted from the drive, fell asleep on their couch shortly after we arrived and proceeded to sleep for a full day. I hung out with the family, hiked in a nearby park and played a game with them called Blockus.

When Chuck woke up, he demanded we go to the grocery store so he could get ingredients to make crab cakes, and then, when we returned with the food, he fell back asleep, so Diana Glassman had to make them. I didn't know until afterward that she followed a strict vegan diet, so I felt awful that she had to handle and smell the crab all day. I don't even think Chuck ate any, so they went in the fridge to stink it up. I tried helping with some yard work to show my appreciation for letting us stay several nights, but I think I made more of a mess than anything. Diana helped me get off my duff on hikes.

Shortly after we left, I found out she was battling cancer. We spoke a few times, and she had such a positive outlook. In 2017, as we pulled in front of that night's club in Reno, I got a message that she had passed away. Chuck was in a bad mood, as a meeting with his sister hadn't panned out earlier in the day, but I didn't want to keep the knowledge from him. Selfishly, I think I didn't want to grieve on my own. I sat next to him at the bar, ordered us each a shot of whiskey and a beer and told him the awful news. We toasted Diana through tears. Sure, I had only known her for a few days, but she was a stand-up person with a wonderful family.

Our West Coast run of dates ran up and down and up and down Route 5 in heavy traffic. In Eugene, the club tried to charge us for room rental when the promoter didn't show up. In Everett, Washington, we got shorted. I think that was the night they tricked us into thinking we had a hotel room, but by the time we knew better, they were off the grid.

As I was eating at the club and perusing Twitter, I saw someone had tweeted that they would buy a drink to the first person who came to the show and introduced themselves. I peered around and realized the guy was sitting at the next table over.

"Doug?" I asked.

Doug Miller glanced up. "Yeah."

"I saw your tweet. Glad to meet another Chuck fan."

"Yeah man, I see you're eating, but do you mind if I sit down?"

I welcomed him.

He was a realtor, a family man, and a huge baseball fan. He had visited every Major League park to see a game—and tons of minor league parks as well. I, of course, told him Jacob's Field (Progressive Field) is the best.

Chris Cornell, vocalist for Soundgarden, had embarked on his own solo tour, so every time we'd pull into a town, we'd see billboards and ads for an upcoming show, sometimes for the same night. It was tough for Chuck to see one of his old friends riding such a huge wave of success, as he didn't even have lunch money. Not that Chuck got angry, but maybe a bit jealous. Especially since Chris performed "Nothing Compares 2 U," made famous by Sinead O' Conner—a song he had long wanted to cover.

The following day, we drove around town trying to track down a batch of shirts at a FedEx location before heading south to Portland for a show. When we arrived at the club, we discovered the main support had dropped off the bill, the chalkboard outside had Chuck's name spelled wrong, and an all-weekend metal fest occupied the club's larger room.

Our set was still chaos to me. To Chuck it was the status quo. Who needed set lists or songs that ended when they were supposed to end? We were still throwing in random bits of this and that to see what worked and what didn't. One tune, "King Arthur" by Cement, always went over well. It's a forty-second-long song that Chuck did on his own until we kicked in together during a start/stop outro. We would sometimes drag out the chaotic noise for several minutes, much longer than the actual song itself. It wasn't preplanned, so each night, the song sounded different. Chuck would try and throw me off or make me hit my conga when he refrained from playing the note. I won't ever claim to be a professional percussionist, but I got good at the fast-paced drum rolls, and I could get some cool sounds out of my conga at times.

That night we stayed at Chuck's old friend, Leo's house. Leo is a big, tall, strong, humorous dude who had once (or twice) saved Chuck's life. Chuck told me that he and Leo were out and about, and someone stabbed Chuck. Leo pulled Chuck from the crowd and got him to a hospital.

I fell asleep to them catching up and watching a documentary about Bob Forrest and Thelonious Monster. After Portland, Chuck started calling me Leo by mistake, because he said I reminded him so much of his old friend.

The last day out west, we got into Seattle early, around noon. I took off to explore while Chuck headed to the Capitol Hill area with his friend Amy, who had printed fliers for the show.

Outside the venue, I was chatting with Chuck and Mathew Murphy—a fan who had traveled a ways to see the show—and Chuck's eyes went wide. He called out a hello to a man approaching.

Mark Bowen, the guitarist for Faith No More when Chuck had joined the band, approached with a goatee and a flat cap. We asked him if he'd come up and play with us. Wisely, he proved too smart for that, ha. They caught up and talked about their time together in the band. From what I gathered, Mark never saw himself as a permanent guy in Faith No More, as he had other projects, and it wasn't his main thing.

The band had so many people come and go as they evolved, but they named a song after him, so he must've made some sort of impression. Chuck always told me the lyrics were kind of everything Mark was not. Chuck saw Mark as a standup dude, "an ethereal, cerebral guitarist." Mark sent me a version of the song he had recorded himself, performing all the instruments and singing. It has a laid-back, psychedelic feel Chuck would've loved.

As I set up our equipment that night, one eye on a TV showing the Cavaliers in game seven of the championship, Chuck poked his head through the front door, right next to the stage.

"Hey. So, listen. Someone asked me if I wanted to smoke a joint, so I took a hit, and then they told me they laced with something. I think PCP. I can't play, dude."

I saw the craziness in his eyes and genuine worry, but I had no idea what the fuck I could do in that situation. I froze. My heart rate rose.

Chuck grinned. "Eh, just kidding. We ready?" He giggled.

I exhaled and called him a few names, which I'm not ready for my kids to learn yet. "Yeah, we're set up. Let's play."

"Eh, give me a few minutes. I'm gonna smoke." He closed the door before I responded.

The Cavs won their first championship. I blubbered like an idiot. No one there cared, but I floated over the moon. I met a super-nice couple before the show who originally lived in Beaumont, Texas but stayed out here now. They rooted for the Cavs with me. After the show, Chuck and I snapped a photo with them; that is my favorite photo of me and him.

The next morning, we started a forty-nine-hour journey straight to Cleveland by stopping at a dispensary so Chuck could get one last peek at all the marijuana Washington had to offer.

Chuck sucked to drive with. To take the wheel, he needed super-strong coffee, snacks, tea, music blasting at an insane level, and smoke breaks every thirty minutes or less. It's next to impossible to get any rest as he drives because he speeds and swerves and talks on the phone and anything aside from responsibly operating a vehicle. I remember once on that trip waking up and feeling seasick only to find Chuck speeding in circles around a truck stop, because he couldn't find the exit to the street.

"Chuck, it's a truck stop. There is no exit."

It took a few more spins before he believed me.

He never understood the difference between an exit or a rest area, and he had some of the worst intuition about which exit to take for gas, restrooms, food, or coffee. We could pass three exits in a row with huge signs for the multiplex everything-under-the-sun places, but he'd wait to pull off at the dark exit with a gas station that had closed in '83.

The only time we considered detouring on the way home was to see The Devil's Tower, but it sat another hour off Rt 80, and neither of us wanted to add more time onto our journey. We arrived home on Wednesday, the morning of the parade for the Cavaliers. I tried to get downtown, but it was a mob scene. I settled for an awesome afternoon nap on the couch with my daughter.

That weekend, Chuck and I loaded into a van for our show outside South Bend, Indiana. The three-hour trip took six hours due to multiple accidents. Donn Wobser was coming to the show, and we kept calling each other with various ideas to avoid traffic, but nothing worked. They closed Rt 80 in two spots and then had us get back on only to detour back off.

One of the openers asked Chuck to sing a version of "Chinese Arithmetic" with them. Chuck typically said *no* to these requests, since he hadn't performed or practiced those songs in years, but since it wasn't "We Care a Lot"—the song 99.9% of the people wanted to do—he said *yes*.

I remember a couple guys from one of the openers being dicks about how Chuck hid in the corner with his band rather than being social with the fans. Little did they know that the people he hung with weren't in his band, just friends and fans. They topped off their ignorance by leaving as soon as they finished playing and talked trash online, which hurt us the following year when we tried to book anther gig in the area. Btw, your band sucks.

After the show, they hosted karaoke downstairs. We hung around drinking a bit and watching. Chuck didn't think highly of the spectacle. Within a year, however, his opinion would change.

We drove home that night.

"Chuck, we have to make more money. This leg bankrupted us."

"I know. I can't believe we had so many days off."

"I'm worried about July. There's only a few dates booked. I need to make money."

He groaned. "Add it to the list of shit I need to deal with."

"I'll start putting out feelers to see if I can add more shows."

We got home, and I went to work. Paul Simisky helped us fill three nights; the band Dead by Wednesday got us a few shows, and we got an email that saved our tour.

I called Chuck. "Hey, this club on Long Island is offering us $1,500 to play a Tuesday night. They asked that we play a free show at a record shop the day before."

"Really?"

"Yeah, I'm going to call and feel them out, but that'll cover our rental and gas and a couple hotel rooms for sure."

I communicated with the club, giving them as accurate a feel for what size crowds we were seeing, and I even offered to take less or not headline if it would leave more to help them promote the show, but they declined, comfortable with the deal.

Chuck slept the entire seven or so hours to the first show—a free appearance at a record shop in Kutztown, Pennsylvania. The town had a sizable college, but being July, all we saw were tumbleweeds as we arrived. Chuck slept until the moment we went onstage. The storeowner had hired a recording engineer to capture the show for a possible seven-inch vinyl release, but I guess Chuck's lack of socializing torpedoed that.

Not that he didn't mingle. After our set, he signed autographs and took photos with whoever asked, but he climbed back into the car as soon as the club cleared. I accompanied the owner and promoter for food and a beer, but I got a separate check.

We drove that night to Philadelphia to stay with my buddy Terry and his wife. I laid on the floor, inches from their brand-new puppy and four cats, who had no interest in sleeping.

We did three dates with Dead by Wednesday, and I talked to them as much as I did Chuck. They were doing their first dates with their new singer, Rob, and a new guitarist, Marc Rizzo of Soulfly. I could watch that dude play for hours. Their drummer, Opus, was the band's driving force and a great dude. He actually played guitar on this run.

After the dates with them, Chuck and I had two nights in New Jersey. These were the first nights that felt like people cared about what we were doing. The crowd at Dingbatz in Clifton got loud and rowdy, making seventy people sound like a few hundred.

Anne D'Agnillo—of "Anne's Song" fame—brought her husband, Rick, and a few friends to see us. They helped run the merch booth, boosting sales five-fold.

After the show, I floated on air to a bar run by Anthony, the singer of the band Long Gone Day, who were playing with us the following night. Stephanie, the band's manager, invited us to stay with them at their hotel. We met them there in the afternoon the following day in Long Branch, New Jersey. She helped us organize our merch, roll our t-shirts for better storage, and gave us a small blackboard to post our prices rather than using the paper scrap with handwritten scribbles.

Johnny B. Morbid invited Chuck to cover "As the Worms Turns" with them. They performed it closer to the Patton-era version, but Chuck knocked it out of the park in front of a stunned and appreciative audience. After the show, David Austin posted a video he had taken with his phone and commented, "The moment must've been special, as even Chuck's conga player taped it."

Jane's Addiction were playing fifteen minutes down the road that night. Just like Chris Cornell's tour shadowing ours in June, here was another group of guys Chuck grew up with, playing in front of thousands as he performed in bars.

Once again, the energy felt awesome, and we carried it back to the hotel, where we stayed up until the sun rose and got locked out of our room. The motel ran out of cups, and I'll never forget Anthony drinking coffee from a bowl.

Chuck and I stopped by the convenience store from *Clerks* before driving into New York City.

Chuck lit a cigarette and glanced around. "It's too fucking hot."

It was one of only two or three times I had ever heard him complain about heat.

"We should go see a movie. It'll be air-conditioned in the theater."

"Maybe."

We walked to Thompkins Square Park and found Doc Holliday's, a bar that definitely wasn't air-conditioned. I checked the movie schedule, but the only thing both of us had any interest in was *Ghostbusters*. Now that we had drinks though, a movie felt less appealing.

Chuck told me stories about various trouble he had gotten into with Flea from the Red Hot Chili Peppers and how every time he saw Anthony Kiedis he felt like he had to reintroduce himself because "it seemed like Anthony never remembered me. It was the same way with Angelo from Fishbone. Norwood and I grew up together, so we were cool, but Angelo …"

I mentioned something about the disdain between Faith No More and the Red Hot Chili Peppers.

"Hell no!" he said. "I love those dudes. I love Flea. I loved Hillel."

And that's when the shit hit the fan.

I don't recall if the news came via text, an email, Facebook message, or a call, but somehow, we learned that the club on Long Island had canceled our Tuesday show. Bye-bye $1,500 guarantee. Bye-bye budget. I know I say that a lot in this book, but get used to it, 'cause this isn't the last time.

We started scrambling to figure out what had happened, but everyone told a different story. The club wouldn't call us back. The guy who had initially contacted us stepped away, not wanting to be involved.

I wrote a nasty post on Facebook, which pissed off someone who claimed one thing, while Chuck told me a different story, and I remembered different details. To this day, I don't know what the hell happened. I get it that presale numbers might've been low. Again, we never expected that big of a guarantee, and we would've happily finagled something to keep the show, but we never got that option. Every club and every show comes with positives and negatives, risks and rewards, but the shenanigans they pulled felt dirty. The tour could've ended that day.

Greg Prato, an author responsible for a dozen books on rock music, stepped in. He had a buddy who ran a bar on Long Island. We switched our show there and then had about two days to promote. Chuck met with Roddy Bottum, his former bandmate in Faith No More, while I explored New York City. I wanted to see Lora Zombie's art opening that afternoon, but I got turned around and knew that by the time I would cross the correct bridge, I'd miss the show. Just as I could never survive in Chicago with all the food options, in NYC, I'd constantly be rushing from concert to art show to book reading to whatever—so much cool stuff in one place.

Our free show that Monday at the record store didn't bring out the crowds, but once again, aside from the store ordering VUA albums to sell, it appeared no one knew we were coming, and no one had promoted the appearance. I know in this day and age of social media the artist is expected to help, which we did, but that doesn't mean a promoter gets completely off the hook. The store didn't receive fliers, presale tickets, or any info from the club.

As I loaded in, I met King Chivas. His real name is … I have no idea; I call him King to this day. He knows a lot about wrestling, and he plays bass. He ended up joining our ranks the following year.

Greg Prato had begun work on a book about Bad Brains, so he and Chuck set up time to talk down the road.

The following afternoon, Roddy joined us as we headed to the rescheduled concert.

Roddy is laid back to the extreme, casual, and he sported a disarming smile under his NY hat. He fits the exact stereotype I had been spoon-fed of every southern California surfer. Though I have no idea if Roddy has ever ridden a board himself, my instincts tell me he could've had a roll in *Point Break*, if interested.

He and Chuck had messaged back and forth about playing a song or two or three together. I had suggested the Imperial Teen song, "The Beginning," as I felt Chuck and I could do the backing vocals and follow Roddy's lead on the instrumentation.

As we pulled into the club, Roddy said, "I was thinking about the song, 'Butch.' by Imperial Teen. Does that work?"

With no strategy, no planning, and no soundcheck, we flew by the seat of our pants, like always. Chuck and I had nothing to lose. Our show had already been canceled. No one had high expectations, so we couldn't really crash and burn. For Roddy, he risked us making him look like a fool if we stumbled onstage.

The crowd got amped. Not only did they get to meet and hang with Anne, of "Anne's Song," but the keyboardist and ex-vocalist of Faith No More as well. And me too, of course.

Roddy grabbed Chuck's guitar and sat on a stool.

He admitted to the patrons, "I've never sat on a chair and sung into a microphone and played guitar to a crowd of people in my life."

I stood next to him, legs shaking. I'd heard the song a lot but had never played it before. And, yeah, I hear you. *It's just a conga, so who gives a shit?* You're right, but I was still nervous.

Roddy continued, "This is my very first time. I've never done anything like this, so bear with me."

The crowd cheered.

Roddy said, "No, it's gonna be great—I shouldn't say that. It's gonna be awesome. Thanks, you guys." He played the opening four notes and then paused. "Hold on, wait."

I felt like I was onstage with two Chucks.

He continued, "You know how you go see a band and they play the opening chords to a song and it's familiar to everybody? You hear that first chord, and everybody goes, 'Oh ya!' It's a big recognizable thing. I know you don't know this song, but it would help me—"

The crowd cheered, and a few people said they knew it.

"Oh, you do?" Roddy asked. "Okay, cool. Well, I'm just asking you all, when you hear these first opening chords that I play, if you could all do that, just, like, scream like you know it well. It would make me feel, as a performer, more welcome and more comfortable. And, I think, I'll do a better job if that goes down." He started over. "I'm going to play a song by my other band, Imperial Teen. It's a song called 'Butch.'"

The crowd cheered.

"You kind of jumped the queue a little bit, but it's cool. We can still do this. So, it starts like this."

He played the opening riff, and the crowd roared.

I felt certain the percussion came in after the second time through the riff, but Roddy started tapping his knee after the first, and I thought maybe I had missed my mark. My throat tightened. I couldn't breathe, but I waited.

A moment later, I joined in as we launched into the song. Now, launched is probably too boisterous of a word, us being an acoustic act and all, but we were on our way—however you want to word it.

Roddy has a great voice—calm, powerful, relaxing—and yet his lyrics are pointed, intense. When we reached the bridge, Chuck leaned over my shoulder to add backing vocals. We hadn't discussed us singing at all, so I was petrified Roddy would get pissed if I joined in. Chuck was his buddy and could get away with it. Me, I was just a dude he was tolerating because I helped Chuck. I had no perceptions that this made me jumping in okay. The problem was Chuck forgot the words.

During a buildup, Chuck attempted to sing one word, and he was off time. He must've felt nervous or bashful, so he quickly retreated to the back of the stage. I thought if Roddy heard the out-of-nowhere singing, he would turn and just see me. Thanks, Chuck.

We reached the refrain and again Chuck stood at my side, and once again he froze. I tried to mouth the words to him—damn I wanted to sing that part; it's so catchy and fun to belt out. Chuck disappeared behind me.

During the breakdown, I nailed the part I wanted to nail, so from there I thought everything else was gravy. I joined in singing at the end, figuring the worst they could do by that point is finish the song and tell me I sucked. Speaking of the end of the tune, I was having so much fun I had forgotten to count along to know when the ending was coming—and that's assuming Roddy would play it just as it sounded on the album.

I watched him for a clue as I sang and drummed and soaked in the excitement from the crowd. We ended clean. Awesome.

Afterward, we brought up a couple people from the crowd for a train wreck of a rendition of "Bizarre Love Triangle" by New Order.

With Roddy, Anne, and their friend, Jean, watching the merch booth, we had the best night yet on the road. I think our best night we had ever.

After NYC, we got into a groove as we played some weird venues: a hair salon, a sushi bar, a private party deep in the woods that got shut down during a storm, and finally, a ski lodge. Seventeen shows in eighteen nights. It did our chemistry a world of good. It felt like a real tour. I felt like a musician, almost.

The last show of the run we opened for Thee Ice Picks, a fun surf rock band, and Daikaiju, one of the best live acts on the road. I couldn't believe how smooth things had gone. Two months without a hint of drugs; we sold some t-shirts, and the club in Burlington, Vermont gave us a room, dinner, and drinks.

Chuck suddenly had to get home. He insisted we leave right after we played and then cut our set short.

He gave me the old, "Get us out of the mountains, and then I'll take over."

We took off around midnight, twisting and turning down the foggy road. Chuck snored the whole way into New York, only waking once or twice to scream in panic when he opened his eyes and couldn't see pavement in front of us.

When we switched driving duties, I was drained. I fell asleep almost instantly. I woke up a short while later to find us parked in front of a random house. Chuck snored in the driver's seat.

"Fine. I'll take back over, but, dude, I didn't even want to leave."

"Huh?" He woke up. "No, I'm good. I just wanted a smoke."

He got us back on the road, and I fell back to sleep.

Thirty minutes later, I awoke to find us stopped again, this time on the side of the highway.

"Chuck, get out of the car and let me drive."

"Okay." He shrugged. "I wanted a quick break, but if you're ready, go ahead."

The day after we got home, Chuck's family called me to say they had busted Chuck doing drugs.

CHAPTER SIX

08/2016:
New Re-Beginnings

Working with Chuck always meant dreading the other shoe to drop. I hate to say it, but the thought never left my mind that further disaster waited around the next corner, ready to derail everything. Even as Chuck and I pulled up to Faith No More's practice space, I had my doubts that a rehearsal would happen.

Can you blame me?

Chuck tended to shoot himself in the foot as the best things were about to happen. He shied away from the biggest moments, like when he fell apart in front of thousands of prospective fans while opening for Korn and blamed technical difficulties. Over the years, he stockpiled various excuses to justify these self-sabotaging events to protect his reputation and, even more important, to safeguard his fragile ego.

I've often said I could write a book full of the various times I've watched Chuck squander opportunities, end friendships, betray business partnerships, and even alienate bandmates all to avoid the stress he puts on himself—well, here we are, right?

But Chuck's neuroses became a part of his persona, his style. His weaknesses and nerves bled into his art, naked and genuine. He could sing about anything and yet listeners picked up on his doubt, his hopelessness, and his desire for acceptance peppered within the thinly veiled gibberish he often claimed had no organized meaning.

I think that quality, above all else, proved why he and I stood outside a chain-link fence in Oakland, California calling for "Billy!" and "Mike!" to let us in.

Faith No More didn't earn a following because Chuck wowed audiences with his golden pipes. Mordam Records didn't sign the band while Chuck hustled and outworked singers from other bands. Chuck didn't carve out a career in music due to his good looks and pleasant attitude. He was a blue-collar everyman who climbed onstage to couple his nerves, paranoia, and absent-professor spaciness with a David Bowie-esque rock-god persona. He constantly battled against the internal screams telling him he wasn't good enough, and no one, save perhaps Bowie himself, could relate to his contradictions.

Chuck is rocking a pair of well-worn Dickies, a t-shirt he's worn for about a week straight, and a long-sleeved flannel, proclaiming, "It ain't about pretty"—part of his sister-in-law's girl-power-themed skateboard fashion line. It's been his attire for most of the summer. Not surprising, as he only brought a half-full book bag packed with one other pair of pants (that he claims he can't find), a second undershirt, clean (I assume) underwear, and a few packs of smokes. He and I just completed a two-day trek across the United States—Cleveland to Oakland—blasting Led Zeppelin the entire way, and even with gaining three hours due to crossing time zones, both of us are exhausted.

We left on Saturday, August 13, later in the day than I had planned due to the typical Chuck nonsense, like he lost all his guitar picks. As soon as we reached the highway, the skies opened and dumped huge raindrops on us as we traversed the western farmlands of northern Ohio. It didn't let up until we took a break on the Illinois border.

We took a three-hour detour, so Chuck could stop at a diner in Denver someone had raved about.

Chuck parks wherever he wants. In this case, he parked across the parking lot entrance to the diner, blocking anyone who wanted to eat. He also left his door wide open. Oh by the way, he didn't even eat, because all he really wanted was to stop at a pot dispensary he had liked the last time we were in town. #DickMoveMosley

The best part of the midsummer drive was exiting the mountains into Cali, where the humidity finally relinquished its grasp, and it felt like the temperature dropped thirty degrees in …

Wait, skip back a few paragraphs. Did I say we're practicing with Faith No More?

Yes, I'm exhausted, but I'm also mired in a fog of disbelief. They are my favorite band of all time. No teacher, friend, job, religion, or family member shaped my formative years more than this band, and I'm about to get welcomed into their private sanctuary.

It's Tuesday, August 16, 2016, at 11 a.m. Though we took a wrong turn or two along the way, Chuck and I manage to arrive on time, a rarity for us. Chuck, of course, hasn't charged his phone, so we can't call the guys to let us into the gated area.

I'm leaning against our rental car—even though it's molten hot underneath California's summer sun—because, a week earlier, I busted my knee in a mosh pit at a Dog Fashion Disco concert. Chuck is having a field day, calling me "Gramps," "Gimpy," and "Hop-along." Up until the day before we left,

I still wasn't sure I could physically get my leg to bend enough to fit in the car. I borrowed a pair of crutches from my mom's friend's sister and wore a brace to hold the kneecap in place.

A car pulls up. Chuck and I exchange a glance, hoping the driver isn't looking for trouble, as we seem to attract it. Unfortunately, the driver loves causing mischief.

Chuck says, "Hey, Roddy. I forgot the code to the gate."

Having shared the stage with him on a song and having slept at his house last month, you'd expect some of the butterflies in my stomach to dissipate, but … uh, it's *Roddy Bottum*!

Roddy notices my crutches. "What happened to you?"

"Oh, these are just for decoration. It's the new fad in Cleveland."

"*Whaaat?*"

He calls over the fence. A moment later, Mike Bordin opens the gate for us.

We enter a parking lot lined by plant life that wouldn't last a month in Cleveland's temperate climate. It's like being on the set of *Star Trek* when they're taken to a secret base on an alien planet. Figures, I left my phaser at home for this trip.

Chuck and Mike hug and catch up as I grab my book bag and a water bottle. Roddy steps inside the practice studio to unpack a brand-new keyboard he got for the two shows the members of Faith No More will be playing with Chuck this week.

Mike extends a hand to me. "Where're you from?"

"Cleveland."

Mike grins. "Then you probably know Chris Andrews and The Spudmonsters."

Shocked how obscure names like those just rolled off his tongue, I raise my eyebrow. "Wow, yeah. I don't know Chris personally, but I go way back with that band. Actually, Eric

[Mathews], their drummer, also drummed for Chuck's band VUA for a time."

Mike nods. "And, of course, you have The Phantasy. Is that club still around?"

"Ayup." Normally talkative, I'm completely floored this is happening, so excuse the lack of quality conversation on my end, folks.

Mike has an inquisitive expression that makes talking to him easy, like you know he actually cares what you have to say. "Does it still have that pirate ship inside?"

Faith No More played there thirty years ago. Since then, Mike has played thousands of shows around the world with Faith No More, Ozzy Osbourne, Black Sabbath, Korn, and Jerry Cantrell, so the fact he recalls a club on the outskirts of a city like mine speaks volumes for his attention to detail and passion for what he's doing. Either that or he has someone feeding him info via a small earpiece, and I'm on some *Truman Show*-type reality program.

The rehearsal space sits in a warehouse sectioned off into several smaller units. As far as I can tell, Faith No More have the only private entrance and parking. The ceilings are high and bare, save a few decorations, so I can't imagine it was an easy task for Bill to record an album in here. Perhaps they installed temporary soundproofing? I notice a small enclosure behind Bill's rig that could be used as an isolation booth. From what I remember reading, Mike Patton recorded his vocals for their latest disc, *Sol Invictus*, at his own studio.

Jon Hudson, guitarist of Faith No More since 1997, sets up an elaborate pedal board as we enter the purple-walled practice area. He makes a point of standing up to exchange hellos with both me and Chuck before returning his attention to a maze of connector cables and effects pedals.

This will be his first time playing many of the older songs live. Now, joining a band and bringing your own style is tough enough, but, learning guitar riffs from a back catalog of forty-plus songs that at least three different guitarists had written and striking a balance between honoring their input while offering your own, is next level. And, remember, this band thrives on changing styles from album to album, and they revel in incorporating various genres from song to song. Go ahead and tell me how this guy isn't top notch again?

Mike Bordin and his friend set up an emerald-green drum kit, which Mike mentions he's only played once before at an in-store appearance at Amoeba Records in 2015. They played a four-song set, including one cut from the Chuck Mosley era—"As the Worm Turns."

Bill Gould arrives riding a vintage-looking motorcycle (truth be told, I know absolutely nothing about them, so it could just as easily have been built that morning). He's wearing a shopworn helmet that, without a doubt, has seen some serious action. He blows through the room with a rapid word for everyone. The mood shifts when Bill enters, no doubt about it. Not negatively, but … it's almost like when a well-liked teacher enters a classroom, alerting the students who have been hanging out that it's time for class. Bill commands an intense presence. Though he is friendly and genuinely interested in catching up with everyone, Bill wants to finish the work on his plate first. He heads to the far end of the room to examine his bass rig.

As he tinkers, Mike—

(Author's note: Through the years, the press, his fans, and his bandmates have called Mike Bordin Puffy—even earning the nickname a mention in the lyrics to "Cuckoo for Caca." However, Chuck asked me not to call him this as Mike didn't like the nickname. I managed not to call him that once throughout the week, a fact I'm

proud of as I am terrible with names, and I've been calling him Puffy for thirty years.)

So, as Bill tinkers with his bass amp and Mike sets up his drums and Jon checks his pedals and Roddy unpacks his keyboard, Chuck paces alone, stewing and second-guessing.

My stomach, already fluttering with excitement, clenches. When Chuck has time to overthink things, it often trips him up. And practicing with his old band represents *the* ultimate thing for him to overthink.

You see, Chuck has suffered from recurring nightmares since his firing from Faith No More back in 1988. In the nightmare, the band asks him to join them onstage to perform, but he blanks on all the lyrics, and he hides behind some amps rather than face the crowd. For a guy who has had decades to ask himself "What if?" *ad infinitum* while reading in the press what a great move it was to dump him, this is poison.

According to Chuck, the dream's most haunting part is the look of disappointment Bill gives him while shaking his head. The reasons for that are many. Bill and Chuck's friendship originated well before Faith No More. The two punk rockers soaked up L.A.'s exploding punk scene during its prime, and, maybe even more influentially, they witnessed the aftermath as punk splintered into dozens of new directions. Hell, they helped shape that second (third?) wave of punk. Bill is a friend and a surrogate older brother as well as an ex-bandmate. Seeing how he's the *de facto* leader/dad of the band, Chuck also has an urge to please him and make him proud. Chuck has an ego, so a part of him also wants to perform so well that Bill gets forced to question whether sacking Chuck was a mistake.

He's never had a better chance than this week.

Over the past twenty-eight years, Chuck has joined Faith No More onstage twice, with varying degrees of success. I already mentioned San Francisco in 2010, and the second happened in Detroit on May 8 of 2015. While driving to that show, Chuck texted back and forth with Roddy to let him know he was coming. He dangled out there that if they wanted him to jump onstage, he would. Roddy said, "Sure." Chuck suggested the song "Mark Bowen," because it's one of his favorites, and he and I had just that week finished writing an essay about that song for inclusion into the anthology *A Matter of Words* from Scout Media.

After they decided Chuck would sing, the nerves hit so bad that he asked me to turn the car around, because he became convinced he had left his front door wide open.

Faith No More had performed "Mark Bowen" on occasion since they reunited in 2009, so Roddy texted a confirmation. I expressed worry that it was a tough song to pull off live, as only a few scarce musical cues existed between the verses and choruses to keep track of the vocal placement. Chuck scoffed at this, but he had a hard time keeping up when I played it a few times in the car. We all got a little nervous.

For brevity's sake, let's say Chuck's performance underwhelmed, even though his fans in the crowd, like myself, were almost in tears seeing him onstage with Faith No More. To showcase how nervous he was: my wife had to help him redress because he had put on the white stage uniform on backward.

Bottom line—Chuck stands here at practice after years of buildup, and I can see he's feeling it. Jon moves Chuck's mic to the center of the room, so everyone can hear him … assess him … judge him.

I sit back and watch it unfold, content to take a back seat after months of stress keeping the tour going, content to witness my own personal concert by my favorite band of all time. *Ho-ly* shit.

Chuck wanders toward the mic but then retreats toward a piano bench to bury his face in a notebook to study lyrics.

Jon stands, flips a switch, and presses a pedal or two and his guitar comes to life. It's a thick, ballsy sound, yet clean. He noodles a few riffs from the *We Care a Lot* songs, peering at his pedals with furrowed brows.

One riff is the intro to "Greed." Now, I am terrible at song titles, so even though I'm a huge Faith No More fan, I sometimes mix up song names or even give them my own, but "Greed" is one of the tracks I have the hardest time remembering. In fact, Chuck and I spent a few hours on the drive across the country trying to remember what it was called while listening to it.

I know Faith No More fans are reading this dumbstruck at my forgetfulness. Inexcusable, sure, but here are my excuses: My *We Care a Lot* CD sported several scratches, which caused major skips on "Why Do You Bother?" and made "Greed" almost unlistenable. For the younger readers, you'll have to imagine our Neanderthal world, back before the internet, when every song wasn't bootlegged for your pleasure.

And the other major reason is the title has nothing to do with the song's lyrics or music. Faith No More are notorious for this, right? "Cowboy Song," "Zombie Eaters," "Faster Disco," "New Improved Song." Who the hell names these tunes?

Anyway, what I want you to take away from all this is that Jon sounded good. I mean chills-up-the-spine good. Though he noticed something I didn't, as he still studied his pedals with frustration.

Roddy turned knobs and flipped through menus on his keyboard, searching for the right sounds for each song. Bill wandered over to investigate the keyboard and mentioned his friend had a similar model. He showed Roddy how to trigger some of the effects: sustain, chorus, and another that gave the notes a wavy feel which fit perfect for one of the tunes.

Mike tested his kit, adjusting the cymbals as he played until comfortable with the configuration. He pointed out to me that he had omitted his ride cymbal and could see the other guys much easier.

I asked why he didn't have it.

He said, "No ride cymbal at all on *We Care a Lot*, so I just left it off."

Around then I realized something felt *off*. Bill had retreated to his amp, having situated Roddy while Jon and Mike warmed up, but Chuck still sat by himself, absorbed in the words from his youth.

And it fell quiet.

I don't imagine the band that has created some of the loudest, most abrasive rock music endures much silence during practice. But it wasn't just the lack of sound.

Bill slings his bass over his shoulders and plays a bit, staring down. I notice him flick sideways glances at Mike and then Roddy. Mike tightens a cymbal in place, but he's watching Chuck across the room. Jon, Roddy, and I chitchat.

And then it really hits home. As nerve-racking for Chuck as this event is, the guys might be facing their own nerves, stress, risks, and doubts about playing with Chuck again as well.

For me as a fan, the shows represented a once-thought-impossible chance to see a side of Faith No More that splintered before I became aware of their existence. For them, they had years of unfinished business, pent-up aggressions, lawsuits, antagonistic press clippings, and the risk Faith No More took at bombing onstage for the first time in decades. Reviewing Chuck's last appearance with them, it wasn't a big leap to imagine a scenario that played out closer to Chuck's nightmare than one where him and the band clicked so well the crowd lost their minds.

Though, Mike Bordin shot down this theory when I asked him how nervous he was to share the stage with Chuck again.

He told me, "Not at all."

When I pressed, he added, "The thing to remember is, we'd played with him at two other shows by that time, in addition to hundreds of past shows. We were well aware of how he'd be, and we were fine with it."

Bill felt the same way. "I wasn't too nervous actually. All we needed to do was play together. If someone wasn't prepared, it would've been on them, where back in the day, it would've been on all of us."

So, again, I apparently was the only one stressing. Maybe I need to talk to someone about that?

Bill, still peering down with occasional glimpses at his band mates, asked, "So how do we want to start this thing?"

Mike shrugged. "Chuck, are there any songs from the list we sent that you feel strong about?"

Chuck still avoided eye contact while staring at the notebook. "Nah, man. I'm good with whatever."

I leaned forward. "So, the original list we got from Tim (Moss, the band's tour manager) had seven or eight songs on it, but then Tim texted another list as we drove here with twelve or thirteen on it. We've been, well, Chuck's been practicing the ones from the old list, so maybe start there?"

Chuck stands, shaking his head. "Nah. Whatever, man. Just start playing, and I'll work it out. Might take a few passes with some of the other tunes to get the lyrics down, but I will." He giggles. "Eventually."

The quiet returns as each of the guys retreats to his corner.

Jon drops onto his knees, pulling cables and muttering. Apparently, whatever he heard earlier still bugs him. I recognize a few of the effects pedals, but his set up is way beyond the one I plug in for Chuck prior to our shows.

He pushes the board aside and grabs a smaller backup board. With that installed, he stands and riffs.

Roddy asks about the *We Care a Lot* reissue, which they'll release in a few days. Bill motions to boxes stacked along the wall to the right of the entrance, and they discuss some of the details of cobbling it together.

They talk until Mike interrupts to ask again about how to begin. It appears every time someone in the band asks a question, they all look to Bill, expecting the final word to come from him.

Instead, he shrugs and says something about doing whatever feels right.

The anticipation boils to the surface, but none of them appear ready to take the first step, until Roddy plays the first notes to "As the Worm Turns." Instantly, the guys focus. Mike tightens the sticks in his hands and shuffles on his throne. Billy slides his fingers to the first note's location; Jon clicks a few pedals and waits, and Chuck steps to the microphone, notebook tossed on the piano bench.

"As the Worm Turns" was one of the first, if not *the* first tune Chuck recalls singing actual lyrics for with Faith No More. It has become a cult classic, often appearing in setlists since the band reformed. They even rerecorded it with Mike Patton in 1992.

The song has a clean piano-line intro that gives way to a synthesized sound just before Bill slides his bass, howling like a caged animal, and the drums snap to life. The guitar riff is simple, the bass driving, and the drums feel restrained for such a huge and heavy song.

Chuck watches with excitement and wonder as his ex-bandmates play. As they all groove together, he says something like "Good God." But I'm not 100 percent sure, as the PA system in the room is no match for the thunderous band.

One of Chuck's challenges with these old Faith No More songs will be to hit his cues. With such a long intro, he runs the risk of coming in too early or getting distracted and missing his mark. Either one can be disastrous on these tunes that focus more on repetitive groove than on powerful, dynamic, loud-then-quiet-then-loud peaks and valleys. It doesn't help that Chuck's vocal patterns often run counter to any drum fills that mark the start or the end of a section.

He glances at me, unsure if he missed his mark, but I shake my head. As the cue approaches, I nod his way, but Chuck has recognized it. He's off and running without my help.

Bill's head sways back and forth. Jon appears calm, nodding slightly. Mike hits his drums hard, man, even at practice. Roddy must still be unsatisfied with the sound he's chosen as he peers at the various knobs on his new keyboard. Singing the first words correctly and on time has relaxed Chuck a ton.

I hear him calm down enough to croon a few lines, sustaining notes longer than normal to showcase vocal control he didn't possess while singing for the band. He'll be the first to tell you that he wasn't a vocalist then, just a fill-in guy who normally played piano and keys. With the PA not up to the challenge and no monitors present to let Chuck know how he sounds, he overcompensates by singing louder than he typically would, almost yelling. The vocals sound slightly distorted, but they cut through the music with a clear message: *Chuck is back*. On the album version of this song, the final vocals have Chuck singing, "*Oh-oh*," but today the vocals escape as a relieved, proud, excited yell.

The guitar rings out; Mike Bordin hits a few cymbals, and Chuck gasps for air, less from the rigors of the song and more from the emotions of the moment.

"Good," Roddy says. "That sounded nice."

Chuck grins but plays things cool. "I've had a little practice on that one."

Roddy returns to finding sounds, this time playing the intro to "Crab Song." Chuck suggests they play "New Beginnings" next. He confessed to me during the trip here that he planned to sound way better singing that song this week than he ever had back in the day. To his credit, he nailed it in the car. Remember though, Chuck is prone to greatness with no pressure on his back.

Bill noodles at his side of the room, and I'm not sure if it's anything to recognize or him simply feeling out his strings. Either way, a surge of adrenaline bursts, hearing his signature tone, up close and isolated.

It's a shame these guys don't get to enjoy the songs and these moments the same way I do. To them, it's work, and baggage is attached to each song.

Mike isn't ready for the momentum to backslide, so he hits a four count on his crash cymbal to alert everyone to play "Introduce Yourself," a galloping punk-rock tune with that quirky Faith No More twist. This song wasn't on the original list the band had sent over, thus Chuck hasn't practiced it, but there's no way he won't give it a go now.

Though he turned his back, expecting some time to prepare for the song he had requested, he swings around and starts singing. He missed the first few words, as the lyrics start with the music.

It sounds sloppy and awesome, like the guys have loosened up.

The short-length song ends as abruptly as it started. Now none of them want a break.

Bill peers across the room. "Want to try 'Mark Bowen?'"

Chuck's jitters return. Here is the song he screwed up the last time he played with them. Here's a song sung at the top of his vocal range—a song that can make or break the mood.

The guys nod and get set.

It's like they're all playing while holding their breath. Hell, *I'm* holding my breath. I brought my tablet to edit a short story as I listened to practice, but I sit on the edge of my seat, praying for this song to work. Let Chuck shine.

About halfway through the song, I see it. Bill, still looking mostly at the floor, sneaks a peek at Mike. Mike glances at him, and they share a quick nod. They both in turn look at Roddy and Jon. Chuck sounds good. Chuck knows the lyrics. Chuck is staying on-time.

For the first time, the doubt I harbored of these shows working feels not only possible but likely. Hell, if they sound half as good as they do now, the crowd is going to go nuts.

As the sound of the keys fade, Bill confirms how I interpreted his glance to Mike with a simple, "Sounds good. It sounds really good."

Jon nods.

Mike stands from his throne and agrees.

Chuck says, "Thanks," and then shuffles his feet. "On 'Introduce Yourself,' I missed a part. I don't have that written down yet. Can we run through that again? And maybe—"

"Listen," Bill says. "Go up there and do what you do. Bring the emotion and the attitude. You can get all the words wrong as long as you bring those. It sounds really good. It feels good. Do you feel good?"

Chuck nods.

Bill shrugs. "Then we don't need to do it again. Let's move on."

I watch as everyone takes in Bill's feedback. It acts as a permission slip, an encouraging word, and an ultimatum. At once, the guys are on the same page. They're twenty-five, gearing up to play to an unknowing audience, and they have every middle finger pointed up, begging for someone to tell them they're not good enough. The guys let Bill's words soak in, and they release any worry about how the crowd or the press or the internet will react to them playing lesser-known songs with a lesser-known singer. Chuck allows himself to shelve some of the hundreds of excuses and neuroses that normally dictate his every move. He surrenders and succumbs to the current sweeping the band toward an appearance at the Great American Music Hall.

When I discover later that Bill is the eldest child of a pretty big family, his authoritative guidance makes sense. He drives this band, guides this band, and though he lords over its legacy, he is more open and connected with the press and fans than almost anyone else with a similar status in the rock world.

The guys plow through another three or four songs, only stopping to repeat "Crab Song"—the set's opener—to confirm its structure.

My phone rings, and I recognize Tim's number. I step outside.

Tim says, "Hey, I'm running late. Did you guys make it and everything?"

"Yeah, even on time. The guys are playing. They've gone through half-a-dozen songs thus far."

"How's Chuck holding up?"

"He's relaxed now. There were a lot of nerves at the start, but I think it sounds great. They're playing 'Greed' right now, and, standing outside, it sounds—Hell, I don't want to say it, but, better than the record."

Tim knows what dealing with Chuck is like. I could tell him that Chuck arrived an hour late and he was hopping around the practice space, pretending to be a kangaroo, and Tim wouldn't bat an eyelash. On the flipside, he also knows I'm an old friend/advocate/bandmember with Chuck, so my view skews toward propping him up.

"Alright, I'll see you in a bit."

I hear his noncommittal response. Tim wants to hear from the guys that things are going good before getting excited.

I decide to stay outside for another song and soak it up with my big dumb fan-grin on full display. When I go inside, I grab my tablet and edit a short story as they plow through "We Care A Lot" and "Chinese Arithmetic"—possibly my favorite song of all time.

Roddy has another discussion with Bill about ways to adjust the keyboard's presets, as he still doesn't like the sounds he has for "Chinese Arithmetic."

The conversation returns to the reissue of their debut album, *We Care a Lot*. Bill noodles a bass line I don't recognize, but it sounds distinctly Faith No More. Roddy studies Bill's hands as he plays; Roddy's brow furrows as he also tries to place the song. Pressing a few keys and adjusting through sounds, Roddy finds a groove with Bill, but I still don't think he knows what they're playing. Bill nods as if Roddy is on the right track.

As they play, Roddy asks, "What is that?"

"It's 'Intro.'" Bill changes the notes slightly.

Roddy watches a moment and plays again. "What's that? My hand just went there and played this, but I don't know why."

Bill nods. "Exactly, 'cause we used to go into this." He plays something else.

The duo play along, and Bill half-jokes that they should play this during the encore. The other suggestion is "Pills for Breakfast," an instrumental from *We Care a Lot.*

As we drove to California, Chuck requested I play that song several times. Chuck felt inspired to write lyrics and vocal patterns for it. He told me that he wanted to ask Bill for a shot at recording vocals for it.

Instead of working on either instrumental, the band plays "Why Do You Bother?" It sounds massive, dark, and awesome. Then again, just hearing the song without the CD skipping sounds great to me. Roddy fumbles with the keys during the intro, unsure of himself or the sound, but he quickly finds his rhythm. Chuck, having waited thirty years to play this song again with his friends, attacks the microphone, hoping to make Bill, the song's sole author, proud. Chuck loves this song.

It ends with drums, guitar, and bass hypnotically grinding the same single chord over and over, while the keys slink through the wall of noise, eerie and foreboding. Chuck barks and croons along, improvising. It's cathartic, a release of so many emotions—the perfect song to end the set.

With one last flurry of percussion, the band halts.

Roddy says, "Don't push your voice too much. It sounded good though."

"Yeah," Mike agrees before focusing on structure with Jon and Bill. "To me, it's more powerful when you guys do the single chord thing only at the very end, after I finish my pattern."

He plays a bit to help explain where in the song he means.

Billy, chewing on a pick or something else small, says, "So don't do the single chord until later ..." He nods as he processes. "Okay."

I ask Bill if he ever thought about singing the song himself, considering he wrote the music and the lyrics.

He says, "I've heard my voice recorded. That would be a *no*."

Roddy starts naming songs he's notated as a possible set.

Bill asks, "What do you think about 'Chinese Arithmetic' instead of 'The Crab Song?'"

Though I'm happy to have found someone to champion getting "Chinese Arithmetic" into the set, I can't imagine not hearing "The Crab Song."

Mike adds, "Yeah. It's a lot more fun to play."

Roddy says, "It would be good, but, you know, when I saw that show (at Mr. Beery's the previous month) that was a moment. 'The Crab Song' really sounded great."

"Really?" Bill shrugs, his pick still in his lips. "Then let's do it."

And just like that, the matter is settled.

Mike Bordin says, "You guys want to try 'Anne Song?'"

Roddy says, "I don't know 'Anne's Song.'"

Mike chuckles. "No?"

Roddy asks, "How does it go again?"

Bill says, "It's A-Major to G."

Mike Bordin counts out, "One, two, three, four …" and he and Bill play. They try to explain the song further, but the first few notes were enough.

Roddy says, "I remember. Muscle memory."

He fiddles around to find a good sound while commenting something about the weird songs, like "The Jungle," sounding really good. He says "Anne's Song" is one of the *weird ones*.

Bill offers that the sound Roddy is looking for has a *choiry* sound. Mike plays the guys the original drum pattern for the bridge, which never worked until they adjusted the snare hit's placement. The pattern sounds very similar to "We Care a Lot."

The band discusses a change in the song—"F-Sharp to G"—but Roddy assures them that he'll get it as they play. They launch into the tune, still sounding unlike anything else out there. Chuck admitted to me that the song isn't one of his favorites. After some prodding, he revealed it had more to do with the surrounding baggage rather than the song itself. His vocals sound subdued, mellow; though, after the intensity of "Why Do You Bother?", everything sounds mellow.

They finish the song and discuss a bit before taking a break.

Tim Moss enters. I can tell he's trying to read the room, as we're all sort of standing around. He put a lot of work into organizing these two shows to promote the reissue, and I know he wants them to go well. He says hello and still can't seem to tell if everyone is happy or disappointed or tired or what.

He asks, "You guys all right?"

I don't know if Bill reads the situation the same way I do, but Tim looked uneasy and bummed when Bill said, "I think we're done," without specifying *done with practice* or *done trying to make it work* or whatever.

He asks, "What are you working on?"

Bill removes his bass. "We ran through the set, and it sounds good."

Tim asks, "Yeah?"

Mike, Roddy, Chuck, and Jon chime in with agreement.

I'm happy to see and hear Chuck enthusiastic and positive. It's so hard for him to admit when something sounds good. It's so hard for him to have fun.

Tim leans to the side, so he can see Mike's face behind the kit. "Everything good?"

Mike confirms.

Tim exhales. He explains timetables and some show details as I pop outside to answer a text from Donn Wobser. I tell him he'll never guess where I am at that moment.

After a moment, the guys come outside to stage a quick video announcing the surprise that they'll be joining Chuck onstage in a couple days. One thing Chuck is great at is being a goofball in front of the camera, so when they have him hold up his phone and pretend to be talking, with the guys standing behind him, they get it done in one take.

I make sure to record Tim taping the guys, and I snap a few photos as the band poses for a promo shot. Why I don't ask if I could jump in and get one with the whole band, I'll never know. Not that I need a photo to remember this day, the time I got my own private Faith No More concert, as it already ranks at the top of amazing stuff I've witnessed. All the stress of quitting my job, touring with the pain-in-the-arse Chuck, and being away from my wife and kids for weeks at a time all feel worth it right now.

Oh, and the best part? We have another practice tomorrow.

CHAPTER SEVEN
08/2016: Dreams and Nightmares Come True

Chuck roped Roddy into covering "Bizarre Love Triangle" by New Order with us during the Chuck acoustic set. We practiced it after Faith No More's band practice. The first day, my knee felt too sore to bother unloading the conga, so I used the box from Roddy's new keyboard as my drum.

Chuck had struggled identifying one note he couldn't figure out every time we played, so he and Roddy worked it out. We decided how to start the song and when the changes should happen, as we couldn't depend on lyrical cues.

At the practice spot, things sounded solid. Roddy found a good key sound; Chuck knew the words, and my cardboard box had a nice snap to it.

Bill walked through practice that second day, taping us via Facebook Live, which I didn't know existed until that moment. He asked me to tape Faith No More's set in San Francisco, since, due to my knee, I couldn't move around much anyway.

Jon taught Chuck a note he had omitted in his "Crab Song" riff, and he lent him a guitar strap, which, I assume, Jon never got back. Now that Chuck had a strap, he could stand while we played, which he did at every show after this, minus the first three shows in the UK.

We pulled up to the club and got rock star parking.

Bill had arranged listening parties for the *We Care a Lot* rerelease all over the world, so he lugged around a laptop to video-chat with people. While they soundchecked, he had one of the parties watching online.

Faith No More had embraced the internet and the social powers it possessed early on, so I asked Bill about the ability to organize the listening parties.

He said, "Technology is crazy. It began with email for me, because, all of a sudden, I could be in regular contact with anyone anywhere, and I made use of this as soon as I was aware of it. These listening parties were an extension of that in a way. I was monitoring all of them through my phone, at a listening party myself! Very cool and empowering."

I asked, "How much trouble would Chuck have gotten into if he had Facebook back in the 80s?"

"I think he would've been fine. I'm the one with the big mouth."

I stood as still as I could, knee throbbing, as they sound checked. I heard the nerves in Chuck's voice as he tried to play it cool.

My phone blew up with people asking about getting tickets. I went outside to get a better signal while texting, and I snapped a photo of the marquee reading, CHUCK MOSLEY AND FRIENDS.

People were gathered outside, trying to get in.

One guy stood at the ticket booth, talking loud enough for me to eavesdrop. "I should be on the list. My name is Jared."

The door person said something about the lists not even being up front yet.

When the guy turned around, I knew I recognized him but wasn't sure from where yet.

I limped over. "Jared?" Then it clicked, or I hoped it did. "Is your last name Blum?"

He is the other half of The Talking Book with Bill Gould.

"Yeah."

We shook hands. "I'm Doug. I play with—"

"Chuck, yeah. I just saw your photo. We messaged a few times back when those shows in Chile happened."

"Yeah, I wish I could've gone. I'll go grab Bill and let him know you're here."

He followed me. "I can probably just get in with you."

Oh, yeah. I was opening for Faith No More.

A long flight of stairs provided the only way back stage, so, as much as I needed to save on beer and food and wanted to hang out with the guys, I only took one or two trips up and down for my knee's sake.

One trip down there I met one of the band's guest roadies.

Mike Bordin said, "Danny, this is Doug. He plays with Chuck."

We shook hands.

He said, "I'm Dan Boyle, I—"

"Oh, I know who you are. Great to meet you. I've been jealous of you, reading about your trips with the band. That's awesome."

I grew up as a Sabres fan, so I couldn't show an NHL player, who spent a long time on another NY team, too much love, right?

I also noticed one of my teen-hood crushes milling about. Not wanting to break her heart by delivering the bad news that

I was off the market, I didn't approach her. I assumed my wife would feel relieved when I told her about my strong will, so her giggles left me confused.

As the crowd filled in, I ran into some familiar faces.

Doug Miller had seen the video announcement, dropped everything and flew down from Seattle. No luggage, no place to stay, and his flight home departed early the following day.

Two coworkers of my wife, TJ and Zach, attended as well. They got a good spot in the balcony, but they didn't avoid work. I conned them into helping me carry the merch and equipment outside at the end of the night.

I noticed someone wearing a Cleveland Indians hat, so I stopped to say I lived in Cleveland. Turns out, they were from Canton, Ohio and played in a band called Kung Fu Grip, who I had seen several times.

As soon as Chuck and I took the stage, things sounded sloppy. His nerves consumed him worse than I had ever seen. He stumbled, fumbled, and jumped around the setlist. By the time we had played two or three songs, Tim Moss stood side stage, asking me how much longer we had.

Chuck launched into "Bizarre Love Triangle," even though Roddy and I had started the song at practice. A few bars later, Roddy raced onstage and joined us.

I nodded to him at the appropriate time to switch parts and then glanced at Chuck, wondering if he knew. He stumbled over the word "confusion," making the whole part confusing. I'm not sure if he got any lines right after that; though he had some humorous ad libs.

I got word from the sidelines that our time had ended before we could play our planned set closer, "Take This Bottle." My head spun. I had wanted to play a good set for a big crowd and not look so chaotic in front of the Faith No More guys. #Fail.

I limped offstage as Chuck began "The Crab Song," like we normally played it. The other guys joined him onstage, and the crowd went nuts.

Tim tapped me on the shoulder and pointed to Chuck. "Looks like his guitar is stuck in his hair. Can you help him?"

I limped across the stage and grabbed the guitar, maneuvering the strap free. I put down the guitar as the band kicked in.

I froze.

Never had I felt that buzz of energy, sound, and magic. I didn't want to move, but I'm too fat to go unnoticed. You can see me hobbling offstage as the Facebook Live stream begins. I took over filming onstage. After a minute or two, Tim asked me to step down, because I was blocking the view of some family and close friends standing side stage.

He filmed the show, as he could move around and go through the club to give viewers a better feel for the atmosphere. The band posted it on YouTube, so I won't go into details from the stage beyond saying that I am still humbled and amazed that an absolute dream of mine came true. In fact, it was better than a dream, as my own mind couldn't even fathom the fact that not only would I see a full-on Chuck Mosley with Faith No More reunion, but that I'd have all access, witness two practices, and open the show while sharing the stage with two members of my favorite band. Not bad for a high-school graduate, blue-collar delivery guy, with no musical lessons, from Cleveland, Ohio.

Though I don't feel the need to give you a note-by-note transcription, I can tell you a few things from my perspective.

Mike Bordin and Billy Gould playing together sound like nothing else I've ever heard. If a cop saw what Mike did to his toms, he might face assault charges. He and his drum tech had to constantly readjust his kit as he beat it down.

Bill scowled and grinned at the same time as he thrashed along, his head banging.

Roddy, Bill, and Mike were set up on the side of the stage where I camped out, so I got a great mix of the three of them.

Bill did backup vocals for a song, and I thought, *I used that same microphone.*

Go ahead and call me a nerd, pathetic even, but every second of that set meant so much to me.

One misperception about Chuck was that his voice often goes out of tune or that he can't hit notes or that his range is limited, and I understand why this is the narrative, but I can tell you that he actually had great control when he could keep his nerves in check.

During the practices with Faith No More, he'd sounded great, belting out a dozen songs he hadn't played or practiced in thirty years, but onstage he reverted to old habits. He shouted rather than sang. Not awful, but it didn't sound as strong as the previous few days. He didn't shout during our sets, so his throat got fried quickly. He held up, but I wanted him to nail certain moments to shut up the haters.

Also, Chuck had a weird relationship with "Anne's Song." He suggested the band not play it, and you can tell, especially at the Los Angeles show, he remained reluctant to sing it. It ended up being a sloppy way to end a great show. I didn't care. It still sounded awesome, and I'm glad I got to hear it.

You could tell the guys had given it their all as they came offstage. As Chuck passed me to head downstairs, I saw relief that his nightmare hadn't come true. The only way Bill would yell at Chuck behind the monitor that night was to tell him great job.

I asked Bill if revisiting these older tunes gave him any new perspective on them.

He said, "What struck me was how primitive some of those songs are—extremely simple and rudimentary, some with as few as a single chord change in them. And, at the same time, there was something very pure about it that caught my attention. It also made me aware how young we were when we wrote them."

I debated taking the stairs one last time to soak up the aftershow glow with the band, but I hesitated. Jared Blum stood next to me, wearing the same expression of mind-blown excitement mixed with the turmoil of a decision he needed to make.

"Are you going down?" he asked.

"I was about to ask you the same thing. I want to, but I also want to give them a moment to themselves."

He nodded. "Yeah, me too."

We both stared at the doorway.

I said, "But damn, I'd love to be there."

"Yeah."

We stood for a moment, each debating internally.

Jared broke the silence. "If you can resist, I will too. Let's give them this moment."

"Damn." We turned away. "I was hoping you were going to say we should go down there."

I've seen a stellar photo of the band taken within those moments. I know family and friends and bandmates and press and NHL hockey players and my teenage-rock-*grrl* crush were down there, but I had hogged the band's attention enough.

We loaded our equipment and merch, along with a few packages Tim Moss asked us to take (more on that later) and Roddy's keyboard into our tiny SUV and headed out for a few drinks with Doug Miller.

The following day, we sped south for LA, stopping to pick up T-shirts at a FedEx facility. Our van overflowed with merch and equipment. Chuck had to ride with a T-shirt box on his lap. Chuck made me remove my Cavs jersey in case we went into the wrong neighborhood wearing the wrong colors. I had already flicked off Oracle Arena and proudly spoke of my World Champion Cavaliers, so I consented.

I said, "The people in the valley are ridiculous, full of innuendo."

Chuck asked, "What?"

"Yeah, they're always making innuendos 'bout my lack of talent."

"What?" Then he shook his head as he caught the reference to his own lyrics. "Oh God." He giggled.

We headed for the Bigfoot Lodge where Bill had set up another *We Care a Lot* listening party and where we might perform a secret set. I got my first listen to the *We Care A Lot* rerelease. Man, that demo of "Mark Bowen" is killer.

Dave Collupy showed up and told me, "Back in the 90s, I wanted to interview Chuck, so I called his label, Dutch East India Trading Company. The girl who answered said she'd check in with him but that he had broken his back two days ago. We scheduled the interview, which took place via phone as he lay in his hospital room in Florida. It was April 8, 1994—the day most of the world found out Kurt Cobain had died."

Dave developed a short film with Chuck in mind as the lead. I don't want to ruin the suspense whether that film got made, but I'll talk more about Chuck's acting later.

Bill and Roddy also made appearances at the party; though Bill called it a night early due to a monster cold. Chuck also had to leave to visit with his daughter, Erica, who had recently moved to LA. I gave him a few bucks for dinner, but I don't know if he bought pizza with the money.

After the record finished, we played a short set, with Roddy joining us once again for "Butch" by Imperial Teen. This time, I felt confident enough to sing along, but the club only had one microphone.

That night, we stayed at Michele Norkon's house. She and Chuck attended high school together, but they hadn't seen each other since graduation. They were very close, but Chuck went off and did his thing, and they lost touch. Later in the book you'll read chunks of things Chuck wrote about his childhood, and he mentioned Michele as one of his few true friends.

She told me, "I often wondered what happened to my shy friend Chuck, but never in a million years did I ever think he would be fronting a rock band. I mean, no way. He didn't even talk in school."

The following day, we got to the Troubadour early for load in and soundcheck. I carried in our stuff, thinking about all the famous/legendary shows that had happened here. I texted my mom to let her know Carly Simon had gotten her big break here, which proved enough to impress her.

I put the merch boxes against a wall, containing the shirts, our CDs, the Indoria CDs, the vinyl, and two of the three boxes Faith No More had asked us to transport. I recounted the boxes. I returned the car to confirm nothing got left there.

I came back and recounted. I checked inside all the boxes.

Tim Moss arrived and asked for the merch. I told him I only had two boxes. We looked all over the club, the parking lot, the van, but couldn't find the missing box. I freaked out. I felt a weight on my chest, and I couldn't bring in enough oxygen.

Chuck had been half-joking/half-serious kidding with them about one of the cases of vinyl ending up with us to sell on the road. I raced around, praying to find the box as I ran the last forty-eight hours of memories through my brain. I recalled standing by the van as Zach and TJ brought out our equipment and merch boxes. I remember rearranging everything several times to make it fit. We had played the show the night before and had unpacked some merch, but I didn't bring in any merch that wasn't ours into the venue.

Did Chuck?

"I might've given a few vinyl away."

My heart leapt into my throat. "Ours?"

"I don't remember."

My head spun. I had either stolen from my favorite band or irresponsibly lost a couple grand worth of vinyl records. Either way, in their eyes, I couldn't be trusted.

I decided that being a scatterbrained dingbat was better than being a thief, so I told Tim, "I have no idea what happened to that third box, but I can't leave here with you guys thinking I would ever steal from you, especially after all you're doing for Chuck. I can't pay you guys back right away, but I promise I'll recoup every record I misplaced."

He said, "Don't worry about any of that right now. Let us get back tomorrow, and we'll do a double check of the inventory."

I still felt awful, but I nodded and joined Chuck at the front of the club to see the marquee.

A guy and a gal outside recognized Chuck.

I shook the guy's hand. "I'm Doug."

"I'm Matt."

I heard the accent. "Where are you from?"

"England."

"Awesome. What are you doing in LA?"

He nodded toward Chuck. "We came to see him."

"No way."

"Yeah. We bought our tickets, obviously before the big announcement, and built a trip around the show."

"That's awesome. I think you might be the only people who bought presale tickets."

We chatted for a moment, and then, after taking photos, I went inside for soundcheck. Matt slipped in behind me as if he was part of the crew. He and I sat on the floor, our backs leaning against the bar as we watched Faith No More soundcheck.

I asked, "Where's your gal?"

He shrugged. "Still outside, I guess. I can't get her or they won't let me back in."

Having someone else to geek-out to about seeing Faith No More with Chuck Mosley was nice. Chuck's voice sounded toast having not stopped talking, singing, screaming, drinking, smoking, and shaking hands over the last few days.

Thom Hazaert arrived—the only time he saw the Reintroduce Yourself Tour live. He had a case of *Demos for Sale* by VUA on vinyl.

Whereas I had known almost no one in San Fran, the LA crowd was full of familiar faces. Mike Hickey from Daiquiri; comedian Neil Hamburger; Senon from Cement; April Springer from the reformed Haircuts that Kill; Bill Metoyer, who produced the second Cement disc; Phil and Garret, who I went to high school with; Chris Kniker from Primitive Race; Jim, my buddy from Cleveland; Ian and Cindy—Chuck's brother and sister-in-law; Andrea, who we had met the previous night and who I had known online for a long time; and a bunch of others. Including Chuck, three members of his first band, The Animated, also attended. Troy, the drummer from Haircuts that Kill, picked up a conversation with Chuck like they had spoken minutes earlier, not decades. With it being LA, there were bound to be some celebrity sightings, and I'm fairly certain one of the Russo brothers passed me. Before I registered it was him, he was too far to chase down, but I wish I could've told him, as a nerd and author from Cleveland, how proud of him and his brother I am.

Gary Jacoby opened, (what a voice!) playing songs from his band, Celebrity Skin. They were one of Chuck's favorite bands. He even toured as their roadie back in the day—1990, I think. Gary mixed in a cover of "S.O.S." by ABBA, and he brought up Roddy for keys on it. He invited Chuck up for a version of "Life's a Gas" by T. Rex. To top it off, Don Bolles, of The Germs and Celebrity Skin, joined Gary for a couple songs. He used Adam's banana shaker.

Chuck and I ended with "Take This Bottle." In the middle of the song, Chuck noticed his friend walking through the crowd.

He said, "Hey, Leo," mid-line.

I felt good about my vocal part, but afterward, Chuck saw a video of it and said, "Glad it wasn't me singing that last note."

I thanked the crowd, collected my conga and walked offstage as Faith No More joined Chuck onstage. I felt bad that the massive applause I received overshadowed the band's entrance. I wish the audience could've showed that same love to Faith No More, so they'd know how great the admiration felt.

I stood, transfixed on the stage and watched them go to work.

With a show under their belts, the band found a slick balance between power and speed and volume and humor and showmanship. Chuck struggled at times, fighting a sore throat and exhaustion, but he held his nerves in check.

I asked my friend, Jim Stafford, about his thoughts on the show. "Brevity may not lend itself to convey the overwhelming range of emotions I felt as I remember watching Chuck hold court with Faith No More one last time."

One of my favorite exchanges of the night came when the band started into "Mark Bowen."

Roddy said, "This is a song about our first guitar player."

Mike gave a four count and started his drum pattern.

Chuck sang, "*Love ...*"

But there was no guitar, so the rest of the band stopped.

"That's how we started it off back in the day," Roddy improvised. "We would just do a snippet and then take a breath."

The humor came off effortless and well-timed.

At some point during the set, I saw Mike Patton sitting on the stairs that led to the backstage area. He most likely witnessed me butcher a verse of one of his songs. Oops.

Like in San Fran, I had only gone back stage a couple times to swipe beers, as getting up and down the stairs proved difficult. One of the times, I passed Mike Patton. I knew he was a big Laker's fan, and I still hadn't forgiven him for ripping on Lebron and the Cavs in 2015 at a Faith No More show in Detroit.

I clapped him on the shoulder. "Hey, man. Go Cavs."

He turned and shot me a glance that can only be described as complete disbelief. "Did you just say, 'Go Cavs?'"

"You strike me as a guy who'd like them," I said and then explained, "I know you're a huge Lakers' fan, but c'mon, the Cavs won. We never win. You guys have like a thousand trophies. Just give me this one."

"Okay." He nodded, still wondering what the fuck I was prattling on about. "You got it."

We shook hands.

He said, "We'll see you next year."

I wanted to say something about the Lakers being five years away from the playoffs, but I refrained. I wonder how he feels with Lebron on the Lakers now.

I walked downstairs, trying to find Chuck to get a photo of him and Mike and I together. After being so timid in Detroit, I knew I'd never have a better chance.

Shortly after, Mike left, as did my second opportunity to interact with my two favorite singers together.

The band, friends, family, and many fans stayed long after the show. The club allowed people to stick around to snap photos, ask questions, sign autographs, and soak up the once-in-a-lifetime thing.

Someone had talked Chuck into getting on a motorcycle and revving the engine in a narrow alley behind the club. I thought of a million ways this wouldn't end well, so, when he got off, not succumbing to the taunts for him to gun it down the street, I was relieved.

Bill climbed on right after, a mischievous glow in his eyes.

I glanced around at members of The Animated, Haircuts that Kill, Faith No More, and Cement and was so happy for Chuck, who got shown a ton of love that night and spent it surrounded by so many people he cared about.

I drove Chuck across the country, helped keep him as sober as I could, got him to practice, and acted as tour manager and booking agent and conga player and merch guy for this run, so, even though I knew the Faith No More camp had to be sick of me by then, I wanted to relax and fanboy out a bit.

I went upstairs and grabbed three beers. Yep, three. I was thirsty. Wanna fight me? I opened one and put the other two in my pockets. One for me. One for Chuck.

Mike Bordin and Jon Hudson were the last guys upstairs.

Jon said, "Hey, I heard that without you, these shows might not have happened, so thanks."

In my head, I played off my excitement that I was talking to a member of Faith No More with what I hoped sounded cool and professional. "Oh, man. I'm just glad it all worked out … *blah, blah, blah.*"

Jon grabbed his stuff and left.

Mike Bordin echoed Jon's sentiment.

I said something to the effect of "Thanks for doing this. I'm excited *We Care a Lot* got rereleased, and it meant a lot to me to see you guys onstage with Chuck again. I know it meant a ton to him too."

To be honest, that might not be what I had said. I had lost all control by that point and was now feeling like Chris Farley's interviewer character from *Saturday Night Live*.

"D'you remember when you played drums on the song, 'Blood?'"

"Yes."

"That was awesome*!"*

I asked him if I could grab a photo with him later and exited the room to pack the merch.

As I worked on this book, I asked Mike, "Did revisiting *We Care a Lot* highlight any songs you feel didn't hold up?"

He said, "More the opposite. I was pleased revisiting them and had fun playing them with thirty years more of experience under my belt."

My adrenaline had helped me completely forget about my knee. I put aside the crutches and darted from group to group, talking, laughing, taking photos. I signed a few autographs myself, which felt odd. I passed walls adorned with Jim Morrison photos.

Mike Bordin called me over. "You still want that picture?"

I snapped a couple on my phone.

Mike said, "So, I hear you're writing a book with Chuck?"

"Yep. It's his autobiography. I'm just trying to guide him along."

"Listen, go easy on us."

I tilted my head, caught off guard.

He continued, "Whatever we did, we made what we thought was the right decision at the time."

I stumbled, wanting to say too much with no time to say it.

He waved and headed off.

Now, let me take a minute and say what I had wanted to say to Mike and the guys about Chuck's book.

Never, in our discussions, did Chuck ever wish any ill will toward the band about anything that transpired. He loved Faith No More and all the members he played with. If his autobiography had been completed, there was no intent to bash them, downplay them, berate them, or cast stones over what happened with his exit from the band. Yes, it hurt him deeply when it all happened, and obviously seeing them catapult to great heights wasn't an easy thing to watch, knowing he could and maybe should have been a part of their explosion into the mainstream. He had regrets and often felt embarrassed when people asked him about his firing.

As Mike said, back then everyone did what they felt was best, and it played out the way it did for many reasons, but he loved those guys. He enjoyed the music and the camaraderie.

Chuck wasn't the best at showing commitment, sometimes going out of his way to appear above whatever band or relationship or job or whatever he got involved with. From my perspective, this was a defense mechanism hardwired into him. Perhaps it helped shield him against facing one of the biggest questions he ever faced in his life. Why was I given up for adoption? Why was I abandoned?

Even though he knew his mother—and perhaps his father as well—he'd had no say in the matter. Just take a moment and imagine how he felt. The two people who are supposed to protect you the most, shape you the most, guide you the most, teach you the most, and love you more than anyone else ever will had given him away.

He never got resolution on this subject, and it haunted him his entire life. On this trip, he had hoped to get some answers, but all he got was red tape and more obstacles. Over time, he built a wall, and he rarely let down his guard.

He told me that he knew he was going to be replaced even before Faith No More left for their last European tour with him. Things were ugly, for many reasons. He had receded when the band needed him to be on his best behavior. He told me he had spoken to a couple of the guys to ask for another chance, that he would break out of his slump of depression and try to not be so needy or obnoxious, but the damage had been done.

He told me a roadie and Jim Martin had gotten into a fight, and Chuck stuck up for the roadie. The band wanted to send the roadie home, but Chuck defended him, furthering the rift between him and the other guys in the band.

Chuck had made plans to stay in Europe after the tour to live and pursue other things outside of music, but in the end, he returned home with the band. Shortly after they returned, he was let go.

I wasn't there for any of this, but I saw his self-defeating patterns and the self-doubt clearly overshadowing everything he did.

The band had tasted their first bits of success. Faith No More was no longer just *a band*. They were a business, a brand, and a product. They had managers, promoters, labels, media, and all sorts of music industry folk pulling at them. Now was the time to strike, while the iron glowed. They needed to get on the road, promote themselves, and work on new songs, but Chuck wasn't being a team player.

Robert Plant handpicked the band to open for his *Manic Nirvana* tour after hearing *Introduce Yourself* and enjoying Chuck's style and sound, only to discover a new vocalist had replaced Chuck by the time the shows happened.

Of course, Chuck went on to create many other quality recordings, but, when he was fired, the innocence of the music business got stolen, the punk ethos shredded. The fun, free-spirited, chest-sticking-out Chuck felt vulnerable for the first time. In some ways, he never recovered. His greatest fear, being abandoned, had happened again, leaving him wondering if he was good enough. It left him wondering why he wasn't loved, even with all his faults and hang-ups.

He was often asked if he regretted how things turned out. No matter what he answered, it felt like he was hedging his bets, not wanting to let people see how gutted he felt.

Whatever happened, happened. I can only tell you what I saw from a distance as he and I grew close.

I love Faith No More—all the records, all the shows, all the memories I have of them through the years have played such a huge part in my life, but I think splitting from Chuck robbed us of not seeing what they all could have done together. I think it robbed us of years of Chuck singing and yelling and bitching and forcing us to see and hear about the world from his perspective.

I asked the band what they learned from writing music with Chuck.

Mike Bordin said, "Explore and evolve."

Bill Gould said, "Well, I was in a band with him before Faith No More, and he taught me a lot about music. He turned me on to a lot of things that have continued with me to this day."

No answers could've made Chuck happier to hear. I wish he had gotten to hear them.

When I asked Bill about his favorite parts of the shows and how he would remember his last concerts with Chuck, he told me, "I thought the whole thing was kind of the highlight. I sincerely believe that what we did was a good thing for all of us. It made a few wrong things right."

The following day, Tim Moss called me. They had found the missing box of merch. Apparently, we had only grabbed two boxes. I had mixed one of them up with Indoria merch, which had come from the same company. What a relief!

Chuck and I hung in LA for a couple days. Everywhere we drove, Chuck had stories.

We'd stop at a red light, and he'd say, "I got in a fight with a biker gang on that corner. I evaded a cop chasing me by ducking down that alley. At one time, I worked in that theater."

The theater, called NUART, sat on Santa Monica Boulevard. Chuck met a fellow employee there named Anne D'Agnillo, an island princess who helped Chuck and Faith No More a few years later when she ran a club in New York City. She told Chuck he could do whatever he wanted to do.

No inch of that city escaped without a story about Mosley. Dammit, I wish he was here to write his book.

I had gotten an email from a booking agent in town, interested in adding Chuck to his roster. We met with him at a flashy building inside a beautiful office.

When we entered the lobby, the security guard looked us up and down.

I said to Chuck, "I don't think they're gonna let us in. Everyone here looks super rich and fancy."

"Eh, those are the lawyers and agents. Everyone who looks like us are probably musicians or actors. That's LA."

The agent gave us a positive response. During the next couple months, I would bounce ideas back and forth with him to get us opening slots on larger tours, but nothing ever panned out.

Before we skipped town, Chuck and Senon had a chance to hang a bit. They hadn't spoken much, face to face, since the van crash during the Cement tour, so several layers of emotions bubbled on either side. Forget that Cement, for all intents and purposes, didn't survive the accident, Chuck considered Senon a younger brother, so the crash left ugly scars.

We raced home, only stopping for shows in Albuquerque, New Mexico; Pueblo, Colorado; and Burlington, Iowa. We had a lot to do to prepare for the UK in a couple weeks, which meant we had too much downtime for Chuck to behave.

CHAPTER EIGHT

09/2016:
Mrs. Bickerson Goes to Jail

Babysitting Chuck Mosley is a twenty-four-hour-a-day/seven-day-a-week job. It has no health benefits, no 401k, and the profit-sharing plan is a scam at best.

One of the difficulties in maintaining order and productivity revolves around Chuck's unpredictable behavior. If you're part of the Chuck Mosley Extravaganza and you think to yourself, or God forbid utter the phrase, "Things are rolling now" or "We're picking up steam" or "Hey, nothing that really sucks has happened to us in a few days," you're fucked. Chuck is about to do or has already done some dumb shit that you just haven't found out about yet.

Let me set the scene.

It's Friday evening. An early September heatwave has Clevelanders second-guessing their desires to prevent global warming. The wife and I put the kids to sleep early, and we crack open a couple beers. We've just clicked Accept on an airline's website to purchase tickets for both Chuck and me to travel to the UK in two weeks for a month-long tour.

After endless setbacks, doubt, and fiscal deficiencies, the tour stands ready to kick into overdrive with twenty-nine shows in thirty days and with some great press to accompany it. Not to mention, the British pound is worth 150% of our currency, so, when we return and transfer it, we'll have earned enough extra to pay Chuck's rent on time!

I raise my beer bottle. "A toast."

My wife raises her bottle. "To what?"

"To you, for helping put all this together. For watching the kids and working your tail off while I go live out my boyhood fantasies onstage."

She nods. "Thanks, babe."

We clink our beers.

Those are the cool moments, the ones that make the crappy drives through Nebraska blasting Iggy Pop over and over and over worth it.

The phone rings.

Before I can finish answering with a greeting, I'm leaning forward in my chair in response to the sound of Chuck's daughter, Sophie, crying.

"I can't find my dad, and I think he's on drugs."

"Oh, fudge."

Except, I don't say *fudge*.

I glance at my wife's rolling eyes. We've danced this dance before.

I swig my beer. "Tell me what's going on."

Sophie proceeds to explain that her father went for a walk with his dog, Fredo, but hadn't returned. She tried calling him with no response. Then, when they did get in touch, Chuck was babbling and not making any sense.

She says, "He was asking me where he was and what house he was supposed to be in."

"Call me if you hear from him, and I'll do the same. Okay?"

"Yep. Thanks. And sorry to have to call you. My mom is at work."

"Who knows, maybe he just decided to wander a bit," I suggest, not believing it at all as I attempt to calm down a smart and street-savvy nineteen-year-old who knows better.

Chuck is no stranger to experimenting with drugs, but the news that he might've fallen off the wagon hit me hard, especially having just purchased tickets to go overseas.

Now to keep things in perspective, preparations for this tour leg started in April, before we had played any test shows or had even practiced. In fact, when I had put out feelers, I still wasn't 100% sure I would be involved in the tour or what my role would morph into.

I researched clubs, opening bands, media outlets, record shops, Faith No More fan sites, and any other outlet that might help us book and promote some shows in the UK. I contacted two gentlemen, Kent Brown and Ian Shaw, who offered bonafide help to get the tour off the ground. I followed up with dozens of other people who had emailed an offer, only to have them either disappear or admit they really couldn't help; they just wanted to talk to Chuck—which is totally cool and something I would've done as well.

Together, Andy, Ian, and I booked shows; rented vehicles; mapped out routes; investigated the visa situation; got new passports; negotiated with clubs about providing dinner and drink tickets; ordered shirts; found hotels or a couch to crash on; contacted and got contacted by numerous bands to open or to open for; worked with Chuck's label, EMP, to duplicate a batch of Chuck's latest release in the UK and get them sent to Andy's house; researched labels overseas for our Indoria release; signed a contract with InfiniteHive from Edinburgh; reached out to good pal, Chris Kniker, to ask for his assistance to get a few Indoria tunes remixed; obtained video from filmmaker Shawn Jones from our show in Harrisburg, PA from July; ripped the audio from one of the tracks to include on the Indoria disc; worked with John at InfiniteHive to redesign the Indoria CD layout; and many other things, so I'm ready to get on the damn plane and play some shows.

I answer my phone a few minutes later. "What's the word, Sophie?"

"Dad got arrested. He supposedly broke into someone's house. He had Fredo with him. The cops are bringing Fredo home and taking my dad to jail."

"Fuck."

And yes, this time I say *fuck*. Then, after getting off the phone and updating my wife, I add, "Fuckity, fuck, mcfucksticks, fucking, fuck, fuck, shit!"

I drink a few beers, my mind racing as my wife and I discuss the situation. If Chuck has fallen off the wagon *again*, how dumb would I be to move forward with the tour? We have a lot tied up in it though, so the conversation naturally moves toward damage control. Now that I think about it, Damage Control would fit way better as a name for Chuck's tour than Reintroduce Yourself.

Do you know who Chuck needs in his life? He needs Harvey Keitel's character, the Wolf from *Pulp Fiction*. You know, someone who can mop up all of Chuck's horrendous decisions in a timely fashion.

My wife mentions that she can cancel the plane tickets up to twenty-four hours after purchase.

I add up the facts. Chuck's in jail. He might've broken into someone's house. He has a prior record, so there's a near-zero chance he'll be able to go even if he gets released in time. Surely, he'll be placed on probation and prohibited from traveling, right?

I told her to cancel the tickets. She got the process done with about ten minutes to spare.

I cancel the T-shirt order. I tried canceling the CD order, but it's too late. I inform John at InfiniteHive and Andy that Chuck might be unavailable for the tour, and we might need to cancel everything. I expect them to flip out, like I feel like doing. Instead, they both tell me to calm down and let things play out. Knowing Chuck's past and the situation, I calculated a three-percent chance he could go. And even if he could, I couldn't ask my wife to allow me to go along and to pay for tickets and stuff to help make it happen.

It didn't surprise me that jail time might be the tour's demise. I mean, Chuck has a checkered past, but I was disappointed nonetheless. During the course of the last few months, Chuck and I had built a good rapport onstage. We had also finished the new Indoria, and Chuck had sounded stellar.

Things had been building organically, even with Chuck's bad reputation and the fact he hadn't toured consistently in decades. When we started, I was prepared for our tour to fall apart during our first show, then the first tour leg, then the second, then the third. And then, when we left to open for Faith No More with no additional shows to bring in any money, I felt assured things would come to a crashing halt. But people loved Chuck. They loved his voice, as unorthodox as it is. They enjoyed his lyrics, dark and personal. The guy could spin a good tale.

But nothing can build with Chuck rotting away in prison.

I spoke to Pip and Sophie several times that weekend, but none of us heard any news. They were understandably angry and considered moving out. How many times can you let someone break the same promises and cause you the same pains before you decide to end things?

A collect call comes in from the county jail.

I spend a moment inputting my debit card info and pay the twenty bucks to activate my minutes. Here I am, paying to talk to Chuck.

He says, "Hey." He sounds exhausted as he offers the usual apologies.

I've heard them before, and I don't care to hear them again. "Chuck, what the hell happened?"

"I don't really know. I left to walk Fredo, and, the next minute, I'm in some strange house and people are yelling and pointing a gun at me."

"What? So, you were using?"

"No," he says, hurt and annoyed that I'd ask. "Hell no."

I say nothing.

"Well, not anything illegal."

"Weed?"

"No, well, not enough to black out from."

"Were you drunk?"

"I don't even think we have any alcohol in the house, except maybe some wine. And Pip has a bottle of schnapps or something in the fridge, but I have no interest."

"Tell me what happened, Chuck. Because I've already canceled the UK tour."

"What? Fuck no. The tour is on."

"How can you tour when you're arrested for burglary?"

He grunts, pissed off. Typical whiney Chuck. He sounds like a spoiled three-year-old when he doesn't get his way. I feel comfortable in saying this because I'm the same. Ask my wife.

"I didn't steal anything, man. I blacked out and wandered into someone's house. No one was home. I went into the bathroom and took a leak, and I came to with people in my face yelling at me. I called Sophie and tried to ask her where I was or why I was there, but she sounded as confused as I felt. An off-duty cop happened to be passing by. He got involved and held me until the cops came."

"And you didn't do any heroin?"

"No, man. I told you, I got scared the last time, and it's over. My body can't handle it."

"Chuck, just tell me if you did. Either way, we probably can't go, so just be honest with me."

"I told you, I didn't do any."

"Chuck, you realize that if you did and I vouch for you again and you get busted at the airport or overseas, I'm the biggest idiot on the planet, right? I just want to help you get your career restarted, but, if you can't handle it or don't want it, just tell me that you'd rather sit at home and do nothing. That's fine. I can go back to my life."

"I didn't do any this time. I took a pain pill."

"Like Valium?"

"Something stronger."

"Soma?"

"I don't know what it was. I got it from my dude. He gave me two and said just take one per day. I took the first one 'cause my back was all jacked up. I didn't feel anything for a while, so I took the second one. Nothing happened, so I took Fredo for a walk."

"You waited a while? Like how long?"

"Thirty minutes."

"Jesus Christ, Chuck. Those heavy pain pills release slowly over long periods. The first one was probably just—"

"I know, I know. It was stupid, but my back was hurting really bad."

I squeeze my phone and clench my jaw. "So, have you been arraigned yet?"

"No. I'm just waiting around."

"Hopefully they'll let you out on bond."

Author's note: I have no idea how that stuff works aside from watching reruns of *Law & Order*.

"Nah, well, the good news is my cellmate has all these law books. We discussed my case, and they can't charge me with breaking and entering or theft because I didn't force the lock, and I didn't steal anything."

I'm sure most of you readers are relaxing now that Chuck's cellmate assured him everything was fine. But for some reason, the lawyer/inmate's words didn't offer me much comfort.

I roll my eyes. "Alright, well, maybe let's come up with a plan to—"

"Oh, hey man. I gotta run."

He hangs up.

I replay the conversation through my mind, wondering how much I believe. Chuck claims no heroin was involved. That's a good thing, if it's true. I can't afford a lawyer for him, and I don't see this getting straightened out in time without one. At best, if they release him, he'll be on probation, right? I think that sounds legit.

Like I typically do in these situations, I decide to call my wife for guidance. Except my phone is ringing again. I accept the collect call.

"Chuck?"

"Hey, yeah. Sorry. I thought I had to go, but I didn't."

"Okay. So, how is it in there?"

"Fucking nightmare, man. I haven't slept or eaten in days. I can't relax. I gotta get out of here. My stomach is all jacked up."

He talks more about some of the other inmates and some drama about certain people getting targeted and attacked. Again, it's hard to discern what's real or fake, as Chuck is prone to say anything to get what he wants at times. He knows I want to help him, so, is he playing on my worry, hoping I'll offer assistance?

He says, "Anyway, Pip is talking to some people, and she might have a line on a lawyer."

"That's good."

"Don't cancel anything. It'll work out."

"Chuck, I had to cancel the flights and T-shirts, man. I can't afford unused tickets."

Chuck sighs, annoyed. "It's gonna work, man."

"Alright. Well, that would be great. I'm trying to live in reality. If you want to continue to stay in fantasyland, go ahead. I need to figure out how to limit the damage when we cancel these shows."

"We're not canceling. I don't miss shows. I don't get too drunk at shows or too stoned, no matter what the press says. I'm not letting this ruin my reputation."

I wonder what reputation he thinks he's protecting, as the unfinished book about him isn't pretty. Trust me, I know—I helped try to write it. That being said, I've shared the stage with him many times this year and saw the heart he brings to each show, even on his sloppier nights.

That's one of the most frustrating things about Chuck. When he is engaged, the talent flows with no effort. He can mumble over a simple riff and create interesting vocal patterns off the cuff, but that's where it stops. He gets bored with the vocal patterns or guitar riffs he creates the moment they happen. This makes second takes, overdubs, and mixing a chore.

I say, "I won't email anyone else, but we need to figure out this shit as soon as possible. I'm going to pick up my kids. I'll talk to you later."

"Alright, man. Just don't worry. I'll prove it to you. I'm focused and ready to work harder than ever."

I hang up and reluctantly put on pants, which aren't needed when I'm at home. I'm an author, not a model. I grab a second cup of coffee.

The phone rings.

"Chuck, what's up?"

"Oh, nothing."

I giggle. Why do I giggle? Because oftentimes Chuck says things in real life that mirror phrases in his songs. "Oh, nothing" and "Oh, really?"—taken from "Anne's Song" and "The Crab Song"—are uttered constantly, and I never get sick of hearing them.

Chuck is what I'd call a stream-of-consciousness writer. He doesn't filter his thoughts at all when creating lyrics. No ultimatum or preconceived message exists when he starts a new song. Whatever comes out, comes out.

I grab the keys and head out the door with my cellphone to my ear. "So, what's new in the last five minutes since I talked to you?"

"What?"

"Dude, we were just on the phone."

"Oh, yeah. I tried calling Sophie and Pip, but they weren't available."

"For what?"

"I'm bored and stressed, man. I just don't want to be here."

I don't bother mentioning how I don't want to be in this situation either. I'm checking flight prices as they rise. If we don't order shirts within the next day or two, they won't be ready in time.

The only positive to the shirts being delayed is that we are still getting offers for shows, so I can add them to the shirt design if they get confirmed. Yeah, I know, why the hell am I entertaining new offers when I'm convinced the shows won't happen? Well, as I said to my wife, "If this were anyone else aside from Chuck, the tour would get canceled, and they'd be thrown in jail. but, with Chuck, there's always a chance."

Now, to be fair, I don't confirm any shows during this time. I keep the conversations alive while concocting new excuses each day as to why we can't commit yet.

"So, you called me to make small talk, Chuck?"

"Yeah."

"I'm paying by the minute for this call."

"Sorry, man. I know. But the calls are short."

"Dude, I've already used up like half the money I deposited, and we haven't discussed anything important."

"You exaggerate everything. It's no more than ten bucks at this point."

"Well, you underexaggerate."

I know that makes no sense.

Once, he caught flak in an interview for saying he didn't care and that he left the caring to me. That's not what he meant. Chuck cared, but he didn't preplan or worry. He just showed up and did his thing and let the chips fall where they may. It drove me nuts. Partly because I knew he could've maximized his footprint and grown his brand quicker by playing the game. Mostly, though, it was because things typically worked out for him without him trying, while my plans always seemed to blow up in my face.

I glance at a budget spreadsheet on my phone. "Look. I just don't want to spend any more money. We need every penny to make Europe work."

"Alright, man. Then I'll call you later."

"Great. But, like, later than five minutes. Okay?"

The next few days follow a similar pattern of Chuck calling without any progress happening. Every time he says the same things: "Pip is working on finding a lawyer; my cellmate has a few strategies; I'm going to get this taken care of and either dropped down to time served or dropped altogether."

Then he calls with some urgency and informs me that if he isn't bailed out by noon the next day, he'll be stuck in jail until his trial. This would make the tour 100% impossible. I have no idea if what he's saying is true, but does it matter?

He has arranged someone to front bail money. As usual, I need to make calls and transfer funds and download apps and learn secret handshakes and meet someone at the dockyard at midnight, etc. to get the money to the correct place at the correct time.

The next morning, I head downtown to bail out Chuck.

From what his cellmate counselor told him, he can talk to a bail bondsman about traveling, as the court won't care where he goes if he appears for his court dates. He also says the court is so backlogged that a summons could take weeks—or better yet, a grand jury could decide to prevent further action. To Chuck, this is like a free pass to abscond, as if nothing happened. To me, it's another opportunity for things to bite us in the ass added to an already-impressive list of options.

Having served jury duty at the justice center a couple times, I'm familiar with the building and the routine. I get past security and head to the second floor.

Now I'm officially a fish out of water. I have no idea how to bail someone out of jail. I approach one of the pleasant-looking women sitting at the desk and explain my situation. She informs me that I need to return to the real world and hire a bail bondsman.

D'oh.

I leave the office, and a guy behind me is trying to get my attention. He introduces himself as a bondsman and says he can help me right then and there. I'm leery of getting some bad deal. According to him, the court regulates costs, so it won't save me any money to shop around. Is this true? Man, who knows? At this point I've accepted so many other stories at face value, I decide to go with the flow. So, underneath a dozen posters telling me DO NOT CONVERSE OR DEAL WITH BAIL BONDSMAN IN THIS AREA, I write a check and sign a guarantee stating that Chuck will appear at his court date, "or else." The threat of "or else" sickens me to my stomach. Unfortunately, to Chuck—the person it *should* rattle—"or else" is like a dare, a starting point.

Chuck calls me two or three times in the fifteen minutes it takes to complete the paperwork and nags me until I get annoyed enough to bark angrily at him. My voice echoes around the marbled lobby.

The bondsman tells me that it can be several hours before they release the inmate, but I paid for a whole day's worth of parking, so I decide to hang out downtown. I brought my tablet so I can write. Ironically, I'm editing a novel featuring a character I based on Chuck. I find a deli across the street. I order a sandwich and some coffee that tastes like it had been brewed during the Reagan administration.

A well-dressed woman sits at a window table. I sit close to her. I typically avoid human contact in these situations, as I like to disappear into my writing, but I want to peer out the window in case they release Chuck. His phone is dead, so he can't call me for a ride.

Luckily, he's easy to spot in a crowd. His unorganized dreads and penchant for wearing filthy pajamas set him apart from most suited, well-groomed folks milling about.

I sip the coffee and wonder who the lady at the window is waiting for.

Chuck calls. "Hey, everything set?" He sounds rough, like he hasn't slept in a week and the only thing in his diet are cigarettes.

"Yeah. I got the bond and did all that stuff. The guy said if it's not processed before lunch, it might be midafternoon before you get out."

"*Daaaaaamn*, seriously?"

"Yeah. But at least it's happening, right?"

"Well, I ran into a lawyer in the elevator when I went up to see the prosecutor. I explained my case, and he echoed what my inmate told me, so I think we're good to go for the UK."

"And what happens if they summon you while we're over there? We can't afford a ticket home."

"They're so backed up, man. It's not going to happen."

"But if it does?"

"By then we'll have money from shows to pay for a ticket."

And that's how Chuck balances his finances, folks. On *what-ifs* and *if-comes*.

Sophie calls. She's downtown to visit someone else at the justice center, besides her dad, but security wouldn't let her enter the building wearing her chosen attire. I meet her at the deli and let her borrow my button-down shirt. Thankfully I dressed up.

Now, I stand six foot two and weight about 300 pounds, so my shirt covers her like a full dress and more. She gets in to see her friend though, so it all works out.

I meander around while she goes inside. When I meet her in a city park area, I wonder what onlookers think as this young gal removes her shirt and hands it to the overweight, bald, bearded dude wearing a salsa-stained T-shirt.

We discuss her father and she opens up about her fears, doubts, and the pain he has caused her. I want to offer comfort or paint a bright future on the horizon, but she's been down this road too many times before. Besides, I'm the guy pushing her dad out of his comfort zone to get him working again. She may see me as an accomplice—or worse, the enabler.

I pass the deli and see the woman from earlier exiting and hugging a man, relief evident on her face. I'd love to know their story. No one comes here without a reason. I'd bet a lifetime's worth of novel ideas play out at the justice center every day.

Within hours, Chuck is home. He's a wreck. I leave him alone for the night to eat, sleep, and straighten out things with his family.

I discuss the situation with my wife and decide to restart tour prep.

Andy and John breathe a sigh of relief heard all the way from Scotland when I tell them things are back on.

We hold off buying the tickets to give Chuck one last chance to leave me behind, so he can make more money on the road without me, but he says he needs me.

I order a conga from Amazon and direct it to be delivered to Andy's house, as I don't want to lug mine through the airport.

The money I'll save not paying to check the conga at the airport there and back more than pays for it.

The next day, I spent the morning prepping for tour so I could write in the afternoon.

Part of being an author—a big part, oddly enough—is writing. No matter what else you have going on, finding time each day to write is of utmost importance. As a husband, father, son, brother, conga player, friend, and movie nerd, time often slips by, so it feels great to sit at my desk knowing I have three to four hours of uninterrupted time to work on a new story. No kids, no wife, no work, no Chuck.

I often find myself juggling projects. Currently, I'm under a deadline to complete a short story within about a month. I knew I'd be in the UK for almost the entire time I had left to complete and edit the story, so I wanted to get started.

Sophie calls at about 1:15 p.m. "My dad's passed out in the bathroom, and he won't respond."

"What?"

"I think he might've done heroin and nodded off. I walked into the bathroom 'cause he had been in there for a while, and he was on the toilet, sleeping. I tried to talk to him, but he's out of it."

"I'm on my way."

My mind races on the drive there. We have the tickets, the vehicle, the tour dates, and I planned on ordering the tour shirts today. If Chuck did relapse, do I have an obligation to my friend to force him into rehab? Should I at least cancel the tour? It seems like Chuck does well on the road. I mean, sure he drinks and smokes, but, away from the daily grind of bill collectors and household frustrations, Chuck seems to find his rhythm.

I enter his house, ready to give him the business—to get physical if I need to. If he did indeed relapse and the scare of the jail time wasn't enough to keep him sober for even forty-eight hours, he needs professional help.

I slam my palm on the locked bathroom door. "Chuck!"

Nothing.

"Hey, Chuck!"

Nothing.

"Chuck, open the fucking door, man. Sophie already told me you passed out and were rambling. Come talk to me."

I hear a sudden rustling and something gets knocked off the sink. Could he be flushing drugs down the toilet? Would needles flush?

I know enough about heroin to know how evil it is and to avoid it at all costs, yet, in my situation, it's embarrassing how little practical stuff I've actually learned about the drug.

"Dammit. I wish he wouldn't have had the wherewithal to lock the door."

"Oh, he didn't," Sophie says.

I push open the door. "Chuck?"

"Hold on. I'm in here."

"I know, Chuck. It's time to come out."

He turns, realizing it's not one of his daughters. "Doug?"

He stares at me, eyes dancing back and forth, as he attempts to process that his conga player is busting in on him in his own apartment.

I advance past him into the disorderly bathroom, checking the surfaces for signs of drug use. I have only the vaguest of ideas of what I'm looking for: needles, spoons, white powder … at least that's what I remember Leonardo DiCaprio using in *The Basketball Diaries*.

Chuck is confused and mad. He wipes his eyes, rubs his temples, and asks me not-so-kindly to get out.

I hold firm and crowd him out of the bathroom without pushing or shoving. I don't want to grab him. There have been enough in-band fights involving Chuck in the past. I know how that ends. That being said, if Sophie, who slides behind us to check the bathroom herself, finds anything, I might lose my shit.

He raises his hands to wave me backward. "Give me space, man. I just woke up, and you're all up in my face."

"Were you sleeping or nodding off?"

"What?"

"Chuck. Sophie says you were mumbling and wandering around the house. You went into the bathroom and haven't responded to her repeated calls or knocks on the door. She's freaked out."

"Why? Can't I just go to the bathroom in peace? You don't have to worry every seco—"

Sophie screams, "Dad, you were in there for a half an hour before I called Doug."

"Huh?" He looks back and forth between us.

I cross my arms and puff out my chest, my lame attempt to appear tough, like the chaperon outside the dance in *Dazed and Confused*. "Chuck, it took me at least forty-five minutes to get here, so you've been in there for almost two hours."

He rolls his eyes. I told you he hates it when I exaggerate, but this is not one of those times. He looks at his phone, screen cracked all over. "What time is it?"

Sophie points to it. "We need to get that."

I snatch the phone from his hand.

"What the fuck!" He shoots me a look of extreme anger. "You're really starting to piss me off. Give it back."

I have no idea why we need Chuck's phone. I try to hand it to Sophie, but Chuck lunges forward. I snap it back and slip it into my pocket.

He growls. "What the fuck? Give me my fucking phone."

He steps forward, but my glance of intimidation or something else keeps him in place.

I ask, "What should I do with his phone?"

Sophie keeps her gaze on her father. "If he got drugs, there's a good chance he texted or called someone about them. Let's go through and see what we find."

Chuck's shoulders slump. He rolls his eyes again. "Go ahead. Look through all you want. There's nothing in there. I just got out of fucking prison, and I have no money. I just charged the damn thing this morning."

Sophie points a finger at his chest. "You were probably in the bathroom deleting whatever was on there. I am so done with you."

I watch Chuck. This comment hurts.

He shakes his head, angry and frustrated. "I didn't delete anything. I was sleeping."

"Nodded off," she says, staring daggers at her father.

"No, I wasn't. I told you. I got out of jail; I haven't eaten or slept in days. Last night I kept jerking awake thinking I was still in jail. Every moment in there, you don't know who's gonna fuck with you. I had my fingers painted with my usual glitter stuff, and I was surrounded by guys who love to hurt gay guys. I was afraid they'd think I was one of them and attack me. Not to mention I'm black, and there's all these racist Nazi assholes in there as well. I tossed and turned all night. I feel like shit. I went in the kitchen and made the first real meal I've had in over a week, and then I went in the bathroom to take a shit and just passed out. Next thing I know, Doug's banging on the door yelling at me, and you're accusing me of doing drugs. Everyone already thinks I'm doing 'em, so I might as well at this point. No one fucking believes me."

I hand Sophie the phone. This time Chuck stays on his side of the room.

I step toward him. "Let me see your eyes."

He peers at me as I move closer. They appear to be dilated, but I have no idea if that's good or bad. I do, for some reason, think it means something, so I play bad cop.

"Chuck, you were passed out, and your eyes are all dilated, man. Just tell us the truth."

"I did." He sets his jaw, annoyed now.

He's been pacing back and forth since we exited the bathroom, and I wonder if instead of heroin he was doing speed or something. I don't remember ever seeing him so jittery.

Fuck. I just wish it was easier to know whether he's using drugs. Chuck is Chuck just about no matter what.

"Chuck, sit down."

He ignores me. "Just let me have my phone."

"No."

He paces a bit more and then sits. That's when I realize the dude is sweating. Yeah, it's an Indian summer in September and we're in the un-air-conditioned upstairs of an old duplex with horrible ventilation, but Chuck hails from LA and is usually comfortable in warm weather.

"Chuck, you're sweating like crazy, man. We all know what that means. Just be honest." I have no idea what him sweating might mean, but I want him to admit if he was using so we'd know for sure. I hope that at some point he'll be fully honest with me.

"Whatever. Shut the fuck up. You came in here with your mind made up already, and nothing I can say will change it."

I sit. "Chuck, could you blame me? You have a long track record of drug abuse and bad decisions. You've lied to me a shitton in the past, so why should I think this time is different?"

He repeats his timeline and pleads his case almost word for word from earlier. It seems to check out. I mean, this guy is flat broke, and he just got out of jail. Then again, I've learned through the years that, like the dinosaurs in *Jurassic Park*, Chuck will find a way.

Sophie returns the phone to me. "I'm not seeing anything."

"Told you," Chuck says, grasping for the phone.

I pull it away and stuff it in my pocket as Pip walks up the stairs.

I fill her in on what's transpiring.

Sophie excuses herself to get ready for work. She now has the joy of forcing a smile for customers for the next eight to ten hours. She barks at her father as she walks out the door, talking about how done she is with all of this, how she doesn't want to talk to him anymore, how he is weak. The anger and threats are a good show, but all I see is a confused and hurt daughter who just wants her dad not to die. She and Chuck are so close. I know this is worst-case scenario for both of them. She slams the door; her footsteps clomp down the stairs.

Chuck sits on one of the couch's arms, and I notice he's stopped sweating. He's also a lot less jittery.

I mention the dilated eyes, so Pip and I check again. They appear closer to a normal size.

Fuck. I have no idea what is going on. Could he have just crashed in the bathroom after his week in jail? Hell, the guy follows an abnormal schedule day to day. It wouldn't surprise me in the least. He sleeps ninety percent of the time we're in the car on tour. He falls asleep at the clubs before half of the shows. The guy is a walking-talking narcolepsy joke.

I also know he doesn't eat at all when he's in the clutches of heroin, and the kitchen shows signs that he has indeed cooked food. That's good but by no means proof either way.

Pip takes the phone and goes through it herself, also coming up empty.

She's seen Chuck in every state of drug-induced haze, and she isn't sure, so I know no way I'd be able to tell.

I try again. "Chuck, if you did drugs today, I want you to tell me right now. It won't affect the tour in anyway. I just want the truth. At some point, I need to be able to trust you. This is your one (after a million other) get-out-of-jail-free card with me. Just tell me what happened."

He repeats the same story, word for word, as he told earlier.

The exhaustion and confusion on Pip's face breaks my heart. She's been through this battle before and has stuck by his side. I want to tell her things are okay. That this tour is building momentum, that Chuck can use it to springboard himself back into the game. He'll be earning again on a consistent basis. But I can't lie to her. She's been lied to enough for a dozen lifetimes.

I head toward the door. "Chuck, I don't know what happened, but I hope what you're saying is true. My inclination is to get you into a rehab facility, but I know you have to pay the bills. If Pip and Sophie decide you shouldn't go, I support them 100%."

"I didn't—"

"Chuck, I don't care. Talk to them. They know when you're lying way better than me. I'll follow whatever they recommend."

CHAPTER NINE
09/2016-10/2016: Rock U(K) Like a Hurricane

There's a character in the book, *The Rules of Attraction*, named Victor who takes a summer break to Europe. Bret Easton Ellis writes that character's story as one continuous paragraph, a stream of fast-paced consciousness. This is how I want to convey our thirty-night stint in the UK.

Since I don't want to rip him off, I'll ask for you to read this chapter extra fast, and I'll keep the narrative to bare minimum details, deal?

We flew out of Cleveland early in the morning, and Chuck was already drunk, having spent most of the money he brought with him on whiskey at the airport. He was mad at me because we had two connections before we arrived overseas. Of course, that was my fault. Luckily, he didn't express his anger until after my father dropped us off.

My passport fell from my pocket as I paced around the Cleveland airport, blasting music to calm me down. It was a miracle that I had removed my headphones the moment my last name got called over the loudspeaker. I rushed to the security booth, collected my ID, and then rushed to collect Chuck for our flight.

Chuck almost got kicked out of the airport in Dublin, Ireland, twice—for lighting up a smoke on the tarmac.

The first time, we had taken a shuttle to a different concourse. As we exited the shuttle, Chuck started smoking. The lady leading us gave him a hard time to put it out ASAP. The second time, airport personnel were leading us to our plane, since they didn't have an attached gate. As soon as he flicked his lighter, an airport employee rushed over.

"Hey!" the guy screamed. "Put that fucking thing out right now! Do you realize everything around us is soaked in jet fuel? You'll kill us all."

Chuck apologized.

The guy continued, now in Chuck's face. "I should throw you out of here."

The guy kept going on, but Chuck boarded, eventually.

Andy picked us up at the airport in Edinburgh, Scotland. He's a pleasant dude with a love of country and rugby and landscaping and his gal and his dog. He performs in a Josh Homme cover band called The Hommesexuals, which pretty much wins for best tribute band name. Second best was Motorheadache.

I had met him online, and he offered to help book some shows. Then, as the tour grew, he offered to host us for our first night, and then he hired on as our driver. Without him, the UK dates go a lot differently.

Chuck slept the entire first day and night, only waking to smoke and complain about his back, which he claims got twisted on the "many" flights it took to get here.

We journeyed out for a drink, hitting two bars, but he almost didn't say a word. He also slipped away "on a phone call," but now I think we all know what he was trying to/did find. Around this time, I reminded myself that I and all other Chuck fans want him to explore all the deep, dark places to create his music—places I'm too scared to go—and yet, I still expect him to operate in the normal world.

The highlight of that first night was sneaking him into the Black Bull Tavern to surprise my buddy, Bob, who had no idea we had arrived in Edinburgh.

During the first show, in Cambridge, Chuck sat while playing. He complained of battling great pain. We met some of Andy's buddies, and Andy gave us a tour of the city, having attended university here. The canal is beautiful. I sat alongside it for hours and wrote lyrics for songs for a band called The Firmary that I am involved with. I found out the hard way that you had to pay to use bathrooms, but it led to a new phrase.

When I went potty, I made sure I "got my fifty pence-worth."

In Nottingham, we avoided the sheriff. I located a club called Rock City, which I had heard about during an interview Faith No More did with Mary Anne Hobbs on BBC Radio back in '97.

Red Rooms was the only club that gave Chuck and I backstage passes.

I slept on a floor next to a toy AT-AT. Andy's phone got smashed when our host for the night tried to move a glass table and dumped everything off it.

Michael Shiraz is everything you want in a friend and a promoter. He brought us to play the Parish in Huddersfield, and it couldn't have been a better show.

That day, a church across the street from the venue had a new bell operator to train, so the bell, loud enough to be heard for miles, rang all day, including during our set. It added a layer of sound that perfectly fit a few songs.

I learned, after too many drinks, that UK hotels don't keep people staffed all night to allow access, so I returned to the bar until they closed at 4 a.m. The bartender lived upstairs, so he said I could crash with him. I fell asleep on a couch, only to be awoken by someone yelling, "Doug!" extremely loud.

Chuck had realized I didn't make it in, and he searched for me, which was touching. We walked down Beast Market Road to our hotel. Best street name ever?

I told my wife, "I'm living a year of Saturday nights and Monday mornings."

As we entered Newcastle via a long bridge, the car next to us blew a tire, sounding like a shotgun blast. The car skidded and smashed the wall on the right. If it had gone left instead …

I toured the city with Ian and Zoe, two big Faith No More fans that I had communicated with online for years. Her being from Australia and he from the city, I juggled between their accents and tried to keep up. We visited a music instrument shop, and Ian played a few keyboards. They took me to Mosley Street and bought me a beef pocket at Gregg's. We played a free show at Trillian's to 175 people.

Andy, who brought along a bass, played with us. With Chuck acting less crabby, they got along. My finger busted open during the set, and I got blood all over my drumhead.

In Glasgow, Chuck performed a four-song solo set at a record shop. John from InfiniteHive attended. He's tall and funny. Frank Quinn, the butcher of Glasgow, arrived in top form. He isn't a butcher, and no one has ever called him that—until just now.

We shuffled to BBC Studios so Chuck could prerecord an interview for the Vic Galloway Show. I swiped the building-entry badge they had given me as a souvenir. I wanted to get involved in the interview, as Chuck and I got each other going; whereas solo, he stumbled and mumbled a lot.

Andy and I handled soundcheck sans Chuck, which happened often. We practiced "Wisdom Comes" by Bad Brains and pushed to add it to the set. Andy requested a microphone, which I thought was mighty forward. Every night, when he soundchecked it, he said, "Dwarf mic. Dwarf mic," and that made me laugh.

Frank yelled out, "I love you, Doug!" during our set. I flashed back to 1996 when I saw Imperial Teen open for The Lemonheads at the Odeon, and I yelled, out, "I love Roddy!"

Will Schwartz misheard me, and asked, "Punk-rock Roddy?"

We stayed at a commune outside of town, and they blasted a Girobabies record all night, which was fine by me. One of the punk dudes who lived there had a voice that sounded exactly like Aragorn in *Return of the King* as he addressed his army outside of Mordor.

September 23, 2016, the nineteenth anniversary of me meeting Chuck became one of the best days of my life. We played the club in Edinburgh—Bannerman's—that I had visited on my previous trip to Scotland, in front of a rowdy crowd. No story in a book will ever communicate how magical of a day that was. Irish Rob, the bassist from The Exploited, handled our sound. He understood what Chuck wanted, adding effects and such from the first few notes. My finger had busted open even more, spraying the crowd with blood every time I hit my conga. The pain got so bad I lowered a second conga that the club had set up for me, so Ian could help me through a song. Our version of "Take This Bottle" received a wonderful response from the crowd. It felt like everyone joined together to sing along. Chuck had mic stand issues, which we turned into a gag. He laughed it off—maybe the first time I saw genuine happiness since we had arrived.

I stayed up with Stephanie Ashford, listening to a French philosopher and an Irish poet argue about humankind's worth and purpose. It was so ... cliché—and wonderful to observe.

The following morning, Scotland's biggest news station reported the country had mysteriously run out of whisky. I never got formally accused, but ...

I tried hiking up the volcano that sits in the middle of the city. Halfway up, my hangover and an oncoming cold decided the view couldn't get any better, so I sat down.

By the time we reached Aberdeen later that day, my cold had gotten worse, and a fever had knocked me for a loop. The promoter expected a good crowd, but that never happened—one of the only duds on the run. Chuck and I argued onstage over something silly, and we looked like assholes. We played with a band called Lords of Bastard that I enjoy. I couldn't even look their bassist, Frazer, in the eye when he told us *good job*.

Chuck and I argued more after the show. "You were joking around too much. You were late with my vocal effects on 'Sophie.'"

I wanted to tell him he had reversed a couple lines, and I had gotten lost, but that happened almost every night, and I still managed to hit my mark. He wasn't really mad about it anyway; Chuck's not like that.

He saw me cough. "Fuck. I better not get that."

I stormed off for the hotel, having no idea where it was. Andy stayed with Chuck—babysitter for the night.

I found Heaven, and it is in Scotland. Though feverish and unable to get out of bed, Inverness proved too beautiful to ignore.

Chuck covered his face as he walked out the door for a smoke. "You better get some medicine for that."

I wanted to yell and ask why he wouldn't offer to get me some, as I obviously was roughed up.

A race happened that day, so I sweated and coughed and shook as masses of people jogged along the river a couple hundred feet away. Andy and Chuck left for the club as I slept, so I almost didn't play that night. At the last second, I woke up and stumbled the mile or so to Mad Hatter's.

A doctor, Angus, bought me a dram of Lagavulin, quite literally what the doctor ordered. We stood back and watched as Chuck joined a group of folk/gypsy-type musicians jamming at their table in the restaurant section of the club. He played guitar and sang, and I wish I hadn't been feeling like death, as I would've enjoyed the night.

Angus told me that he and his wife were in the midst of a move. He expressed worry about his cats at the new place. Even more daunting, he faced the wrath of his wife for attending our show two nights in a row rather than helping at home. I felt so bad that he treated me so kindly, as I figured he would catch my germs.

On our only off day, I had planned to hit a distillery. Instead, I slept off my cold.

I ran into Ian and Zoe in Chester after scoring two rare Faith No More vinyl that I'd never find stateside. They had seen us live four times now and planned on attending the next two shows. They handled our merch booth that night, helping me rubber-band our shirts, which had finally arrived.

In Cannock, we played a great club called The Station, which had old Black Sabbath tour gear as part of their sound system and a barrier between the stage and the crowd. We helped them move it out of the way, as we wanted to play as close to the crowd as possible. The club also had an ancient piano that Chuck started noodling on. A gal named Stephanie sat down with him, and they played and sang—a show before the show.

Both Zoe and Ian had mentioned to me separately about their trepidation over their relationship. Ian lived with Zoe and her kids in Australia, but his visa situation had approaching deadlines.

During our set, I asked if anyone in the crowd wanted to come up and propose marriage to anyone else. I peered out, and Ian's eyes went wide … like, cartoon popping-out-of-his-head wide. They didn't come up, so we continued. After our set, I got off stage, and Ian said he wanted to propose. I told Chuck he had to sing one more song after a quick announcement.

Ian and Zoe got onstage, and the proposal happened, so Chuck serenaded them with "Life's a Gas."

We stayed in a converted horse stable that night, one of the most unique hotels around. Andy slept in the van. He fought exhaustion and burnout after weeks of endless days and nights, long drives, and my clogged sinuses causing my snoring to rage out of control.

Chuck's superpower of waking up moments after we passed a town or rest area to ask, "McDonald's?" remained strong.

Andy would shake his head. "We just passed one. We'll stop at the next one."

Minutes later, "McDonald's?"

"Almost."

"McDonald's?"

Andy, now gripping the steering wheel and clenching his jaw, asked, "There's a Burger King in a mile. Will that do?"

"Their breakfast sucks. I want a Big and Tasty."

Andy would try to find an alternative, but Chuck had fallen back asleep, only to wake up as soon as we passed the next McDonald's. I know, you're wondering why we didn't stop at that one. The times we did, Chuck got mad at us for waking him up.

We played in Cardiff, our only date in Wales, so I wandered off to get the local flavor. Instead, I ate a cardboard hamburger while two locals berated me for being from America and allowing Trump to pull ahead in the presidential race.

Chuck told the drummer from the opening band that night, Stay Voiceless, that he wanted to hire her for VUA once he moved to the UK next spring. He also told me that he wanted to fly me over to continue playing conga on acoustic tours. Flattering, but an absurd notion.

When Chuck ended with "Life's a Gas," the crowd "sang" the guitar parts, getting just as loud as Chuck. Andy and I returned onstage to sing with them. *"... like a priestess. Ba, ba, ba, ba, ba, ba."*

After the show, I ran into Dave Wakeling from The English Beat; though, over there, they simply called them The Beat.

Two guys wanted to take us out on the town for drinks, but one of them passed out in the cab. We dropped them at home, and I stumbled to our hostel. Chuck held court on a porch overlooking the water and a soccer stadium used in the World Cup. He drank some insanely strong beer. Two random dudes chatted us up about *Top Gun* and *Ghost*. 'Murica!

In Bristol, the promoter turned out to be a truck driver who didn't live in the area. He booked us at a venue that held 700 people, easy. Faith No More had played there with Chuck back in '87. We drew about a hundred. Needless to say, we got shorted.

The crowd got a special treat when Chuck's childhood friend, Art Terry, got up with us to play two of his songs. Shona Cutt did a photo session with Chuck at the club and took some stellar live shots. She got a couple of Chuck and I sitting in a staircase, a moment frozen in time I'll never forget. She also got another classic one of me in the foreground and Chuck in the background favoring me with a befuddled expression.

After the show, Melanie and Alastair, a couple with one of the weirdest relationship dynamics I've come across, took us to a rock club in the basement of an old building. I told Art how weird it was to see people dancing along to a DJ spinning Korn and Disturbed and Metallica.

When people talk about smooth, cool dudes, they're talking about Art. He could certainly play Lando Calrissian, if needed. He's got such a welcoming smile and a relaxing voice.

I kept the wristband from a gay bar called The Queen's Shilling, where we danced until 5 a.m. I could see Chuck doubled over in laughter as I owned the dance floor. I am not a dancer, but sometimes, you gotta channel your inner Irene Cara and go for it, am I right? I embraced my "Bear" status to the tune of many free drinks.

I almost got stuck in an alleyway in Basingstoke. I had the crowd sing my dad happy birthday from Cobblestone's in Bridgewater. Aside from the coolness of playing for a second time with Alex James and Death of Rats, Stoke-on-Trent represented the biggest misstep of the tour.

Andy caught my cold. I wanted to help him drive, but I wasn't insured there and I can't drive stick. I knew the miles were getting to him, so I refrained from mentioning the total he had driven the entire month was less than half of our crosscountry two-week trip the previous month.

We arrived in Birmingham to find armed soldiers on every street corner. Apparently, a huge political rally had the city on edge. We stopped by my fellow author Jacob Owen Prytherch's house. We did some much-needed laundry, and Chuck trimmed his facial hair, leaving my clippers behind. Jacob treated us to an all-you-can-eat Asian buffet before we all went to the show. The opener that night was a Faith No More tribute act—weird, but funny at the same time.

Andy Watson took a few stellar shots of Chuck, one of which Chuck hated. He claimed he looked super old in it, but everyone else loved it. While he got photographed, I hung outside on a balcony overlooking a canal full of colorful boats. I struck up a conversation with a few people.

"Hi, I'm Preeya," one of them said. "Where you from?"

"Cleveland."

"Really? I was just there."

"Why on earth where you in Cleveland?"

"I went to a concert."

"Damn, that's a long way for a show. Who did you go see?"

"Dog Fashion Disco."

I almost spit out my beer. "I was there."

"The whole weekend?"

The band and their various side projects did three nights in a row at the Agora.

"Two out of three. I actually blew out my knee the last night and almost missed being at the Faith No More shows with Chuck, because I couldn't bend my leg to get into the van."

The more we talked, the more we found common friends and bands we shared, and I learned a new term. "Lock in," when at closing time, the bar shuts down with people inside who continue to party.

Chuck got up with the openers for a song.

Since we were in Birmingham, we had practiced and attempted "Sweet Leaf" by Black Sabbath, but Chuck chickened out before we got far into the song.

After the show, a gal asked me, "Do you hate Chuck?"

"No, why?"

"You were glaring at him almost the whole night."

"Oh, that's just how we show each other we care. It's, uh, part of the show."

Our hostess played us music at her apartment that night.

She glanced at me. "You have better taste in music compared with the way you dress."

Thanks.

Jim Brown, one of the biggest Faith No More fans on the planet, had come to the Birmingham show, but he had to leave during our set for work. The next night in Bradford, he stayed and spoke to Chuck at length. After supporting us through his FaithNoMoreFollowers group, I was glad we got to meet up.

Sarah and Paul, who we met in Huddersfield, attended. And so did Matt Larkin, the guy who had flown to LA and watched soundcheck with me. He paid admission even though we had him on the list. It felt great to see people not only willing but excited to see us again. Chuck sounded stronger, and we were all more confident with the songs by now.

I wrote a note that night. *Chuck says I exaggerate, but that's 9000% not true.*

In Swindon, it got chilly. I remember shivering through soundcheck. I remember the bathrooms at the club were covered in pornography. I remember Steve, a genuinely lovely man who attended the show with his full-grown sons. They told us about how, back in the 80s, they weren't communicating with their dad—puberty and all—but they bonded over the *Introduce Yourself* album. After seeing Faith No More, they sort of reconnected. I could tell how much it meant to both him and his sons to still be on great terms and seeing Chuck live again.

The promoter shorted us and said he was sad to see Chuck so messed up, even after I explained Chuck always tightened up onstage. Now, again, I remained under the impression that the court case and the jail time and his family's threats could keep him in line. I would've been shitting my pants to face all that trouble, but Chuck? He saw it all as more reasons to do drugs to forget his problems.

I never saw him do drugs in the UK and didn't think he did anything aside from drinking heavily, but now I have my doubts.

The club let us sleep upstairs above the bar, but Andy chose again to stay in the van to watch episodes of his favorite show, *Father Ted*, and avoid our snoring.

At around 4 a.m., Chuck got off the couch and tripped over me asleep on the floor. He opened a window to smoke, knocking something glass off the sill. It fell two floors and crashed. Chuck tried to catch it, only managing to knock over something else in the process.

He said, "Hey man, take the couch. I'm gonna smoke, and then I'll sleep on this chair."

I didn't argue.

When he finished his smoke, he realized the window wouldn't lower. The two of us shivered all night with no blankets. He caught the cold I had recently shrugged off.

Bournemouth is a lovely city on the southern coast of England, and the club, the Anvil, had a stellar sound system and engineer. He had my conga booming off the low ceiling with a thunderous *thump*. I hate that I don't know his name, but the guy's voice sounded like Chris O'Dowd's.

So many people bought Chuck drinks that he passed them to me, two at a time. He stumbled over a slight incline in the floor while holding two double Jacks and a beer, which drenched everyone's shoes. He uprighted himself and then immediately tripped again, dumping an entire beer on me, laughing the whole time.

The folks in Milton Keynes know how to party, now. They showed us a great time, even if our crowd wasn't as big as Soulfly's, who had recently played there. Chuck smoked outside, embroiled in some deep conversation, so Andy and I played along to the Black Sabbath songs the sound guy had pumping through the house monitors as we waited.

After the show, Chuck and I stumbled down enough alleys to lose our sense of direction.

He asked, "Are you having fun?"

"This is pretty fucking cool. I think if we—"

"Ugh, no business talk tonight."

We crashed at the club and watched movies all night with the staff. They had laundry machines, whoa! I bought a dress for my daughter. I don't know anything about fashion, but it's super cute.

I wrote a note. *Either I have six markers in my pocket or zero.*

In Derby, we played at the Hairy Dog that had a sign proclaiming, *Just don't be a cunt*, which I find to be solid advice. Now, Americans, before you riot that I used the *C*-word, know this: in the UK, the word is not as revered as, say, saying *Voldemort*.

Chuck complained all night. "A shady, bearded guy stole ten pounds from me."

The guy had been walking around the club, scamming people with various stories and tricks while asking for money, cigarettes, or drinks.

My wife called me early the next morning. She had flown to London to meet with us. She arrived under the impression we were already in London, and she'd crash with us as soon as she arrived. It was the only time on the road when I had to drag Chuck from bed rather than the other way around.

The Boston Arms, the club that booked us, sat on the north end of the city. I waited for Michele to come up the stairs from the tube. Andy waited with me.

I heard the clanking of luggage on the concrete, and then there she stood, stunning as always, but ... Michele was cross. She expressed her anger toward me for not being there when she arrived, while killing Chuck and Andy with kindness.

"So, be ready," Chuck said. "The London crowds are even more subdued than the L.A. ones."

Not only did the audience prove him wrong, but Chuck sold us short as well. Our set sounded loud, loose, and funny. Michele joined us onstage to sing on "Nameless." I watched her so much that I missed hitting the rim of my conga a couple of times, but I wanted to soak in the moment as much as I could.

I asked the crowd, "The whole 'Arms' thing ... What's the deal with the Boston Arms, the London Arms, the Stratford Arms ..."

Chuck made a shotgun loading noise.

I continued. "Do you guys work out, like, all the time? What's the deal?"

Chuck tried to tell me arms meant guns and protection, but Nessie called out from the crowd, "No, it's for hugs."

I told Chuck, "You're shooting people; she's hugging people. There's a miscommunication here, folks."

Chuck, loving to egg people on, said, "Trump for president."
Boos followed.

I said, "Did you say, Trump or *Chuck*?"

This led to a crowd chant of, *"Chuck, Chuck, Chuck!"*

Andy and I conversed while Chuck fiddled with his guitar and drank one of my beers.

Then he said, "Arms are for hugs. I get it now."

Update: October 27, 2019

I have cobbled together a live record that may or may not see the light of day, and the exchange above about arms and hugs and guns is included. What I noticed in this banter is that at one point I say, "The Cleveland Arms" and without missing a beat, my wife calls out from the crowd, "Looks like those Cleveland Arms need some work."

My wife, always looking to prop up my confidence.

The night ended with a two-song encore. Chuck took his best stab yet at the Bad Brains song. "Bob Forest" killed. We tried for our new extended outro with Andy and I pounding away over Chuck's cloud of feedback, but my conga danced around too much to hit it squarely, as the rubber tips had all disappeared from the metal rack that held it. I wish that set had never ended.

Blackpool reminds me of the Jersey shore of England. Tons of people-watching opportunities presented themselves, as tourists from all over the globe gathered in the city to partake in the various amusements in town, including a boardwalk carousel and a tower that you can climb for a good chunk of change. We stayed in a haunted hotel that night with a leaky faucet and electrical plugs that had been installed upside down.

The following day, with only a can of Irn Bru to fuel us, we mingled with the real world and spent a couple hours trying to find sparkling nail polish for Chuck.

Eventually, when we did eat, Michele ordered chicken potpie. "This was probably good two weeks ago when they first made it."

Manchester—does anyone call it Madchester anymore? The city felt huge after Blackpool, Milton Keynes, Bridgewater, and Basingstoke. In London, we didn't get the city's full scope and scale, since we only saw its northern edges. The overcast, dreary, cold, and rainy weather gave us the stereotypical England as depicted on American television.

We parked alongside the venue around noon. A few people waiting for Chuck approached with vinyl ready for autographs.

Frank came from Glasgow, so I wore a makeshift Frank for Queen shirt and gave it to him after the show. Sarah and Paul also attended—their third or fourth show on our tour. Jon Duggan flew from Ireland again and told us we could expect to see him in Paris as well.

We enjoyed sounding like a well-oiled—or at least well-liquored—machine, but all of us had hit a wall of exhaustion, and each of us took a turn with that nasty cold.

The version of Chuck and Michele singing "Nameless" that night brought me to tears. I hope a recording of that exists, but I hope not a recording of us trying "King Arthur" and "Bizarre Love Triangle," as they both got mashed together in some chaotic bog of eternal stench.

After the show, we hung out until the last possible moment, as we had to check in to our hotel by midnight. Frank jumped in our van, and we arrived with two minutes to spare. The hotel bar stayed open until 2 a.m., and we didn't want the bartender to feel lonely, so ...

In Norwich, we explored the market and ate bad Chinese food. We played with a band called The Bloodshake Chorus, who put on a hell of a show but probably lose money each time they play to afford all that fake blood. During their set, I scrambled to order our ferry ticket for Paris.

Someone in the audience heckled Chuck. The banter played as amusing, until the guy got belligerent and demanded we play "We Care a Lot." Chuck handled it well, telling the guy we would play it if he came onstage to play the guitar and sing and if he paid us five hundred bucks. After the show, the guy cried and apologized to Chuck for being a dick.

I love "We Care a Lot" as much as the next fan, but, as an acoustic tune, eh ...

Stephanie, who we had met in Cannock, got onstage to sing "Take This Bottle," but apparently, she already had (kidding, Stephanie). She has a strong voice, but nerves and no practice made for an interesting version of the song. The whole set felt off that night, and the crowd didn't buy-in like most did. Afterward, someone gave us a subpar review in the local paper.

The UK has some amazing beers, and I attempted to try them all—bitter, sour, cider, porter, and stout alike. That night, I bought my wife a cider she still hasn't forgiven me for.

She took a sip and put it back on the bar, a scowl on her face.

I rolled my eyes. "C'mon, it can't be that bad."

I sipped and regretted it immediately. It was the only beer we didn't finish the whole trip.

We hit the bar pretty hard and then spent a good chunk of the night trying to find a man named Shaunie at a Tesco, but we failed. Angry about not finding a party, Chuck got in the hotel elevator, mumbling, "Billy Idol gets it. Why doesn't anyone else get it?"

This was one of his favorite movie lines to quote from *The Wedding Singer*.

Our last day in England happened in Canterbury, an old village with so much history. That day, my wife and I celebrated our tenth wedding anniversary by exploring the city. A massive church, the Canterbury Cathedral, left me dragging my jaw on the ground. The grounds around the building appear equally as stunning. Not as stunning as my wife, of course.

We played a wonderful pub called The Lady Luck in front of a packed house. A female patron spoke loudly while we played. It continued for a chunk of the set, until Chuck stopped midsong to address the chatter. The funny thing was, he wasn't even referring to her when he stopped. He had picked up on another conversation a couple were having at the back of the club, so he asked them about their chitchat.

And just like that, our twenty-eight shows in the UK ended.

To put into perspective the insanely bad luck that shrouded Chuck—he told *Quietus Magazine* he had "Charlie Brown luck"—I offer this: Since 1914, the British pound has always, *always*, held a much higher exchange rate than the US dollar. Two times in history when the pound's worth has dipped close to even with the dollar. 1985 (right as Chuck started to tour with Faith No More), and, you guessed it, EXACTLY WHEN WE WANTED TO EXCHANGE OUR MONEY. The country was exploding with inner turmoil over the Brexit vote, costing Chuck and I several thousands of dollars in the process.

People often say, "You can't make this shit up," but, until you've rolled with Mosley, you can't truly comprehend the extent of those words.

We boarded an early morning ferry and left for one last concert in Paris.

CHAPTER TEN

10/2016-06/2017:
Houston, Rehab a Problem

On October 15, 2016, I found myself crying onstage before the last-planned show of the Reintroduce Yourself tour. I had ducked behind my conga and fallen deep into a bottle of Jack. Chuck had traded show beers for the brown liquor. The stage wasn't more than three feet from the ground, so people could clearly see me balling. I couldn't stop.

I'm not anti-emotion nor am I a tough guy, but I tend to contain my tears for reading *Locke and Key: The Guide to Known Keys* or witnessing Mogwai in concert.

This was the last day of the tour though. It hit me that somehow, someway, we had completed every show and goal we had laid out earlier in the year. We did it with minimal support, outside or inside. We did it with minimal experience. We did it with zero budget, no new release to push, or a PR company involved. We did it with Chuck shooting himself in the foot, over and over, creating obstacle after obstacle. We fucking *did it*.

After that night, I faced returning to the real world and finding a real job again. Not because of any lack of desire to keep going but due to Chuck's inability to fly straight and limit the chaos enough to make money rather than hemorrhage it.

So, yeah. I cried out my sadness, my stress, my relief, my sobriety, and my excitement and my pride.

Chuck and Andy joined me onstage, and we flew through a blur of a set. We played fast and loud, and the crowd responded, so we cut loose. As I wiped sweat and tears from my face, I thought, *This is a great ending to our book.*

Screw the people who would say our tour didn't move the needle enough. Forget the people who would ask where the new music was. They had no idea what a miracle it had taken to get this thing off the ground. We reintroduced Chuck to the world with ninety shows and ended with a stellar set in Paris.

Sucking in the dank basement air as the show ended, I waved to the crowd. I picked up the Jack and resumed chugging. I packed our equipment (big thanks to John Duggan for the power adapter that saved the show, BTW) and sauntered into the crowd, grinning like an idiot. I passed Chuck surrounded by fans waiting for him to sign records and take photos and swap stories and listen as they spilled about their problems and health issues and life battles. We nodded to each other, and I disappeared into the smoke and lights and chaos of the after party.

This was the ending. Chuck was back.

The following morning, Chuck flew home alone, and Andy drove our rental van to Edinburgh. My wife stayed with me in Paris for two days to celebrate our anniversary, take in the Eiffel tower, verify the rats in the bushes do run the city and to visit Shakespeare and Co., a bookstore shown in two of my favorite movies, *Before Sunset* and *Midnight in Paris*.

I worked on a new outline for Chuck's book, starting and ending during that night in Paris. It had a romance about it, a balance. It had a positive finality. I had given it my all, and my wife had sacrificed all year to make ends meet and to keep the family and the tour together.

Chuck still had legal issues to work through, but he had Thom Hazaert to rerelease the second Cement album, a booking agent in Los Angeles working tirelessly to keep Chuck on the road, and Chuck had reclaimed his swagger. A VUA reunion swirled in his mind, as well as a long period of sobriety. Good work all around and a collection of stories to share for the rest of my life.

Then I received an email from the booking agent who had signed Chuck, saying he might have some dates as early as two weeks away. Well, hell. How can you end the book in Paris if bigger and better things happened right after?

I fell into the trap of procrastinating on the book until it could have the proper ending as well, but the winter shows never materialized. We spun our wheels, waiting.

Chuck took a bus to Sacramento, California, to record vocals for Primitive Race's new CD. Not flying had put a strain on their budget and on their recording schedule. His role also expanded to encompass lead vocals on the entire disc, so he didn't finish all his parts in one session.

Part of the problem was that Chuck had become convinced he couldn't lock in lyrics or even vocal parts until he got into the studio's vocal booth and could hear everything through good headphones. While I understand the sentiment—and I do know how tough it was to listen to music with any peace and quiet around his house—to me, it's just another example of his tone-deafness when it came to wasting other people's time and money.

This wasn't a band with label support and big merch sales to overcome the extra expenses. Chris Kniker funds that whole ship, and he had just expanded his family with their first child.

Chuck and I spent endless hours together in tour vans and hotels and clubs with nothing but time, and Chuck made almost no progress on the PR stuff then. The mumbles from the first session sounded cool though. Simple, effective, maybe leaning too much on the instrumentation for melody and pattern, but his lyrics took a dark, personal tone that I thought fit right in line with the music. Chuck really dug the stuff too. He mentioned it in each subsequent interview, excited for people to hear it.

Chuck attended court to face his breaking-and-entering charges. The judge sentenced him to probation, and Chuck had to check in for drug tests downtown.

"I can't survive in there. It's not an option. I like my routine. And the food isn't even really food. No, I can't go to jail."

In December, we got word that Dug Smith, the singer/drummer we had played with in West Chicago, had died. He was younger than me. Though we had only met that one day—one of the worst of the tour—I had enjoyed Dug, and we had kept in touch via Facebook. Prior to his dying, he had posted a cryptic message, so I reached out to him. He sent me a thank-you message and said we'd jump on the phone at some point to talk. It's hard not to look back and wonder if I had pushed to talk sooner, it would've been enough to change things. Mostly, that's ego and guilt talking.

Mandy, Dug's sister, asked Chuck to play a memorial show for her brother, and Chuck agreed.

"I'll take a bus or train out there, so you don't have to lose money on the trip."

"I'm sure we'll find a way for me to lose money somehow," I said. "If you get the date set, I can book shows around it to lessen the losses."

"She said it'll be on a Saturday."

Whatever money and momentum we had brought home had long been diminished, and we still had Chuck's legal issues to face. The longer things dragged on, the more my wife and I got comfortable with the idea of seeing the tour through. Not for any noble sense. Not for any notions of getting rich. Simply put, we invested a lot of time, money, and effort into jumpstarting this jalopy, and now we wanted to ride along as it zipped down the highway. I needed to be a part of it, rather than cranking the engine and giving it a push.

In February, I sat in a courtroom to support Chuck. I was under the impression his probational officer had scheduled this meeting with the judge to determine if his rehab stint would be in-house or out-house.

"If the judge asks for anyone to speak on my behalf, would you?"

"Of course. The whole breaking-and-entering thing sucks, but you've been good since the fall. This judge doesn't seem like a hothead, so you're in as good of a spot as could be expected in a situation like this."

"Yeah, well …" Chuck started to say something, but his attorney arrived.

The judge asked Chuck to stand and explain what had happened, which Chuck did, leaving me more confused than when I had arrived. Apparently, Chuck had failed a drug test since we had gotten home, a few days before his original sentencing. He got arrested and thus missed a court appearance.

His explanation, something to the effect of, 'I knew I might've failed a drug test, so I stressed out. When I stress out, I do the dumbest thing possible for that situation, and this time it was doing drugs, which caused me to fail my next test.'

The judge inquired about another time, within the last week or two, and Chuck had a similar response. By the time their talk finished, I couldn't keep straight how many tests he had failed and when those had been, but my belief that Chuck had stayed clean since the previous summer obviously felt naive and foolish. I flashed back to the day Sophie had called me to get Chuck from the bathroom, to the days in the UK when he slept hours on end, to the crabby exchanges we had about petty BS, and I realized how much deeper his addiction ran than I had understood.

The judge immediately passed his sentence, and I was relieved I didn't have to speak up because, at that moment, my blood boiled. Not that he had done drugs, but that he had lied and lied and lied and lied about it. I felt upset that he couldn't trust me enough to confess that he had slipped up, again and again. All the AA meetings we attended, all the talks we had, all the regrets he mentioned, all the changes I thought he wanted to work for, and all the times he snuck around behind my back—that's what angered me.

Chuck earned fines, house arrest—including wearing a tracking monitor on his ankle at all times—and three drug tests at the justice center each week. He also now had a long, suspended jail sentence hanging over his head if he slipped up any more.

I don't typically take many photos of Chuck and I, but I snapped a shot of us outside the courthouse that day, freezing on the way to my car. Though livid and betrayed, I felt relieved that Chuck hadn't been incarcerated, because I knew that might have killed him. Also, it wasn't often that we both wore button-down shirts and ties.

Chuck and Chris Kniker struck a deal for Don Debiase, one of the nicest people in rock music, to record the Primitive Race vocals at his studio in Cleveland. The dude is a huge Star Wars nut, which always sits well with me.

With Chuck on house arrest, he had to get preauthorization each time he wanted to leave the house. This made recording complicated. I escorted Chuck to the studio to maximize time he would otherwise spend on a bus headed across town.

During one of the recording sessions, Chuck ran into Chris Zitterbart, who operated the Agora—a club located in the same building. He mentioned that Dog Fashion Disco planned to return to Cleveland for a weekend run of shows and that we could open one of them. It became one of the first confirmed shows we had for the year—and the last show Chuck ever played.

The recording went well, mostly because Don has the patience of a saint.

Chuck stood at the mic, take after take, stumbling, mumbling, fumbling, and layering one oddball take over another. "Can I try that again?"

I had seen him do this with VUA and Indoria, so I knew the drill, and Don caught on quickly.

"Yep." Don clicked his mouse. "Here you go."

He never pressed Chuck. He only made things comfortable and offered feedback here and there. He was thrust into a weird spot as he really wasn't the engineer, mixer, or producer of the track, and yet, he had been tasked with bringing out and capturing a top-level performance from a guy nervous to even sing full tilt.

Don swiveled his chair toward me. "He sounds good."

I nodded. "But he's still holding back."

"Compared to where we were before, it's night and day. A lot more confident."

I have this OCD thing where, when nervous or bored, I start to find patterns around me and count them. I remember staring at Don's floor tile and counting—a lot.

I said, "Well, he's starting to remember lyrics. I see him glancing at his notebook a lot less. He's getting there, but I don't know if it's quick enough. He already recorded some of these tunes in California, so you'd think he'd just zip through, but it's almost like he's back to square one and starting over."

"I'm just trying to keep him on track. I've got a million takes on some of these songs. It's a mess, and I'm leaving for tour soon."

In the booth, we hear Chuck swear. "Can I do that again?"

Don swiveled back to his computer. "Yep."

Chuck asked, "How does it sound?"

"Good. You're still straining on that one line."

"I'm trying out different lyrics and words in there. That'll get cleaned up as I finalize stuff."

"Here ya go."

He clicked the mouse and swiveled back to me. "So, I leave—"

Another swear. Chuck came in late.

After a couple more takes, Chuck says he's coming out of the booth. "Maybe, can I try this guitar line out?"

"Yeah, but can you stick to vocals for right now while the mic is set up for them? I didn't realize you were doing any guitars."

"I'm not. Not for this, for that other stuff."

"Well, we could—"

"I'll grab a smoke and we'll figure it out. I gotta make a call anyways."

Eventually, Chuck returned and treated us to a good ten minutes of one side of a phone conversation. He grabbed his guitar and noodled one of the new tunes. "Don, can you play what I did so far on the new one?"

"Yeah, which one first?"

"'Mr. Smith.'"

"This one is about a guy we met last year. Dug Smith."

I nodded, "Yeah, I remember him."

"You do? From Chicago?"

"West Chicago. That's a day and night I'll never forget. He was a cool dude."

Chuck checked some lyrics or notes in his book, still fumbling on his guitar as we listened to the song.

"That's a cool vibe."

"Do you think Mandy will like it?"

I nodded, having only met her briefly and spoken to her on the phone after Dug passed, but I felt like even if she didn't dig the song or the lyrics, she would love the fact Chuck Mosley had penned a song dedicated to her brother.

"And this is another one that came out right after that first one. They are sort of similar, so I dunno …"

The second song, aptly titled "Song 2," sounded as simple and mellow and introspective and personal and relatable as the previous song.

"Do you like them?"

"They'd fit right in the set with 'Sophie' and 'Chip Away.'"

The recorded demo versions of "Mr. Smith" and "Song 2" were raw, a little hesitant, and the tempo, since he didn't play to a click, had a liquid feel, speeding up and slowing down. Chuck rerecorded some of the vocals during that session, and he might've redone all the guitar; I'm not 100% sure. Don and Chuck added the sounds of rain and thunder during and in-between the songs, making them connected as one long tune.

Chuck liked that effect, as they were written back-to-back and had the same tone. He described them as *cousins*, much like the songs, "King Arthur" and "King Arthur's Cousin, Ted." He enjoyed themes, lyrics, and emotions cropping up in different songs in similar ways. One example I can think of:

Chuck said, "In 'R n' R,' I say, *Like the time you tried to teach your nephew to walk.*"

"Don't you say *fart*?"

"No. Well, I wanted to, but they fought me on it. I first said the line in 'Chinese Arithmetic,' and then it came up again. Just slightly different."

The lyrics included in the booklet of the cassette—yes, cassette—has *fart* listed for "R n' R" and *walk* listed for "Chinese Arithmetic." Also, in one song, he says *nephew* and the other, *cousin*—but you get the idea, right?

I enjoyed both new songs and felt, even though I wasn't part of writing them, I had helped get him to a space where he felt comfortable writing again. I did suggest a change to "Song 2," as it had his stop/start/crash-to-a-halt/restart pattern, but he held firm on that one.

"They're dramatic pauses."

There was a method to his madness at times. Given how strong the crowds responded to this song live, he had it right.

Chuck had planned having Don's dad add some guitar on a cover of "Old Man" by Neil Young, but I don't think they ever got far enough in its recording to make that happen.

When we had returned from the UK, Chuck had assumed he'd polish off the Primitive Race vocals in a couple days. A few months later, the album still didn't have finished vocals.

In March, I went through the various emails and messages we'd received from people interested in bringing Chuck to town. We certainly had enough to piece together a couple short runs while waiting for legal things to straighten out. I contacted bands we'd played with, clubs that had treated us well, and a few promoters from the previous year to get the ball rolling. I couldn't confirm dates, as I had no idea how long rehab intended to keep Chuck off the road. I also didn't want to interfere with our booking agent's plans, so I established the places we wanted to hit and then kept everything in a holding pattern.

The response from people told us all we needed to know—they wanted us back. Even through all our issues and addictions and limitations, we had struck a nerve. Luckily, we had a booking agent who had mentioned some promising stuff on the horizon.

Then we got an email stating our booking agent, who technically had never booked us a single show, had grown too busy with other clients and could no longer invest time in us. Derp. It hurt but didn't surprise us to learn he'd had a tough go of finding people willing to give Chuck a chance. Get in line.

The extra work I put in for the previous month justified itself, and I wondered where we could've been if I had started booking during wintertime and gotten us on some of the spring and summer events we craved.

If there's one thing I get angry about when thinking about Chuck's situation and how things transpired, it's that he never ever gave himself or the people around him enough consistency and confidence to get into a groove. With Chuck, you always walked on eggshells that he'd either get bored, change his mind, get arrested, lose his phone and disappear for a month, or worse. Any and all progress came only after monster effort and surviving several setbacks. Booking each tour leg, designing the shirts, even settling on sticker colors left me feeling like I had boxed Mike Tyson. Many things got left on the cutting room floor due to tiny hiccups and indecision.

The bonus of booking ourselves was we now controlled the dates we played and where we went, for the most part. We focused on making money rather than covering the whole country. No more cross-country trips with more off days than booked concerts. No month-long tours. Stick to the Midwest as much as possible. No shows that pose a legit risk to lose us money. No bills we don't fit on. No forcing the issue to fill a date if something quality isn't happening. But I think we broke every one of these guidelines within a week of making them.

A musician/promoter/good dude from Oregon, Ian Boynton, contacted us. Ian had a friend organizing a large-scale event coinciding with the upcoming solar eclipse in August. His friend had a cleared a field in the high desert of Madras, Oregon—the place NASA deemed as *the* location to watch the eclipse.

Now, I don't think either of us were overly excited about the moon blocking the sun, but the combo of heading west and playing a cool outdoor event sounded much better than another show at another dive bar. We expressed interest but knew we'd have some major gaps to fill to afford a trip there and back.

As the first batch of dates took shape, Chuck put his foot down and said he wanted to add a third person to our group. He said that ever since we added Andy on bass, he couldn't hear the music without it anymore. I enjoyed having the added instrument to the lineup, but I had hoped to make it work longer with just the two of us. Of course, Chuck called the shots.

I put an ad on Craigslist, *Bassist or keyboardist needed for non-glamorous touring,* figuring honesty served as the best means of communication at that point.

Four or five people responded the first week, and we ended up auditioning two of them.

Joshua Nelson, a local multi-instrumentalist who had a powerful voice and a great attitude, met with Chuck on a day I couldn't, for one reason or another. Chuck told me it went well, but Joshua had some scheduling conflicts at the end of the summer.

John, the next tryout, came, and we had a good jam, including playing a newer not-yet-titled song. It's a long song that ends with a lengthy, fast, repetitive riff and ended up titled "Relocation." Fun to play when it's working, pulling teeth when it doesn't. John handled Chuck well, even as Chuck revealed all his dark secrets of troubles with drugs and the law.

I cringed, expecting John to get uncomfortable—maybe even take his name out of the ring—but he nodded, and we kept playing. He had several obstacles between his multiple music gigs around town but told us he'd love to hit the road.

Chuck checked in to rehab, expecting a thirty-day stint.

"They might let me go early when I explain I've actually been sober for like seven months—well, eight really. Wait. Well, aside from the stuff in January. And February. But still, it's going to be like five or six months by the time I'm inside for thirty days."

Rehab forced us to turn down a few good shows in April and May and drop the pursuit of a rad opening slot the first week of June. The promoter of one of the shows proposed another date for us to open a three-band bill in Pekin, Illinois. Chuck's last day in rehab, if he flew straight and was telling the truth, would be June 9—the day of the show. We said *yes* to the concert, and Chuck talked to the facility about getting released the night before, so we could have enough travel time to make the five hundred mile trek. Nothing like cutting things close.

He also got weekend passes after a month residency, so we could practice, as long as he managed good behavior.

Chuck stayed in a facility about thirty minutes from my house. I got to know the route well, as reason after reason for a visit presented itself. One time, however, the point of my visit revolved around something positive.

"So, I'm working on a couple new songs."

It was late, probably nine or so, certainly I feel like it was after visiting hours, but there I was drinking a Kool Aid-type juice in a break room with Chuck. He looked good, mostly due to recent weight gains filling out his previously skeletal frame. I typically don't notice that stuff, but receiving hundreds of live photos from the previous year made it hard to ignore.

Most of his roommates were attending a group meeting he had decided to skip, so they had us move to a different building with proper supervision.

He said, "I prefer the Saturday group session, because the counselor who leads it makes the meeting way more tolerable. She actually listens and gets what I'm going through. You might know her. She's involved with the local music scene in some way. Like, her family owns a club or something."

"What's her name?"

"*Uhhh …*"

"Never mind."

"I haven't had songs come out of me like this in a long, long time."

"Awesome. Can't wait to hear 'em."

"Yeah?"

"Of course."

"Can I make a call first?"

With Chuck, there's always something brewing. In this case, he needs my phone to reach someone on the outside as he's not allowed to have his cellphone or make outgoing calls.

Now, within this month or so Chuck had spent in the facility, not a weekday had passed that Chuck and I hadn't talked three or four times. Weekends were tougher for some reason, but his passes started soon.

I slid my phone across the table, nervous that one of the guards would catch me. Chuck made a call.

As he spoke, I remember sizing up the guards, guessing which one Chuck had persuaded into letting him sneak phone calls. Conducting business equaled a big no-no, and yes, I take the blame for allowing it to happen, even knowing it might stunt his rehab. Though this call ended up being to his sponsor, Kristen—a great influence and addition to his life.

He hung up the phone. "Let me grab my guitar."

He went into the common area and searched a couch and a chair before returning empty-handed.

"Shit. I must've left it in my building."

"All good, man. I have some booking stuff to go over, a few T-shirt design questions, and—"

"Oh, shit. I need to grab another notebook. I've got something you've got to see. Let me ask the guard if I can go grab it."

He walked off and spoke with the big dude with dreads and then took off down a hallway. I waited for a good twenty minutes before Chuck returned.

He handed me one notebook and held another. "I've got a bunch of lyrics in there, but I need you to write down a phone number off one of the pages."

We scrolled through and found it, and he told me who he needed me to call.

He ripped out a piece of notebook paper, a mischievous grin spreading across his face. "I think we should start our own company. Booking, promotions—all that stuff. This will be our logo." He put down the paper, giggling like a little girl.

I'll describe the image the best I can, but it may also appear in this book, if only because I know with 2000% percent surety that Chuck would have wanted it included.

As I wrote that last sentence, I sighed.

My wife asked, "Are you okay?"

"Yeah, just ... Do you know where that pink notebook I have of Cris's?"

She led me to a basket by the garage door and retrieved it.

I opened it and removed the paper containing the image I'm talking about for her to see.

"Your exasperated sigh makes a lot more sense. How does that image still exist?"

I scanned the "logo," quickly glancing at Chuck.

A cowboy dude filled most of the page. Normal enough, until I noticed he sported a hook for an arm and a penis that stretched to the ground, touching his shoes. Then I saw a soldier cut in half at the waist, intestines pouring out as he reaches for his rifle. His left foot stretched downward to keep his balance on a large scrotum hung upside down. A cannon fired an old-style black ball over several pyramids in a desert. A pterodactyl swooped down, holding a baby in a sack in its beak. A grenade blew up, and a crescent moon sneered down at a wolf standing on top of a house, howling, with one hand up his own ass and the other touching his flamethrower penis.

As I studied the page, Chuck doubled-over in laughter, only because tripling with laughter is not possible. He fell out of his chair and howled along with the wolf, and I shook my head.

"We want to call it Wolfpack Productions."

"Who's *we*?"

"Mike and Cris and me. They are both out now, but they're cool. Mike and I have been talking about starting a podcast. Do you know much about them?"

"I mean, the general concept of—"

I noticed him searching the ground around us. "Fuck."

"What?"

"I forgot the guitar."

"You were gone that long and didn't grab it?"

"I got distracted by the picture."

And … he laughed again.

I rolled my eyes, a gesture that has become all too common when dealing with Chuck. "I'll hear them next time."

"But I really want you to hear them."

"Let's focus on what's coming up this summer."

I asked him about life inside. Chuck had made a couple friends and met many others he found bizarre. He enjoyed telling me about people weirder than him, but I could see the nagging in his eyes. His thoughts were elsewhere.

"Man, I'm going to go see if he can let me get the guitar."

He stood and asked, but the meeting had finished, and they wanted Chuck in his building.

Luckily, since he had someone on the inside giving him phone privileges, I heard new stuff shortly thereafter. And it sounded great. One song became four, became seven, became eleven or twelve new songs.

Chuck told me at one point, "I had to shut off the creative flow before I got overwhelmed and started to forget songs."

Between booking, managing, and promoting, my days filled up fast, and I fell behind on other personal things. I had set aside my fiction writing—a staple in my life for years—and that stung.

I posted a general call for help on Facebook. I knew Chuck fans existed in social-media world, and maybe one or two of them wanted to champion Chuck's cause.

Anne D'Agnillo mentioned a few names from Chuck's past, like Bob Forrest, who still worked in the music industry and might be able/willing to get things rolling. I spoke to one of these people, who manages a band I have liked for over twenty years. He knew Chuck from way back when and knew his reputation. Since Chuck couldn't talk on the phone during the week, when normal people conducted business, I had to cook up excuses to postpone things until the weekend. A few people bought it, many others didn't, and the rest knew something was amiss but didn't want to pry or push too far lest they learn something they'd rather not know.

In my opinion, Chuck's actions and his rehab stint had cost us at least a few promising outlets to help aid his comeback. And even as he dropped the ball and hurt everyone around him, he urged those same people to follow his vision.

Now that he had gotten me to add a third member, Chuck needed to push his luck. He brought Cris Morgan to the table as a second guitarist. With the lineup ballooning to four, the limits of what we played certainly expanded.

I had booked over fifteen shows under the impression the two of us, crammed in a small SUV like last year, comprised our group. I had then booked another fifteen to twenty shows with us traveling as a three piece. That meant renegotiating for more food and drinks; it meant a bigger rental vehicle; it meant more gas; it meant that much more effort to find floors to crash on or more money to book a hotel room; it meant more equipment to lug around and set up and maintain; and it meant splitting our tiny guarantees into pieces.

It did sound cool though, playing the tunes from the previous year in practice and hearing the added elements. Cris had an ability to pick up notes, riffs, tones, and add style quickly. As we rehearsed, he got comfortable and went off on his own tangents, layering in atmosphere, emotion, and some cool lead parts. This proved a blessing and a curse, as, even though Chuck had added Cris to be "the real guitar player," Chuck still wanted all the attention and the solos.

Cris preferred playing what Cris wanted to play. Sometimes, even if that fit from a technical standpoint, it didn't make the most sense for that song or part. And when you alter what you play each night, it can throw off the other people onstage who might or might not expect to hear something different.

I sound like a hypocrite saying that, as I love bands who weave in new parts and improvise live, but keeping Chuck focused and on-track onstage proved difficult the previous year. When you introduce more distractions, that job grew exponentially harder.

At practice, on stage, or whenever Cris has his guitar out, he wants to noodle. The stuff he plays sounds great. The guy can riff and riff and riff, and he has quality vocal patterns too. However, sometimes you need to concentrate and let the others around you focus. Chuck had ADHD times ten, so, when he stopped to explain parts of a song or when he started a new song, anything—a bird out the window, a mouse farting, or noodling on the guitar—threw him off and flustered him.

On the flipside, Chuck lived in a sandstorm of chaos and distraction. The television in the corner blasted at top volume; his phone vibrated nonstop; he would yell into the kitchen for Pip; and a farm's worth of dogs and cats ran around, barking and purring and pooping and begging and generally occupying the exact space you need to stand by your instrument. Somehow his distractions helped him focus. His chaos made perfect sense to him. I never figured out if that had any legitimacy or if he lived his entire life oblivious to the tornado he constantly surrounded around himself.

We got together a couple weekends in May, preceding our first batch of shows. Cris, Chuck, and I became three of the people going, and we auditioned a few others during those weekends. I, of course, felt overwhelmed by nerves since we didn't even have a band, let alone time to practice new or old songs to get tight by June 9.

May 13—I have a recording of a blues jam that, I think, Cris started along with one of the first recordings of "Blue Heart," a bluegrass tune that reminded me of Johnny Cash. Chuck had been playing a different tune, called "Nirvana," since it reminded him of the band. When he stops, I asked him to play that other thing he had played over the phone for me.

Chuck starts and stops a few times, finagling lyrics and phrasing, and you can hear him searching for the right range in his vocals. He had a deep rumble that gave the song such a downtrodden feel. Even with the awkward exploratory delivery, the song gripped me right from the start.

He stopped midsong. "*You were running … comin' round* … Fuck. Fuck!"

I said, "Lotta *fucks* in the lyrics, man. You gotta lighten up."

He continued the song, ignoring my goofball commentary.

Cris and Mike both found excuses to talk to Chuck's daughter, Sophie.

Chuck told Cris something to the effect of, "You can either date my daughter or be in the band, but not both."

We practiced on May 20 and 21 at Chuck's place. The heat and flies and pets and chaos made practice a nightmare, but the energy of playing new songs felt awesome.

By this time, I think Cris and Sophie were talking regularly on the downlow.

During practice, we found out Chris Cornell of Soundgarden had committed suicide. We were all shocked. Chuck was angry at Chris.

Chuck told us about the last time the pair had hung out, at one of Cornell's concerts. Cornell had made a mistake early in the set, and Chuck said Chris let it eat at him all night.

I thought about the previous year, seeing Chris Cornell's name in lights on all the biggest clubs' marquees and of how jealous I was of his position. They always say money and fame can't cure depression.

We played an untitled song, referred to only as "I Don't Know," with an oldies summer radio-hit vibe to it. Within the song, Chuck had referenced Stevie Wonder before singing a line from "More Today Than Yesterday." When we recorded the song on my phone the second time, I saved the file as "More Than Yesterday."

On the twentieth, Joshua couldn't make it, so we practiced with two other people. The first guy called himself Darby Crash, but Chuck made sure to let me know he wasn't *the* Darby Crash.

His real name was Jay, and he had met Chuck through Chuck's sponsor. Jay lived over an hour away, near the

Pennsylvania border. Though shy and despite his equipment not working, we had a fun couple of hours playing. Jay came off as nervous, genuine, and hopeful. I hated leaning away from him due to equipment and transportation issues, but Cris, who was mostly a lock to come out with us, also lived about an hour's drive away, to the south, and had limited resources and no car. Getting Chuck around and throwing him a few bucks was one thing, but to have three dudes in the band all needing me to step up felt like too much.

On that same day, John came over and played. Again, things went well, and the new stuff now flowed with him holding down the bass. I found communicating with him easy, even midsong, and I think it came from the constant gigging he does, whether original music or covers.

On the twenty-first, we worked with Joshua and Cris, our focus mainly concentrated on the new songs. "Blue Heart" consumed a large chunk of time as Chuck tried to walk Cris through the solo he had running through his head. Cris tried several different styles, but Chuck wasn't feeling them. I heard some stuff I really liked and fought to give Cris the reigns to create his own solo.

On the recording I have from that day, Chuck instructs Cris to "do like a hesitant kinda thing. *Dar, dar, dar, dar, dar, dar, dar, dar, dar, dar, dar, dar, dar.*"

Mouth-guitar always sounds cool, but it's hard to type.

Chuck listened to Cris attempt to follow the instruction and then said, "You'll kinda get the feel when we're playing." He turned to me. "Is it recording?"

"Yep."

Before I could finish my short-word answer, Chuck had already started playing and then quickly stopped. "Let's slow it down."

The reason I add that nugget is to showcase another tendency of Chuck, both endearing and beyond frustrating. He's the only one playing. He sets the pace. And yet, he stops and says, "Let's slow it down." At practice, it's amusing, but onstage, when he waits long enough for us to start and then he stops to adjust, he totally throws everyone else under the bus.

Relistening to these early recordings though, I can hear the excitement in my rhythm. I totally got lost in the songs and sped up as I played, happy to contribute.

Cris plays drums and anything else he can get his hands on, so I certainly experienced a rising amount of nerves and jealousy as I saw him and Chuck grow super close. They had a connection through rehab and drugs that I could never relate to on any genuine level. They had both lived in California and both approached music in a similar fashion. Both are songwriters. Not to say I don't write songs, but … it's different. Cris and Chuck discussed Cris playing drums rather than guitar, which always hurt. Again, I knew I wasn't a permanent solution. At some point, if things went well, I'd need to get replaced. Obviously, the sourness in my gut every time this got discussed showed me that I had become more attached than even I wanted to admit.

As we reached the guitar solo, Cris played a clean riff reminiscent of a surf rock "Munster's Theme" sort of vibe. He had an electric guitar and a busted amp, which makes it hard to visualize how things sounded. He had a thin but loud tone that cut right through Chuck's small-amped acoustic, making timing difficult.

When Chuck played "Mr. Smith" for the first time at one practice, I banged along; although, he had originally demoed it as a guitar-, bass-, vocals-only tune.

We played it a few times, and I asked him if he had any feedback or wanted any changes.

He said, "No. It's great. Like usual, you just slid right in. You know that if I hear something I don't want, I'll tell you."

We ran through "More Than Yesterday" a few times and discussed various titles for it. Cris had either inquired about Stevie Wonder's real name or had known the correct answer—Stevland.

We thought that sounded cool, but I suggested the altered "Steveland," and the name stuck. I had helped Chuck name another song, "Ericalution," a couple years earlier, combining Chuck's explanation of the story/lyrics along with his eldest daughter's name. He already had a song called "Sophie" and wanted to make sure they each had one.

As an aside, I love the cover art for the "Ericalution" single. It followed a simple, often-used design of the evolution of man but with a clear Mosley twist.

My parents, who watch my kids twice a week, had us over for dinner. I played a few recordings from recent practices I'd taken with my phone. My dad and mom both enjoyed "Steveland," though my mom said, "I wish I could hear and understand his lyrics better."

My dad asked how we had named the song, and I walked him through the story.

He looked confused. "But Stevie Wonder didn't write 'More Today Than Yesterday.'"

"What?"

"That's a Spiral Staircase song."

"I'm pretty sure Stevie's version is the hit though."

He wasn't convinced. "They made it a hit themselves. Sixty-eight or '69, I think."

I shrugged, listening in my head to Stevie Wonder sing it. "I dunno. I only know Stevie's version."

In truth, I had only heard the song a few times, and it had probably been years since the last spin. Maybe it was in a commercial or movie I had seen, but that's about all I could remember.

I looked up the song. As usual, my dad had his facts straight. Fine, they did it originally, but come on, I had never heard the name Spiral Staircase before today, so I doubt their version was *the* version everyone knew. I searched the internet for a good video of Stevie Wonder performing it. Nothing. I looked for when he had released the single. Nothing. I looked for any evidence he had ever performed that song. Nothing.

This mystery quickly escalated into Mandela Effect territory. At the next practice, I mentioned this to Chuck, who I felt certain would help me set the record straight.

He paused, eyes distant. "Stevie didn't do that tune?"

"Not that I can find."

"Shit. I swore it was him, but I do remember the name Spiral Staircase."

"My dad said he likes 'Steveland', but you're going to have to update your lyrics."

From then on, Chuck replaced *"Stevie's on the radio …"* with *"Staircase on the radio…"*

Thanks, Dad.

For the final weekend of practice, we retreated to Joshua's house on the southeast side of Cleveland. He and his band had claimed Joshua's basement as their practice spot and recording studio, so the set up worked great and boasted a thousand less distractions, aside from a fallen tree from the neighbor's yard that had unfortunately busted Joshua's fence.

We worked on some of the previous year's setlist, but Chuck didn't want to waste time with songs he played solo, like "Sophie" and "Chip Away." Unfortunately, I think this contributed to neither song getting included heavily in the 2017 setlists. And really, the solo stuff made less sense with three dudes hanging out and waiting rather than just one. Chuck, of course, found a great song to make everyone wait anyway.

He wanted to cover "Nothing Compares 2 U," made famous by Sinéad O'Conner but written by Prince. Chuck had his own version that slowed down the song and added an extra-long noise guitar solo. It fit his vibe and the set, but Chuck wanted to open with it, which I thought was a terrible idea.

Continuing to call his tour the Reintroduce Yourself Tour meant people would still show up expecting to hear Faith No More tunes, maybe even the entire *Introduce Yourself* record. This meant metal dudes in Carcass and Metallica shirts, waiting for headbanging rock music rather than our brand of distorted acoustic rock. So, when we opened with a nine-minute ballad, it had people scratching their heads wondering what the hell they had gotten themselves into. Chuck, of course, loved those moments.

I thought the quicker we captured people's attention, the more they would stay and the more they would drink, making even the smaller crowds tolerable by the people paying us to come and perform.

Anyway, he stuck to his guns and often would pull out that song to begin.

"This is still our soundcheck. The actual set starts later."

Certain nights, people sang along and/or chuckled, and it fit. Other nights, it went over like a "lead" zeppelin.

I should've snapped a photo of the sneer he would shoot me as he started singing it, knowing how it boiled my blood. Whenever possible, I would exit the stage or sit and drink while he meandered through it. In those moments, I became an audience member and could appreciate his performance better.

Another huge change was the exclusion of "Bob Forest" to end our set. It's one of my favorite Chuck tunes and always made for a grand finale as, even when we messed it up live, we managed to make it a memorable spectacle. The main reason it got demoted was to make room for this new, long, meandering psychedelic tune Chuck had written.

That song and "Bob Forest" shared many similarities and were equally daunting to pull off live. When we jammed it at practice, it typically ran fifteen to twenty minutes long. My conga part didn't begin until after the third verse. When it started, the song didn't stop until our arms threatened to fall off. The tune built from a slow, folk tune into a monstrous speed demon of psychedelia, Chuck's echoing vocals and squealing guitar bursting from the speakers like a non-filtered glimpse into his maddened mind.

Again, when it hit, watch out. When it failed, damn, watch out.

Chuck headed back for his last week of rehab; Cris and Sophie connected further; Joshua packed his GoPro camera; and I prepped us for a three-day jaunt.

Ready? Nope. But we didn't have a choice.

CHAPTER ELEVEN

06/2017:
The Cris Mosby Boys Ride Again, For the First Time

Someone gave Chuck an ancient MP3 player with about twenty-five songs on it to pass the time in rehab. He had no ability to add or update songs, so, by the time we drove eleven hours to Pekin, Illinois, we had every song memorized, even if none of us wanted them stuck in our heads.

Our first mini-tour leg of 2017 had officially begun to the sounds of Katy Perry, Portishead, Stereolab, and Lana Del Rey. Chuck pretty much only ever listened to music with female vocals. You could play thirty albums for him with no reaction, no sign that he's even listening. Then throw on a Dresden Dolls song. Before the first chorus, he's asking who it was and falling in love.

The four of us got out of town without much issue, but the drive took longer than expected due to every inch of Rt 80 covered in orange barrels throughout Indiana. Pekin sits on the outskirts of Peoria, home of Jim Thome, so we also got a good dose of Illinois traffic.

Initially, Justin, the show promoter, had added us as an opener for two other more-established bands, but they both had dropped off last moment. I can't remember the official story, but it had something to do with one of the bands running a Kickstarter campaign and needing to finish a recording to appease donors.

Either way, instead of a thirty-minute set, we were headlining, and two locals had been added with no time to promote. The crowd, sparse but loud, made us feel welcomed by arriving early. One couple, who had driven from Iowa, were stressed as they hadn't heard we were no longer opening. They had only secured a babysitter until like eleven; we were set to go on at ten or so.

Jerry, the sound guy, bucked the stereotype of grumpy soundmen. He was friendly, helpful, and worked with us, which immensely helped the show. Now having said that, we've also had total jerks capture our sound great, but man, it's just easier when you don't feel like you're totally ruining someone's life by showing up.

As a low-tiered band, you try to get along and stay out of the sound person's way. Or, if they're cool, you work with them to experiment a bit, give them some freedom and have a blast.

My own self-doubt and insecurity with having the new guys along had me reflecting. My jealousy about them stepping in without going through anything I had endured still remained, but it's not personal.

Again, last year—and the previous eighteen or so years—I had done a lot for Chuck, and the sacrifice and commitment I had made the previous year, along with all the hours and work I had put in had only managed to get me into a position that I now had to work harder and see less reward while other members came and went and got paid X-amount without lifting a finger, sacrificing anything aside from time and risking nothing aside from being in a car while Chuck drove.

I had a blast playing with Chuck but could only imagine how fun it would be not worrying about promotion, booking, transportation, merch, budgets, hotels, keeping promoters happy, or anything else aside from waking up, drinking beers, and playing a show.

We took the stage, which had a barrier in the front with no good way on or off, and Chuck started stumbling, mumbling, fumbling even worse than the previous year's shows. He warned me I'd have to tolerate some more of his neuroses, as he didn't have drugs, booze, or weed to help him cope. When he did play, his tempo was way fast. We zipped through songs when we weren't stopping and starting, stopping and starting.

I goofed on "Blue Heart," reversing my beat at the beginning somehow. By the first verse, I had things straightened out. Chuck added a long talking intro, explaining the song that became a staple during the set.

"It's a Blue Heart, not black, 'cause then it would be dead. It's been broken, stepped on, lied to, hurt, but it's still beating. Blue Heart."

As we played, most of the crowd exited. At first, I felt mortified, like we were bombing, even though I thought we sounded pretty darn good for a first show. Afterward, I spoke to several people who assured me that Pekin wasn't a late-night town, and folks weren't used to staying out late. I also noticed most of the out-of-towners had left, needing to get on the road. Again, we played about four hours later than people had expected.

For me, it marked the first time I placed my conga in the traditional drummer spot, behind the singer and band. Why did that matter? Well, first off, most of the mid-song changes happened by me watching Chuck's fingers. This is especially helpful on the nights his tempo/timing/structure of songs get loose. From behind, it was harder to watch his fingers, so I relied more on his head bobbing and shoulder sways.

Chuck and I also had relied on fun banter to move the show along and make it a little more unique, city to city, and staring at his back made it hard to bounce off him in the typical way. He also got nervous enough that he'd forget to talk to me like he normally would. We interrupted each other a few times and missed a few opportunities to settle down, I think.

After the show, a father and son told us great stories about discovering and enjoying Chuck's music. The son—sorry, I forgot his name—told Chuck we reminded him of a stripped-down Pink Floyd, which Chuck loved. He often mentioned them in interviews after that.

The guys got their first taste of sharing a room with Chuck; TV on blast, door slamming once an hour so Chuck can go smoke, waking up at 5 a.m., and worse, they had to handle my snoring.

At 10 a.m. the following morning, I found myself wandering around a Walmart parking lot, waiting for Chuck to return a pair of Dickies he'd bought earlier that morning because they didn't have the big pockets he preferred. I paced while talking on the phone with Gabby Glazer of Luscious Jackson. She had heard from Anne D'Agnillo that we wanted to secure a show on a Tuesday night in Brooklyn. She knew a spot we should try. Random moments happen in my life that leave me perplexed with how they ever came together, and that was certainly one of them. Thanks to Gabby, we got the show.

We headed south to St. Louis. The bar we played, Red Fish, Blue Fish, was in the St. Charles area, north and west of the city proper. We pulled into a strip mall, realizing we had over five hours until showtime. Chuck and Cris, maybe Joshua too, went to shop for the right kind of Dickies while I checked out a local record shop run by Phil, the guy who brought us to town. I found a ton of stuff I wanted, and, for you Clevelanders, I confirmed the rumors that The Michael Stanley Band were also popular there too.

The promoter bought us pizza, which the club had made. Oddly, the people at the club ordered pizza from somewhere else as they made pizza for us.

Cris had gotten Chuck a delay pedal to replace one that had broken. As the anti-gearhead that Chuck was, he removed it from the box and turned the nobs all the way up. The previous night, it had caused some confusion and thrown us off. Joshua sat Chuck down and gave him a tutorial on the pedal, and they found a couple settings that matched the sound Chuck wanted.

Chuck did an in-store appearance at the record shop. A few people attended to get autographs and photos, including Alison Masson—the driving force behind Metal Babe Mayhem. Again, anytime a group of metal fans came to see us, it made me nervous. Sometimes it worked out fine and they appreciated what we did, while other times we saw the disgusted expressions that we weren't melting faces.

Bro, it's an acoustic tour …

A guy named Nick arrived early and hung out late with us. I loved the people I met playing with Chuck. Nick is a dude just living life, man.

The bar had an odd layout, with a couch area up front near the stage on the righthand side. A group of people with no idea who Chuck was or apparently how loud they were talking sat there. It didn't help that Chuck spent no less than ten minutes talking and fumbling with his guitar before we played "Bella Donna," and then I counted with my phone recording that he started and stopped the song about a dozen times. It went something like this:

Chuck dicked around until Cris and Joshua got antsy. They started playing "Wisdom Comes." I joined in. Chuck started singing along before stopping because he felt we were playing too fast. We were.

Then he noodled around some more until I asked, "So?"

"*Sooooo* ... Hey, um, hello. Hi. So, is there some intro music?"

"What?"

"Err, not intro music. What do they call it? You know, when the band comes out onstage and they play, like ..." He made some distorted drum-and-bass groove with his mouth.

I used my radio announcer voice and said, "Ladies and gentlemen!"

Cris started playing "Mahna Mahna"—The Muppets song, not the band called Menomena—and Joshua noodled around.

The crowd went from excited to politely paying attention to murmurs to no one watching, aside from Nick.

He clapped.

I saluted. "Thanks, Nick."

"Oh, boy." Chuck searched the crowd. "Um, good evening. My name is Charles Henry Mosley the Third, and, uh, this is Cris. It's only his second time onstage playing guitar."

I piped in. "Usually, he's just dancing."

Chuck said something about it being an audition for Cris and then added, "If you think he's doing all right, just tell me after the show."

The exchange got a few laughs and claps and would've been a great way to start, but Chuck still felt nervous, so he went into a monologue about all our upcoming shows, half of which he had no idea when and where they were.

"I have really bad stage fright. I always have. I'm not making that up."

A guy, sitting on the couch, yelled out, "It's probably Parkinson's."

Chuck took it in stride, strumming his guitar. "No. It's nervousness, I swear to God."

I said, "Chuck, that dude is really big. Don't mess with him."

Though, by the end of the show, I wanted to.

Chuck asked, "Why? Was that bad?"

"No. Just play a song."

This drove me mad. Absolutely crazy. I understand Chuck felt nervous before we played, but he also insisted on beginning with a song he started, usually singing right off the rip. Time and time again I suggested the band start and he joins us so he didn't have the opportunity or the control to hijack the crowd for ten minutes while waiting to feel ready to play.

Chuck told the crowd he wasn't sure if he needed to pee before we started, but he decided just to start. He sang the first word of "Bella Donna" before stopping and said, "Yeah, and I'm losing my voice. Please forgive me for all of my shortcomings." He clears his throat. "I'm not doing that for you guys. I'm doing it to clear my throat."

By this point, the din of the crowd is loud as a chunk of the people have tuned us out in favor of talking with the other bar patrons. People are returning to the bar to get their second drink since we've started, and we haven't even played a song yet.

He played the opening note and let it ring out. "Stop shaking inside out," he mumbled to psych himself up. Starting again, he got through the song's first seven words. "Can I just get a little more of myself in the monitor?"

Joshua asked, "More vocals?"

Chuck nodded. "Yeah, vocals. That's what I meant. I think I'm singing loud, but, if you guys can't hear me, just let him know." He pointed to the soundman. Chuck started the song again. *"Yesterd—"* Stopping again, he said, "And the starting-and-stopping thing will end soon, okay?"

I made a sarcastic coughing noise.

Ignoring me, Chuck started again. *"Yesterday morning—"* He stopped again. "I promise I won't do it anymore."

Started. *"Yester—"*

Stopped. "Sorry that thing distracted me."

I rolled my eyes. "Three strikes, Chuck."

This time when he started, Chuck sounded strong. He had confidence. He had emotion. He was vulnerable. Onstage, we fell in line and delivered to a crowd that no longer cared. Their conversations, laughter, clinking drinks, and indoor smoking drowned us out.

As we played, we won some of them back, and the crowd gave us a supportive applause by the time the song reached its first break.

Chuck thanked them and restarted the song but sang the wrong line.

He stopped. "Wait. That's wrong."

He started.

We finished the song, and Chuck said, "Thank you." I don't remember anyone clapping aside from Nick. About nineteen minutes into the set and we had one song under our belts. Not bad for Mosley work.

We hit them with "Death March" next, and we were off and running.

The set hadn't really gelled yet, and I take the blame for that. I didn't understand how different things would be with four dudes, how much potential for expansion and improv and, hell, I didn't realize how much noise an acoustic band could really generate. Not to mention we were all learning the new songs.

Chuck still had unwritten lyrics for some, and others had parts he still wasn't sure of the guitar riffs, but I think I tried to simplify what we were doing too much and maybe I held onto the intimate vibe we had created last year. I had dug it, warts and all. This new thing had an edge and a groove and an untamed psychedelic element lurking, waiting to get unleashed.

As I contemplated my place with the band and how the setlist I had fought for now felt wrong, I forgot to turn off Chuck's vocal delay we used for our version of Cement's "Living Sound Delay." He started "Blue Heart," heard the delay and, to his credit, didn't stop the song. He played it off and gave me a chance to shut off his pedal before continuing.

After a few more songs, Chuck glanced at the setlist and read the titles. "Okay, no. Maybe. Yeah, but we'll see. Oh, alright. Fuck it."

I said, "Russian Roulette with the setlist?"

Chuck giggled. "I know."

"Where's Mosley going next, everybody?"

His giggle became a hearty chuckle.

"We don't know," I said, totally honest.

Chuck looked at his guitar to see where his fingers should go. "We'll see."

I loved when he had genuine moments of levity. He had a different laugh. For a guy fighting demons, twenty-four seven, those moments were rare, but damnit, we had some, and they are a big reason I tell myself the tour succeeded.

He started singing, "Nothing Compares 2 U."

Every time we played it, I think he expected a big crowd reaction, but that rarely happened. The song, at least the first verse or two, were hard to place the way he performed, because the tempo dragged. In a club full of five hundred Mosley fans, this tune would've killed. Everyone would sing along and talk about it the next day at work, but people don't want to hear downer tunes at the dive bar, man. They want excitement. They want a beat. They want reasons to buy shots.

He did a portion of the first verse, but he backtracked when it got zero response. "Or I could go like …" He played, "Old Man."

I can't remember if we had ever practiced it with Joshua. Hell, I had only played it a couple of times.

Chuck spent a lot of time avoiding decisions for various reasons. On this tour, his indecision with who should play on what song hurt us daily.

For example, he had moments he wanted to play "Old Man" by himself, other times he wanted the band along for the ride, and at even other times he only wanted us to play on certain parts. These thoughts confused and distracted him so much that it even affected the live show.

That night, midsong, he stopped playing. "Eh, you guys can take five."

Then he changed his mind, and we played more of it, but I could feel his split decision weighing on him as we played. He heard things he didn't like from us, and he let that damper his performance.

The middle of our set leaned far too mellow during those early shows of 2017. Again, not knocking the songs but rather commenting on the places we played and the audience's expectations of us. "Chip Away," "Song 2," "Mr. Smith," and "Nothing Compares 2 U" all in a row really lowered the energy. Maybe at a wine bar it would've killed?

"Come Around" was one of the most fun songs to play in 2016, but it felt muddy with the added pieces and lack of practice. I kept falling out of my groove due, I think, to the added instrumentation playing closer to the recorded VUA version. Or maybe I just wasn't playing something that really fit the song's structure. I left it off setlists after a while, but I missed playing it.

I went outside for fresh air and to put some space between Chuck and myself. It was only our second show, and I was already frustrated that he sabotaged our set each night before we had a chance to goof up ourselves. I sat down, leaning against the strip mall's brick wall and checked the time. It was too late to Facetime with the kids, but I had spoken to them earlier, so it was all good.

A guy who had parked his motorcycle right outside the door told me, "Good luck with the rest of the tour." He revved the engine, blowing exhaust right in my face and drove off into the St. Charles night.

I moved farther from the club and sat by myself for a while. Was I still the right guy for the band?

Having asked myself this question a lot throughout the previous year but then accomplishing so much, I got caught off guard that I might still feel out of place. Why wouldn't I be? With Cris and Joshua involved, the band could achieve a certain amount of groove and tempo control, along with concealing Chuck's wild play. This put pressure on me to step up to their level and raise the bar rather than drag things down to the sloppy depths of the previous tours. Again, I am not a percussionist, so even taking the stage took a certain amount of naive ego. I had to play the part and believe I could play the part without really ever facing the question of *could I* or *should I* play the part.

I had rarely thrown things off with my rhythm. I mean, I kept the beat simple and focused on tempo and leading Chuck along rather than flashy fills. I often told people that a monkey could do my job, and that was true—though I wouldn't want them driving the van.

Joshua came out to check on me. I followed him into the club, and we got drinks. I ordered a whiskey and ginger. He got a root beer something. If I remember correctly, it was a root beer-flavored beer they brewed themselves and mixed with moonshine. Though I don't know what was in it, I know Joshua got a bit tipsy. Right, bud?

The after-show buzz for me is super strong, whiskey or not. Though we played to a half-interested crowd at a strip mall bar on the outskirts of a city and our performance had sounded shaky, I still walked offstage feeling like a million bucks. I am addicted to those moments. I will never experience enough of that buzz to satisfy me. It's empowering to know you performed something that caused a reaction in complete strangers.

That rush of ego made finding a bent piece of metal, possibly someone's earring, in my drink all that much more enjoyable. To ride that high and get a swift reminder that you weren't worth enough to the bartender for her to check your glass, really encapsulates what it's like to tour at our level.

I still have the metal, if someone needs it back.

If the earring wasn't enough to bring me down to Earth, the bartender telling me how crappy this night had been for tips and that she wished she had called out sick that night certainly did.

The best part of the night, and one of the tops of the tour, happened at the surprisingly affordable hotel. Joshua had managed to drink several of the root beer drinks, and he was feeling the buzz by the time we were ready to crash.

He sat next to Chuck on the bed. "Man, I just want to make sure you're happy."

Cris and I giggled from around the room as we watched.

"Chuck, it's your vision. It needs to be what you want." Joshua put his arm around Chuck.

"It's great. We sounded fine." Chuck stood to go outside to smoke. "Just watch the first verse on 'Blue Heart.' There's three lines not just two. And remember on 'Bob Forest' to ride the A and watch me for the change."

I settled to the floor in the corner as close to the air conditioning as I could get.

Joshua continued, even without Chuck in the room. "Do you think he liked it?"

"Yeah, man. It's getting there." I pulled my hoodie over my shoulders.

Joshua stood. "I just know I made a few mistakes, and I want him to be happy with everything. I want him to be glad he brought me along."

"Okay."

Chuck returned and the dialogue continued.

"Chuck, you sure things were okay?"

"Yeah."

"But I just want it to sound like your vision, man."

I don't remember word for word, but it sounded similar to what I just typed, along with Cris and I giggling and saying Joshua would feel it in the morning.

Joshua sat next to Chuck on the bed and leaned his head onto Chuck's shoulders. "You sure everything sounded good?"

Damnit. I was too tired and amused to take a photo or video of the situation, not to mention I didn't want to embarrass Joshua, but now I wish I had so badly—only because I know Joshua more, and Chuck got such a kick out of it too.

The following day we headed for Indianapolis. Cris and Joshua slept the entire drive while Chuck and I reflected at being the experienced road dogs assuming the role of parents to our green kids touring for the first time. Typically, Chuck and I rode up front and did most of the driving, so it became easy to feel like the parents even though we were barely adults ourselves.

I drove the first few hours, but Chuck asked to take over. It was rare for him to actively want to drive, but he had received new mixes from the Primitive Race camp, three of each song, and he wanted to listen to them.

I dozed off to the hard rock blasting from the speakers, thankful for a chance to recoup. We also planned to head home to Cleveland right after our show that night, so I knew I needed to stay rested.

It didn't last long.

"Oh, shit!" Chuck yelled as I felt the car weave. "We're just about out of gas."

I sat up. Yep, the gaslight was on. I searched the map on my phone for gas stations. Apparently, we were in the Twilight Zone of gasoline. The next station on the map lay about twenty miles ahead; the closest was about six miles behind us.

"I saw an exit and thought about stopping to use the restroom, but I noticed the light right after we passed it. I'm not sure how long it has been on."

We exited at the next stop, nothing but fields as far as the eye could see aside from a few trees. Chuck pulled an 80's action movie 180-degree turn, dust and small pebbles flying behind us as the music continued to heighten the moment.

Whichever mix Primitive Race chose, I was excited to hear the final disc.

We reached the correct exit, and Chuck almost missed it. Again. He flew up the ramp and turned left—into oncoming traffic. A truck headed right for us. We both screamed. He swerved, just missing the middle barrier separating the road. He raced into the gas station, both of us still frozen with fear. He hit the brakes.

My heart raced, and my breath couldn't come quick enough. I turned in my seat to verify everyone was okay.

Cris cracked his eyes. "We there?"

Joshua didn't even stir.

As I pumped gas, Chuck exited the gas station, flipping something in the air that made an electronic insect noise. The unsettling nature of the sound only grew when coupled with the childish giggles Chuck couldn't stop from escaping.

Turns out, he had bought two magnets.

He tossed them up. He giggled. He tossed them up. He giggled. He tossed them up, and I retrieved my camera to capture the absurdity.

We caught traffic in Terre Haute, Indiana, and then realized we would lose an hour due to crossing into the Eastern Time Zone. We had planned to arrive early to ensure the soundman had time to tweak things, as they would record our set.

Drew Fortier, a guitarist, and I texted about meeting up. He happened to be in Indy, visiting his girlfriend. We were supposed to share a bill earlier in the year at the grand opening of Ellefson's Coffee in Jackson, Minnesota, but Chuck, being in rehab, killed those plans.

We arrived and, dude, it got so hot outside, the heat zapped my motivation real fast to do anything.

Adam, who ran the studio and venue, had ordered a stage for us. They constructed it while we loaded in. Our soundcheck took a long time due to feedback issues with the vocals. The sound guy was convinced Chuck's vocal pedal was to blame, but we had danced that dance before. In the end, it had something to do with phantom power and other things above my pay grade. All I know is that we didn't check our sound or practice a new song we wanted to try due to the delays. I also realized there stood a great chance that my weight might send me crashing right through the stage.

So much for the pounds I had lost in the UK. (Hey, so I want to insert a joke about weight and pounds and the British currency here, but I feel bad joking about money knowing how hard my wife worked to keep us afloat while I stretched our accounts and my weight stretched my waistline.)

Matt Mosley (pronounced: Mahz-ley) drove from West Lafayette, Indiana for the show. Though he pronounces his name wrong, I told him, "Today, you're officially a Mosley."

Matt told me later that Chuck had introduced me as "Doug, my partner in musical crime, and trust me … What I get away with is a crime."

We stood outside, and he told me about being a Marine, about his wife (all good things, Yung-Yi Chen), and about the dissertation he was working on for school.

Why were we standing outside? Well, I get claustrophobic inside the venue before the show. Like, I don't know where I belong pre-show. A "backstage" room had been set up with water bottles, but I hate hiding from the crowds who came to see us, even if there isn't a crowd. Also, Joshua had taken up residency across a few chairs in there, and I wanted him to sleep so he could hopefully play with us that night. Manning the merch booth provided another option, but people walked in and out, so it felt too warm. I wanted to avoid eye contact with Adam, as no one was coming to the show, and I felt guilty. I always do, even though I promoted to the best of my ability.

I think I get so claustrophobic because, at that point, there's nothing else you can do to draw people to the show aside from

Twitter and Facebook. Maybe I'm not even claustrophobic. I might just be antsy, nervous before the shows. I don't feel nerves onstage, and the antsy energy only seems to happen when the crowd is small. I dunno, man, maybe I just need a distraction.

The stage managed to hold me up, probably losing money for people in Vegas, but the combination of its shakiness and my back pressed against the wall made for a tense show on my part.

Another example of Chuck's stage fright happened that night as he told the crowd about how he had written a song about Dug Smith, who had passed away in December. He explained we would play it soon at a memorial for Dug, so we needed to practice it. As he finished his banter, he realized "Mr. Smith" wasn't next on the setlist. Instead of changing things up, like he did almost nightly, he tried to convey, poorly, that the next song wasn't the one he had just been talking about. He played "Song 2" instead.

We played "Relocation" for the first time live, though I don't think it had a title at that point. Chuck called it a few things, and most of the titles included *Re* at the beginning.

He told some people, "It's called 'Relocation' because the song starts in one place, but it takes you somewhere totally different by the time it's done," or some reasoning close to that.

After the show, I wanted to rush us onto the road, but Chuck had a few beers he wanted to finish. Adam showed us this swinging instrument he had bought on a recent trip to Australia, which sounded cool, but I worried Chuck would find a way to fling it into a car window or something.

When we did finally leave, Chuck had to eat right away. I know, you're wondering why I would fill a novel with stories about going to McDonald's, but Chuck found a way to make every moment unique on the road. We got our food in the drive-thru, but Chuck realized we hadn't gotten our full order. I pulled around again, but the line wrapped around the building. Chuck exited the car and stood across from the cashier's window and stared until they noticed the dreaded dude sporting a surly expression. It took a good ten minutes, but he explained to them we got shorted some food.

He returned, puffing out his chest at his accomplishment, only to realize we still needed one more fry.

Against my whining protest, he went back and repeated his actions. This time it didn't take quite as long, but I found it much funnier now that I had lost all hope of getting home without the confusion and delay that comes with Chuck.

Recalling my days working at Wendy's, I wonder what I would've done had I seen Chuck staring at me through the window late at night.

We had survived our first test. Cris had passed his audition. Now we had two weeks before our next run to smooth the kinks and really hit the ground running.

The next day, I texted Chuck. *Union Hall capacity 150 is available July 25th but we need to find 2 locals to open and help bring folks before they will confirm. If you know anyone in NYC that plays music and has fans now is the time to call them.*

His response, *Ask Anne?*

Again, I couldn't resist quoting Chuck's own lyrics back to him. *She said, do whatever the hell you wanna do. Now, is the time, where you can do anything …*

Ha ha ha ha fuck u!

It always feels like we should've been more on top of things to start each run, but stuff piles up. Booking shows, renting cars, auditioning new people, helping Chuck work on the Cement re-release, scheduling and conducting interviews, transcribing the interviews Chuck scribbled on paper, learning new songs, Chuck and Chris from Primitive Race debating song titles, negotiating with several people on recording time, and ordering T-shirts. Oh yeah, and trying to avoid deadbeat-husband status as well.

Joshua couldn't go on the second batch of dates due to him officiating a wedding for a close friend. I contacted John, the other bassist we had connected with, to update him on when we would practice.

He responded, "Oh, you wanted me to go on that run too?"

"Uh, what?"

"I thought I was just going on the long run in August, so I booked other gigs, and I have a doctor's appointment on the twenty-ninth."

I said, "*Sheeeeeeeet*," but I wasn't referring to those things you put on your bed.

CHAPTER TWELVE

06/2017-07/2017:
Ah, Mr. Fortier,
Just in Time for the Reckoning

In Cambridge, someone smart once said, "Necessity is the mother of invention," but, in Cleveland, Chuck and I realized, "Shit, we need a bass player, fast, willing to hit the road with us for nothing and with no time to practice."

However you say it, it boiled down to some quick thinking and a little bit of luck to patch us up in time for leg number two.

Drew Fortier, who lived six hours away in Chicago, offered to come with us as a guitarist.

I texted Chuck to let him know to call Drew.

He responded, *What's his last name?*

Fortier.

Hmmm, French.

Explains a lot.

Pretty boy.

Yup.

Chuck asked Cris to switch to bass and … *Boom!* We had a band, but no way to practice.

Chuck, Cris, and I convened on June 21st after I picked up Chuck at his old rehab facility; he had attended a meeting.

My note that day says, *Stopped at Drug Mart. Stopped at Mega Mart. Dicking around ... Dicking around. Tough to get in a groove. Love the new song, but the middle part is looong and boring.*

A running gag all year was what to name the band, since we only went by Chuck Mosley when booking shows. During the last run, we had jokingly referred to ourselves as Chuck Mosley and the Self-Helps. I had given us that name because Chuck always threw out these sage motivational life affirmations from time to time, and I think he knew enough of them to write a book. That day at practice I changed our name to Chuck Mosley and the Clay Pigeons, because he shot down every idea we shared, sometimes even before we had finished explaining them.

This called back to my first band, Fromandafly, when our bassist, Chris, would do something similar—using the neck of his bass as a gun to literally blast ideas from the sky.

Five days before we needed to leave for our next run, Drew let us know he had to travel to New Jersey to play guitar for singer/songwriter Stephen Shareaux. Not only would he pass right through Cleveland, there and back, but he had confirmed a meeting with a filmmaker in town for the trip. Drew asked the director to meet him at Chuck's house, so we could jam a few songs with Drew.

Thom Hazaert and Stephen Shareaux wanted to visit the Rock and Roll Hall of Fame. Somehow, Waylon Reavis got roped into picking us up in his insane tour van. His band, A Killer's Confession, is on Thom's label and had recently released their debut.

The first time I had seen Waylon perform live he covered the intro to "The Crab Song" with Mushroomhead, like we did at our shows.

The Rock Hall's basement floor displayed several rows of mannequins donning outfits that a variety of musicians had worn through the years. Chuck, Pip, and I passed sign after sign declaring, *Do not touch displays. Alarms will sound.* This is Mosley we're talking about. To no one's surprise, when we reached an outfit David Bowie had worn, Chuck reached out and felt it.

No alarms sounded.

Pip mentioned the signs to Chuck.

"Really?"

Pip pointed to one of them, a couple feet away.

Chuck's cheeks flushed. We glanced around to see if security were coming. They weren't. We hustled away, because, you know, Chuck could easily blend in with the crowd.

Stephen Shareaux and I got separated from the others, and we discussed, naturally, rock music. I told him about how my Uncle Don had exposed me to music from an early age and how, for my wedding, he had gifted my wife and I with a ton of music.

Something in my expression caught Stephen's attention. "You okay?"

"Yeah." I fought back tears. "My uncle passed away earlier this year, and it just hit home again while I talked about him."

"Must've been a cool guy."

I nodded. "A true fan of music who spread the word about it whenever he could."

I motioned around the hall. "Heck, he lived this. He saw almost every band honored here."

Thom snapped a few photos of Chuck, Cris, Drew, and myself that became the *de facto* band photos we used to promote the tour before we had even played a show together.

Rumors of Stephen Shareaux twerking have spread, but, what happens in the tour bus, stays in the— Yep, he totally twerked, and it was hilarious. I'm thankful we didn't crash, as I'm not sure how we would explain why Stephen wasn't buckled.

A few days later, we left stupid-early to drive to Chicago. Chuck had this habit of waking up, and he'd ask, "Is that the Mississippi?" if he saw we were passing any sized body of water.

He asked in Indiana, Delaware, Nevada—anywhere and everywhere. Whether we crossed a river, a brook, a rain puddle, or the ocean, he would still ask. I laughed every damn time.

We met Drew at a bar where he worked so we could cram in one practice before we played that night. Even with the impending show hanging over us and being tired from the travel, we had a blast with Drew.

We quickly incorporated a Bane impression—the bad guy, not the band—and between the four of us, we added about a million "That's what she said"s" into our conversation.

Chuck relaxed quicker than normal, enough that when I told him I wanted to go live on Facebook, he didn't even offer up a delay or any excuses.

At one point, Chuck got a phone call. He approached the front area of the bar, and the three of us kept jamming. Drew played the outro to the Faith No More song, "Epic," so Cris and I joined in.

When Chuck returned, he listened to us play for a few bars.

He asked, "Is that the Chili Peppers?"

Drew, Cris, and I burst out laughing. Chuck was dead serious. He had no idea. After guessing a few other band names, he asked who it was. When we told him, he laughed along with us rather than being annoyed.

Later in the practice Drew played it again, and Chuck added a layer of feedback/noise guitar over it.

Chuck clicked off his delay, letting his guitar ring out. "That sounds cool. We should totally do that."

"Epic" represented the ultimate "what if" for Chuck, so it was cool to see him not only embrace the song but have a little fun with it.

Sadly, after Chuck tricking me and being dishonest in the past, I always had to second-guess his words and actions, but hanging out with him during the summer of 2017 helped me remember the sober side of Chuck. The fun, relaxed, go-with-the-flow Chuck always made life more interesting. The buzz of new music, the growing anticipation of our tour, excited bandmates, and the summer offered the possibility of real growth.

We played a free practice/show that night at Livewire. Though we had only announced the show a couple days earlier, I think things turned out okay. I put extra pressure on myself as an old friend of mine, Dee, and Mark Vasquez, the bassist for one of the best bands around, Ideamen, came to see us. We were loose. The show had a new vibe with Drew around. I think it was Cris' first time playing bass live, but I could be wrong.

And that's another aspect of Chuck that can't be overstated. He rode with the people around him, even if it was the last thing he wanted. Whether from outside or from self-inflicted circumstances, Chuck blended it all into one group and lead with, "It is what it is. Let's roll."

How the hell did he operate that way when everything—his family, his bandmates, his budget, his health, his future, his legacy, and his celebrity status—all hung in the balance?

From the five hundred drummers/percussionists he knew personally or that he could have easily contacted, I stood at about 498 in terms of talent and experience. Obviously, the other stuff I brought to the table raised my profile a bit overall, but a million great reasons exist why I shouldn't have been on a list of consideration.

Chuck embarked on his first full-band solo tour with a medical device salesman playing conga, a young drummer he'd just met playing guitar, and a vocalist/keyboardist who answered a Craigslist ad for bass which promised only misery and disappointment. None of who had much touring experience or any clout in the business.

Then, with three shows under our belt, we moved Cris to bass and added another guy who we practiced with once—that day. Sometimes I got disappointed in our performances, and other times I ask what miracle happened that we made it through certain sets.

I slept on a concrete floor that night in a friend of a friend of a friend's basement.

The following day, we hung around the guy's house because FedEx were delivering Chuck's next batch of shirts. It was hot and rainy, but I spent most of the morning outside, paranoid to miss the deliveryman. (Ask the band Daiquiri why I'm so paranoid or revisit the chapter where I mention chasing a Fedex truck holding Chuck's guitar.)

We waited.

And we waited.

The worst part was that the house where we stayed sat a few blocks from a Fedex depot. Every ten or fifteen minutes, a delivery truck passed us, cutting through the neighborhood.

Cris and I called out to the truck drivers as they passed.

"Shirts?"

"Hey, you got shirts?"
Then it branched off to random cars.
"Shirts?"
Then we harassed people walking their dog.
"You the delivery guy for shirts?"
Hours on end. "Shirts?"
Cris' phone would ring. "Shirts?"

Early in the afternoon, we learned the "guaranteed delivery time" wasn't before noon as promised but by end of day.

We left town empty-handed and crabby. The traffic didn't help. The rain didn't help. It followed us almost the entire drive to Rock Island. When we arrived, the club was way bigger than expected—good sound system, great staff, wonderful selection of beers, and, damn, I recommend the burgers—but filling that sized place felt daunting.

Then, the tornado warnings sounded.

The city quickly became a ghost town. We had an early start time, because the venue had karaoke that night, but I don't think the time mattered. It was brutal. The streets appeared empty, and only a few people showed. The tornado watch showed the storm headed north toward Dubuque, but I doubt that had too much effect.

Chuck was in a phase where he took sips of beer but then spit it out so he could get the taste but still say he wasn't drinking. He noodled around for several minutes while talking from the stage to people in the crowd, so I started the show. "Hey, folks. It's a Wednesday night, so just keep the mosh pit safe. Let's all get home safe tonight. There's a tornado outside from what I hear."

Chuck nodded. "There is a tornado."

Someone in the crowd added. "There's a twister out there."

I responded. "There's a twister out there, so we're gonna twist in here. Let's twist again, like we did last summer."

Once Chuck heard someone else be funny, he wanted in on the action, so he said, "Somebody say something so I can say something stupid back."

I said, "Knock, knock."

"That's what she said."

Drew tuned his guitar. Cris, still feeling out the bass, played, I think, a bit of Fleetwood Mac, but I saw Chuck now focused on playing rather than chitchatting.

"I'm having a little feedback issue, but I don't care if you don't."

He hit his strings, his distorted acoustic guitar exploding from the PA, ringing out and around us, loud and full enough to be tangible. Man, it sounded huge.

This was going to be fun. I got ready to play.

Then Chuck went into a monologue, explaining he wasn't drinking and why he had spit on all our shoes. He wrapped it up and said, "Thanks for coming out. I'm Chuck. That's Cris. That's Drew. That's Doug, Mr. Doug, aka Dad, aka—"

Cris suggested, "Father."

I tried, "Bastard."

Chuck answered. "Captain Xaggerate."

He monologued again, so I snored until he played. Good Lord. It was like he knew we had a strict deadline so he needed to push our start later and later to see how long it took until I cracked so he could blame me for making things stressful onstage.

After we played a few somber songs in a row, I wanted to lighten the mood.

"So, for those of you who haven't heard, as of like 8:30 a.m. this morning, Chuck became a grandfather. Round of applause for him and his daughter and her boyfriend."

I added a drumroll as the crowd cheered.

"That's old news," Chuck said. "It was like the first thing I said when I came up here. Where were you?"

"I don't listen to you, Chuck Mosley. Because, if I did—"

"If you did, you'd be here onstage with me rather than at home with a real job."

Chuck 1, Doug 0.

Shortly after this, the building next door caught on fire, so police and fire folks blocked both ways to get to the club. Getting people to attend shows is tough enough, but you add in fires and tornadoes, and, well, that's how you get twenty people in Rock Island on a Wednesday night.

The night ended with "Bob Forest," one of the last times we played it before replacing it with "Relocation."

Chuck introduced it this way. "This is about one of my co-grower-upper wither people I got in trouble with. His name is Bob Forrest. He had a band called Thelonious Monster in LA, and it was *fucked up*, and every night was a total-chaos nightmare. Then, we'd go out after, and that's when everything really hit the fan." He started the song. "Well, I don't know what'cha t—" He stopped. "'Cause we'd get in trouble for shit that each other did and stuff. We'd say, 'I didn't do it' and 'that wasn't me'—"

I interrupted, no longer able to contain my laughter. "Co-grower-upper? What *is* that?"

Without delay, he answered, "It's a farming term. You never heard of it, because you grew up in the city."

"I don't think that's historically accurate, man. I'm pretty sure. I'm gonna call you on this one. Has anyone heard the term co-grower-upper?"

Someone in the crowd pointed out, "Chuck, you grew up in LA."

I said, "Yeah. Your farm in LA." I added a line from *Half Baked*. "Yeah, right near da beach, a-boyee."

Chuck chuckled with the crowd.

"Okay, you got me on that one," he admitted but couldn't let it go without adding, "But it is in the dictionary I just can't think of what it means."

He starts playing, totally goofing up the intro.

In one line of the song, Chuck sings in a much different voice from his norm, and he said, "'Cause that's what he (Bob Forrest) sounds like." He sings the next line normal before telling the crowd, "Now that's me again."

His pacing was off, but everyone laughed and were already entranced by the song. Chuck leaned toward me during a break in vocals and said, "I almost fucked myself up back there."

I thought, man, the song is still really shaky right now, but let's do it.

After the set, Chuck had some people sign his guitar—one who came to the show specifically to talk to Chuck about his troubles with addiction.

Y'see, that's another aspect of this whole thing that gets lost. Many people looked to Chuck for answers, even though he struggled right alongside them. Maybe that's a big reason why they sought him out, I'm not sure. What I do know is he encouraged people and shared all his knowledge and experience in the hopes they stayed stronger than him.

He wanted everyone to get better. He wanted everyone to quit and get healthy. I wish he wanted that much for himself.

Even then, five months sober, and the cracks appeared, even if I remained ignorant of the true problems.

How did I remain ignorant? Man, Chuck was a blast to hang around that summer. After Cris and I drank a few of those Doom beers from Founder's, we all hung out and sang karaoke at the club.

Chuck loved it.

I never thought I would see him loosen up like that onstage. He had a blast. And for the most part, he sounded terrible. It was great. You've never seen Katy Perry's "Dark Horse" sung so off time and yet so entertaining, and don't get me started on the rap part of the song. Priceless.

How he could ramble for ten minutes before playing his own songs, buckling under the pressure of nerves, and yet, with no irony, take same stage in front of the same people and ruin Portishead never added up to me.

I'm not saying his nerves were an act. I'm saying I never truly understood his issues or how to help. And really, when you've got Chuck Mosley singing Patsy Cline karaoke, why would you even try?

The following day, we hit the outskirts of Des Moines, Iowa.

I have mixed emotions about how to approach this show. I'll say it went down as one of the weirder nights, for various reasons.

One, the owner of the club, who had been responsible for booking us, had called the local rock station to complain about them mentioning the show, because he didn't want five hundred people storming his place when it could only hold one hundred.

Two, the sound system was insane, but the sound guy got called away before the show started, so the event almost got canceled.

Three, we drank warm cheap beer in the parking lot, because they didn't own a liquor license.

Four, of the five hundred people the owner expected, about twenty-five showed up, even though we said, "If five hundred people showed, we would play five sets."

Five, the heat beat us down.

Six, people got photographed while sleeping.

Seven, we did karaoke two nights in a row.

Eight—seriously, photos while we slept.

Nine, for the record, Drew sleeps all creepy with his arms crossed over his chest.

The following day, the other guys slept while I drove us back east on Rt 80. The car in front of me swerved just enough to get my attention. I took my foot off the gas.

As I did, the car swerved again, this time more violently. I hit the brakes.

Chuck woke up instantly, another worst-nightmare scenario after his accident in the '90s. He screamed loud enough to wake up Drew and Cris, who also called out as they saw the car in front of us spin in a 360, out of control.

I steered us left onto the grassy berm, avoiding a collision by less than ten feet. The car that had lost control came to a dead stop, horizontal across the highway. I saw the driver panic. She slammed the gas, with the car in reverse, and backed across the highway as fast as she could before swinging it vertical again on the far side.

Oncoming traffic reacted, brakes squealing, horns honking.

I peered at the driver long enough to see her get her breath under control.

I mouthed, *Are you okay?*

Her eyes stayed wide, but she grinned in relief and nodded. *You guys?*

I nodded and hit the gas, getting us on the road before a semi-truck driver had to swerve to avoid us. We talked about going back for her, but I didn't know what we'd accomplish aside from interrupting more traffic.

The drive returned us to the outskirts of Chicago, this time to play the Elk's Lodge 1510—one of the most fun, laid back nights on the tour. They hadn't booked an opener but contacted a stand-up comedian to offend the crowd before we did.

Terrance O'Donnell, who had brought us to town, led us into a kitchen area and poured us a shot of liquor called Malort. I've tasted a lot of different types of drinks, but this …

He told us the guy who invented it had smoked so many cigarettes that he couldn't taste alcohol anymore, so he came up with Malort. That dude had issues. Nasty. Friends don't let friends drink Malort, O'Donnell.

Our set had a groove, uneven and loose, but we achieved our own sound. Drew got comfortable, that certainly played a part, but the Chuck Mosley Band (aka the Cris Mosby Boys, aka Chuck & His Band of Other Musicians) never set out to wow audiences with our musical IQ or ability to shred. We wanted simple songs with genuine lyrics, relatable to all, while not too full of themselves. Somehow, we joked in-between memorial songs for friends lost and introspective tunes about addiction and loneliness and regret and a longing for the past.

After the set, we split up around the club. I headed to the merch table; Chuck signed stuff, and Drew and Cris went outside. A few people murmured that they wanted more songs. We had only practiced a certain amount with Drew, and we'd played them all by that point, but this crowd had shown up and welcomed us. After almost ten minutes of shaking hands and selling shirts, people still wanted us back.

Chuck went up first. He told everyone we were out of songs and that we wouldn't be attempting any Faith No More stuff as a few people called out for "We Care a Lot" and "Anne's Song."

Someone in the crowd yelled for those people to stop. She said she was there for Chuck, not for Faith No More. She yelled out VUA and Cement tunes louder than the Faith No More requests, a sound to behold.

Chuck played "Steveland" solo.

During the second verse, he sings, *"Standing at the crossroads of another state of mind, now it's 2017, and I am almost out of time."*

The line haunted me then, but now …

I joined him on the extended outro section. After a moment of playing, word spread outside that we had restarted. Drew scaled the stairs, followed by Cris shortly after. "Steveland" wound up getting a fifteen-minute rendition and served as a reminder that you never knew when Chuck Mosley & His Band of Other Musicians' sets ended.

Chuck and I conversed on the back porch of Taran's house—our host. Our talk stretched until close to sunrise, encompassing everything we had going on: no money, no solid band lineup, no recording, no label—and those represented our band's main issues. Chuck had another few dozen of his own to discuss. We laughed at our drama and drank to better times.

A few too-short hours later and battling exhaustion, I shoved off for my daily walk, going far enough to get lost. After more and more wrong turns, I cheated and tried the GPS on my phone. As the screen spun, unable to pinpoint my location, I wiped sweat from my forehead and kept going, eventually finding my way back.

Taran owned a semi-trained lizard that he brought to the back porch to get sun. As he ran errands, Taran charged us with watching his pet. I don't even take care of myself, so naturally, I had my reservations. You might not be reading this book to hear about babysitting lizards, but I need to stall. I'm not ready to delve into the following day—the first confirmed date on the 2017 docket, the memorial for Dug Smith.

We got to the club, and all the memories of the crap I went through the previous year flooded back only outweighed by the wonderful yet brief time I had spent with Dug. I recalled pacing the parking lot, livid, confused, and ready to walk away from the tour after learning Chuck had just lied to me so he could borrow the car to hunt for drugs. Dug had asked me if I was okay, and we had hung outside the club, talking shop. He was a *real* drummer, so I let him do most of the talking. I remember my conflicted feelings when Chuck had joined me onstage as I finished setting up our equipment. I remember him telling me, "You know I love you, right?"

I remember believing him.

At the memorial, we weren't headlining, so we cut a few songs from our set. Chuck also said, "No medley."

He wanted me to argue; he was baiting me. Chuck wanted someone to yell at. He wanted a release. Whenever Chuck wanted to get a rise out of me, he tried to cut the medley from the set. It's not that I was married to it—I had never wanted a medley—but I did know that many people attended his shows to see Faith No More tunes they had never seen him perform way back when, so I fought to keep those snippets in the set.

I said, "I'm not going to argue the setlist today."

Then he talked about playing the show solo, but I told him I had met Dug too and wanted to be a part of it.

I suggested, "Maybe you should start with 'Sinéad.'"

He gave me a sideways glance. "Why do you say that?"

"If there was ever a night for a downer of a set, it's tonight."

He studied my face, looking for a trick or sarcasm or something he didn't find. "Maybe."

I kept my distance from Chuck most of the afternoon, as I felt the angst, conflict, and nervous energy emanating from him.

Dug's family set up a painting of him in the back area of the stage, where he would've placed his drums for a show—right where I had seen him a year previous. My conga sat in front of the painting, and—I won't hesitate to be honest here—I turned and spoke to the painting a few times.

I teared up as we began, suddenly feeling the weight Chuck had been carrying for months. We were about to play a song he had written about Dug, for his family. He and I needed the song to go perfectly, even with all the setbacks, new members, and general chaos of recent months and days.

The song sometimes felt shaky live. Chuck would speed up or slow down during the second verse, often causing it to at least threaten to fly off the tracks. Add the emotions and some timely technical difficulties and you had a ball of stress onstage.

Chuck's guitar effects kept shorting out. It wasn't a brand-new problem. He had waited and waited to replace the powered pedalboard he had borrowed from Adam the previous year, instead leaving home with a cheap adaptor cord that gave us problems right out of the gate. By July 1, we had grown accustomed to the annoying set up, but I wanted to rip every cable onstage into a million pieces that night. It didn't help that it shorted out when stepped on, and Chuck always shuffled.

Chuck introduced "Mr. Smith" before we played "Song 2" again. Not sure if it was by mistake or design. The songs were like cousins, maybe even step-siblings. He connected them together as one long song when he first recorded them. From that stand point, I understood why he did it.

When "Song 2" finished, the crowd clapped, but Chuck wouldn't bare any further delay. He said, "Here we go," and began.

At a couple points in the song, my percussion part is simply me rapidly tapping two fingers on the edge of the conga as the music fades. I ended the roll by swiping my fingers across the surface of the conga and away from myself, sort of like exorcising the bad memories, the pain, the stress, and throwing it out as I allowed in the song's positive vibes.

Chuck gave an incredible performance. I recall exhaling and turning to talk to Dug's painting, hoping he appreciated the tune and to thank him for helping me hold it together while I played.

One of the biggest goals we had for the year had been successfully reached and executed, and I don't think I even appreciated it enough at the time, but I know it affected Chuck from that night forward. In fact, I don't think we ever got "Mr. Smith" quite right after that.

Drew, who had driven to the show with his girlfriend, took off for home. He couldn't make the journey with us to Ypsilanti. Just like that, we were a three piece.

On the way into Michigan, we stopped at a rest area and set up in the parking lot for a Facebook live video. Chuck always talked these up big, always had a grand scheme to make hilarious skits, but, typically, the video featured him grumbling too quiet to hear and me inserting show info as I tried to get him talking. On this day, however, outside circumstances and a great ad-lib by Chuck created exactly the feel we wanted to deliver. He stood in front of a semi-truck, clearly not ours, and asked me to start rolling.

He explained we were at a truck stop in western Michigan and gave a briefing on how the tour was going, telling everyone how great our tour truck had treated us … and then it pulled away behind him. He looked panicked. He jogged after the semi and yelled out how someone was stealing our stuff. I followed along, but I couldn't keep a straight face. When he was in the right mood, Chuck could get the whole room rolling with laughter. Seeing him lighten up and goof around was powerful, as I knew how few times it actually happened for him. We did many other Facebook live videos. When he couldn't top the Ypsilanti one, he would just put the phone on the dashboard and film us blasting music and driving along. While maybe not as cool as the slow-motion walking scene in *Reservoir Dogs*, a car full of dudes staring out the window for twenty minutes with pop music blaring was fun to capture.

The next night, the bad news reached us that the bill had six other bands. Luckily, the vocalist for one of the bands wore a cape, which helped lighten the blow. Look, over the last two years, we'd shared bills with no less than five hundred bands, so little bits of character stand out.

I typically don't want to single out people in the crowd, but one woman had danced all night by herself, and this continued during our set. I am not mocking her. I am not questioning her style or her spirit; I am merely narrating the events that I recall the best I can. I watched, wondering what music she heard, gyrating and shaking independent of our music.

I enjoyed our set as a three piece, mostly as it became easier to hear what each of us played without an extra layer to muddy the waters. Not that the second guitar caused all of that, but with less, I almost felt it sounded like more.

Another It's-a-Small-World-After-All example happened when a member of Downtown Brown attended that night's show. He joined us for "Bob Forest," similar to when he had helped out Chuck when they had toured together years earlier.

Later that night, Chuck and I stopped at a rest area shortly after reaching Ohio. We stood around at about 3 a.m. taking stock of the year as Cris slept. We were both glad the memorial for Dug Smith had come and gone. That show had hung like a ball of stress above us for months.

Chuck said he felt great with more time sober. He spoke of leaving behind music for a while to speak to groups of addicts to share his story. He had an urge to teach, to lead, to create more than music. I couldn't have smiled wider.

Chuck wanted to properly record the new songs and have a release soon that we could build off. He admitted he understood how the tour could continue, saw how his solo career had taken on a life of its own.

Loopy from lack of sleep, I suggested, "Tonight sounded cool with the three of us. Maybe we keep things simple and rebuild to a fourth member?"

"No, four is good. We'll have Joshua back for the next run."

In case I harbored thoughts of a retort, Chuck walked to our car. "You want me to drive?"

A few days later, while on vacation with my family, I woke up with an odd feeling in my stomach. Within a few hours, I found myself writhing in pain on a hospital room's floor. Turns out I had my first kidney stone. I won't divulge all the details of my brief hospital stay, but I will brag that through all of it, I kept my sense of humor and told several bad jokes as I prepared for my belly to fall out of my skin.

After a nine-hour drive on July 20, we stood outside the club and watched the line grow by the minute. As the first date of ten shows in ten nights started, we wanted to kick things off with a bang and hoped Philadelphia could deliver.

Of course, the reason we stood outside in the sweltering heat was that no one from the club had arrived yet. The line we watched gathered across the street at a huge club hosting the band, Ghost, that night.

The whole Philly experience turned into a clusterfuck of dropped balls and bad luck. Even my buddy, Terry, who had hosted us for three days the previous year arrived with bad news. His air conditioning had broken. I scrambled for hotel rooms—another hundred bucks we didn't have, gone in an instant.

Philly marked the first time we played with bassist King Chivas. Chuck had talked to him about coming along on bass for this run months ago, long before we had anyone else established.

It felt weird to have two bassists, but Chuck didn't want to go back on his word. Not that I did, but logic and common sense have a place.

King played two songs each night—"Death March" and "Tractor."

He arrived early every show. We typically showed up when we showed up.

I took a few photos of King with the other guys outside the club in Philly. Odd to snap band photos without myself in them but great to see King's excitement.

I did a Facebook live stream outside the club, but the sun drained our energy, and the promoter not returning our call had killed our spirits. We also learned the co-headliner's guitarist had broken his arm, so they had to drop off the bill. Before we had even played a note, the run I felt most confident about trended in the wrong direction. Not that we expected much in the way of payment after the small turnout, but at least the promoter could've shown up to the show he had booked and explained why the club didn't even list us on their calendar or why zero fliers got posted or that he had no intention of paying us even if a hundred folks had attended.

During "Sinéad," Chuck paused. "Oops, I fucked up."

I asked. "Which time?"

"Every. Single. Time."

He also added a new nickname to my repertoire—Judgy McJudgerson; though I think Pip actually came up with it.

We found karaoke down the street after the show, and Joshua blew us away with a song from *Rocky Horror Picture Show*.

The following day, we raced to the Atlantic Ocean.

"Is that the Mississippi?"

Cris, Joshua, and I walked along the boardwalk in Long Branch, NJ, but we didn't have enough money to get onto the beach itself. I wasn't opposed to a stroll, but I felt like I needed some space. At first, I couldn't place it. As the day progressed, I realized Cris and I had spent a lot of time together.

Chuck and he weren't on the same terms as earlier in the year. How could I expect them to be? Cris dated Sophie, Chuck's youngest daughter. He had moved in with the family, in fact. Chuck, a man who valued his alone time and his privacy, now had Cris nearby 24/7. Apparently, he needed space.

Did I care? No, not really. But when it started to affect the shows, I made it a point to pay more attention.

That night we had another one of those packed bills with six or so bands and a couple of them wanted to stretch their sets as long as possible. This annoyed everyone involved and had several people griping. At one point, Cris ridiculed one of the openers, and I tried to get him to stop, as one or two of the members stood a few feet away. Chuck always said, "Don't disrespect my fans."

Now, these guys played in another band, but I think it still applied, even if Chuck might've agreed with what Cris said.

My mood soured because we had played the same club a year prior and had drawn a better crowd. I had expected word of mouth that our last show had killed would help generate more buzz for this year. Nope.

I snuck off to the pizza joint for a few slices. Why did I sneak off? Because none of us had any money, so, every time someone got food, you had to share it, and I didn't want to, okay? I got in the car only to find Chuck already in it. He grabbed a slice and grunted frustration.

"You all right?"

He gave me the usual shrug off. "I'm tired. I'm stressed."

Bills, family drama, self-doubt. He wanted to vent his frustrations over several issues but knew his anger would openly lead to more drama. Chuck felt trapped, like always—too powerless to change his situation without taking heat. So, I listened.

Word circulated that Chester Bennington, vocalist for Linkin Park, had died. He was the second big-name guy, tied to depression and drugs and the small community of rock, who had committed suicide that summer. Chuck wished he had had a way to talk to those guys, especially Chris Cornell, as he had known him. He felt like he could offer proper perspective, given his own experiences.

Pulling into NYC is a thrill every time ... Every. Time. It's not that I love the city—in fact, the jury still needs more evidence to deliberate—but it goes back to something Denis Leary said years earlier about NYC forcing you to live moment to moment. That city is wild and unforgiving, and I'm convinced it's also possibly rabid.

Chuck and I took the kids to Tompkins Square Park to observe a political rally/concert. Anne's stepson, Mathew Stenz, worked the event in some capacity. I had met him while sleeping on Anne's kitchen floor the year prior.

We hung out for a couple hours, a rarity on the road, and witnessed art-punk bands and people from the left and right screaming at each other. Chuck took a few photos with people who spotted him.

That night, we made our triumphant return to Mr. Beery's, the club in Bethpage, NY that had saved us the summer before. Again, the crowd got loud and sang along and hung out and treated us super awesome, but the audience equaled about the same or maybe a few less than had shown the previous summer. I didn't know what else to do to raise awareness or interest in our tour.

I recognized most of the faces from our previous trip, like in Jersey the previous night. Merch sales stalled, almost nonexistent, as the only new T-shirt we had said, *Chuck Fuckin' Mosley*, and most people can't get away with wearing it.

When I started booking shows, Chuck had suggested to try and avoid headlining club shows, preferring to play second to last so we didn't go on super late. Having gone on many times after midnight, and worse, after five or six bands have already played, I felt the same way. The flipside to that though is you need to set up and start playing quickly so you can finish on time. We had often performed shows when openers extended their sets or other delays occurred, delaying our starts and angering fans who drove far to see us. Chuck does nothing fast.

The rest of us would stage our gear and then race to set up as Chuck watched from the crowd. Then, when we signaled *all good* and started to soundcheck, he would sneak outside for a cigarette. We'd twiddle our thumbs until he joined us and grabbed his guitar.

He'd play a few notes, often much quieter than he intended to play live so the sound guy would crank the volume.

I'd roll my eyes. "Chuck, at least turn on the distortion so he knows what he'll deal with all night."

He'd hit his pedal but again hold back, as he only played a second or two. "Is that good?"

Sound guy gave him the thumbs up.

"Okay then. Do I have like thirty-two seconds?"

Before anyone answered, he'd disappear again. Another smoke, a shot, a beer, and then Chuck would grace us with his presence again. In his head, it all added drama and anticipation. From what I could tell, it only annoyed people or pissed them off.

We stayed with Anne and Rick that night in the city. I slept in my spot on the kitchen floor, but the kids opted to sleep in the van. I had learned never to decline bathroom access, a shower, or hot coffee—but to each their own.

We made tracks north the following morning, as our show started early in the afternoon in Portland, Maine.

Before you ask, yes, Chuck made sure we knew how every time he played in Maine, especially with Bad Brains, he got robbed of eating fresh lobster and that this time he wouldn't be denied. I'm not a seafood fan at all, but even I was willing to make a stop and try lobster. And no, we did not get lobster this time around either. Why? You guessed it. Chuck wasted all morning with some BS, so we got there late.

At some point around then, Chuck said, "If Doug was my boss, I would be fired from my job as Chuck Mosley."

That night, we played on the roof of a bar in Portland, Maine. Paulie, of Thee Ice Picks, had helped us get a few gigs again, this being one of them. Beautiful night, appreciative crowd, and an unsteady sound system helped make this a memorable gig. During "Song 2," seagulls floated above us, chirping and honking along to the music. This led to me suggesting to Chuck to call it "The Seagull Song." Not only an apt title, but an obscure play on an unreleased Faith No More tune that has grown into legend over the years.

The PA overloaded and shut off a few times during our set, ultimately ending "Relocation" without microphones or amplification. This wasn't the first time it had happened to us during that song, nor the last, so we started calling ourselves Mosleyhead, the Loudest Acoustic Band in the Land.

Paulie had recently had his first child (congrats again), so, when we stayed at his house, we kept quiet, even when he surprised us with ice cream.

We had an early start the next day.

I goaded. "Rise and shine, Chuck. You've got a movie to film."

CHAPTER THIRTEEN

In Which We Pause Our Tour
to Perform in a Short Film
07/24/2017 - 07/30/2017

Thanks to our friend and filmmaker, David Collopy, Chuck was set to assume the lead role in a short film that day. We had to absorb the brunt of his nerves in the form of crabbiness.

Chuck had a knack for performance, and I thought escaping into a role might provide a fun break from the monotony of the road. Of course, Chuck felt the need to sulk and affect a childish demeanor about it.

"It just feels weird. So, what? Do I play myself?"

We drove to Salisbury Beach, a tourist destination featuring a two-story arcade called Joe's Playland right off the water and enough nostalgia for vacations of the past that you swear you've traveled back in time.

Joshua, Cris, and I walked around the tourist area, a two- or three-block section of souvenir shops, ice cream stands, and cheap pizza places, while Chuck talked on the phone and flipped through a rack of T-shirts at a shop.

I blew into my hands, a feeble attempt at warming them. "I'm grabbing two slices and a coffee."

I waited for the pizza while enjoying my warm water mixed with a single coffee bean. When they handed me a plate with what appeared to hold two cardboard slabs covered with tomato paste and four shreds of cheese, I devoured them.

"That's terrible, but I could eat another ten slices."

My review sold Cris into buying a slice for himself.

David and his crew filmed that morning at another location to complete scenes featuring the other main character played by Daisy Mae Collupy, David's daughter. She portrayed Chuck's fictional daughter, but a pouring rain had put them behind schedule.

With nowhere to go, David suggested we head to the cottage his family rented for their vacation. He forgot to alert them to expect us.

Again, much like similar situations, I love seeing people react to unexpectedly meeting Chuck. Not because they recognize him, but because his overall appearance—the pink dreads, the sloppy clothes, the unfocused yet sharp eyes—often had people unsure how to handle him.

David's family welcomed us into their home and hosted us for several hours.

When the crew arrived, we followed them to the arcade's second floor, which they had reserved to shoot a few scenes.

I'm fascinated by film—obviously, as a writer, I hope to one day help create them. But, that day, I was merely a spectator. Joshua, Cris, and I watched from a distance, snapping a few photos and wishing we had quarters to play a great selection of games.

Eventually I gave in and tried to play Q-Bert, but the controller was broken, so my game lasted about four seconds.

Chuck can intimidate adults, but kids love him. After he and Daisy worked through the butterflies of making their acting debuts, the camera caught some great stuff. I teared up a few times watching them, knowing how much Chuck reflected on his role in raising his own daughters.

David spoke to Chuck about a crowdfunding campaign to help afford the costs of editing and other post production. Chuck hesitated to ask for any more money after making his own money woes public a few years earlier, but eventually he went along with the idea.

After filming at the arcade, we drove down to Salem, Massachusetts to set up for our show and to film additional scenes. The script wasn't long, but the afternoon proved to be, as various lighting issues and continuing bad weather delayed the production.

We recruited author Brian Paone—a longtime friend of both mine and Chuck's (he had even paid Chuck's rent one month in full via Western Union during Chuck's money woes so Chuck wouldn't get evicted)—his eight-year-old son, Everett (who Bill Gould had given backstage passes to for the Faith No More show at Madison Square Garden in 2015—the damn kid at six years old had hung out with Mike Patton, Roddy, Bill, Jon, and Puffy), and their friend, Lisa, to portray fans excited to meet Chuck before his gig. They did great, especially considering how many times they had to redo the scene as, again, lighting and weather forced the crew to adapt.

I also got roped into performing on camera. I played Chuck's hired-gun percussionist named Doug. Obviously, it took all of my acting chops to stretch out into such a fantastical character, so foreign to my everyday existence.

My line wasn't spelled out, but a short description gave me what I needed to improvise: *CHUCK is interrupted once again; this time it's by DOUG, a percussionist in his late-30s, who is there to support CHUCK at the gig tonight. DOUG assures CHUCK that this afternoon's soundcheck gave him a good feel for the songs and that he's really stoked to be playing this gig with him.*

I also added some body motion and wording to imply that Doug battled addiction, and Chuck had offered him a much-needed third or fourth or fifth chance to prove himself.

Chuck claimed to get uncomfortable in front of the camera, but I thought he took the ball and ran—or at least jogged—with his performance. I'd love to have seen more from him onscreen.

At one point, David spoke with his director of photography. "Clearly he's not an actor, but he is a character."

The director of photography replied that Chuck was actually pretty good despite not being a professional actor.

One of the actors got injured, cutting his finger bad enough that it almost halted production. He got patched up, and they managed to finish the final scenes.

For some reason the first band hadn't started yet. I passed the stage and overheard one of the musicians explaining, "I didn't bring my amp head."

The door guy at the club knew someone with equipment he could borrow, but delays like that on a Monday are tough for a crowd to swallow. By the time we had set up, a third of the crowd had thrown in the towel.

David looked tired, after a full day of directing. "Hey, the shoot has gone on extra long, and I need to cut these guys loose. Can you guys frontload the set with the songs we want to film, so we can get it done?"

I thought this sounded reasonable. I rewrote the set.

Chuck didn't agree. "We're not changing. I want to start how we start. We build and build and then come down and then build and leave the crowd saying, 'Wow!' like always."

"We still have dynamic ups and downs. This just starts with the new songs and the VUA stuff David can legally use on film."

"No. I'm starting with 'Sinéad'. Maybe if we cut—"

The club's manager pulled me aside. "Hey, we want all the music done by eleven, so if you start within the next fifteen minutes, you'll still have like forty minutes to play."

"What the fuck?" Chuck said, tired, having hustled for hours on end that day with little break time. "Well, then no medley."

"If you cut the medley, I'll quit."

Wait, what? Yeah, I didn't want to quit nor did I care if the medley appeared in the set. I just didn't feel like playing Chuck's games, especially with the clock running.

We bickered back and forth, both basically saying, "I'm tired and crabby, boo-hoo."

It had been a long day for all of us. I wanted to play and get good audio and video for the film.

I don't recall having a ton of fun onstage. I do recall thinking that I needed to smile for the camera, as I was still playing the role of "Doug," but, every time I got in the flow, Chuck took a dig at me or changed the setlist or goofed up, and I'd get pissed all over again. Here is my official apology to the crew who put in overtime to cater to us.

How exhausted did I feel after the show? I can't even tell you where we stayed, though I drove us there, and Chuck complained about me taking the long way out of town.

The following night, we played in Brooklyn. I won't spend time describing the show, as I want to keep it an intimate memory for the fifteen or so people who had attended. I will say that John S. Hall, who opened, was pleasant and easy to work with. And that, at least, one crowd member thought we were playing at a place called Union Pool rather than Union Hall due to the NYC accent.

Go on. Try it. Union Hall. Union Pool. Hall. Pool. How eight million people can talk in a way that makes those words sound the same baffles and amuses me.

King Chivas got involved in a Twitter battle about wrestling with someone who he considered a big deal. Maybe a wrestler's manager ... Cris, do you remember?

After the show, Joshua, Anne, and I went out for drinks.

There came a point when I sat next to Anne on a stool at a tiny bar near her place, and I asked, "Anne, what am I supposed to do, huh? Chuck's been bugging me since the day that I was born."

Sure, quoting "Anne's Song" lyrics to Anne herself could be considered uncool, but I did it with no regrets.

She raised her glass. "Do whatever the hell you wanna do. Now is the time where you can do anything."

She continued, but I had fallen off my stool, laughing in disbelief.

Our show's highlight the next night in Wallingford, Connecticut was seeing a few familiar faces—Anthony Frisketti, Mathew Grant, and Michael Yarish. We had met all three the previous year when we had played at a beauty salon.

Before our set, Anthony scurried around the club gauging, I assumed, lighting and angles to maximize the quality of his photos.

I set up my conga. "Feel free to roam wherever. We don't care."

"Even if I come onstage?"

"Yeah, just don't block me in case I want to dive off one of these."

Two parts of the stage up front rose a foot or two higher than the rest of the stage. Cris stood on one and mimicked launching into the crowd.

The following day, we drove to Baltimore with high hopes and empty stomachs.

We played a huge, well-known club, which had screened a movie called *Camp Killer* before we played. Shawn Jones, the writer and director of the film, had helped us set up the show and had used a VUA song in the credits of the film.

The drummer from the opener tried to explain to me that due to the club's proximity to the train tracks we were in a no-survivor zone if a train carrying, I think, oil or gasoline derailed.

By that night, Chuck Mosley & His Band of Other Musicians really took ownership of the new songs. "Blue Heart" had a swagger, "Song 2"'s extended distorted outro made the song a bonafide tearjerker, and "Relocation" ballooned into an unstoppable juggernaut.

After we played, the manager and one of the bartenders treated me to my first-ever air xylophone solo on a pool table.

Sleep stayed out of reach that night. Police busted drug dealers and prostitutes all night at our hotel, and whatever they passed as breakfast took years off my life.

We drove north along the east coast. "Is that the Mississippi?"

In Kingston, New York, Chuck had a chance to catch up with Doc from Bad Brains. I knew how much it meant to Chuck to have face-to-face time with him, and that made me happy.

Chuck and I discussed what the two had said, but the highlight for me was the revelation that Doc had texted Chuck some files. I hoped they were the songs Chuck had recorded with Bad Brains that never got released, but Chuck never knew how to operate his damn phone.

Doc, it would be a gift to the fans for those songs to see the light of day. Any chances of that happening?

We attempted our snippet of "Wisdom Comes," but one of Doc's friends played a gig down the street, and he might've left prior to us tackling it.

Chuck said, "Probably for the best that he didn't hear it. Those guys are masters of their instruments. They are a force. No one holds a candle to them."

With that show done, King went back home, and we drove a few hours to stay at Anne's and Rick's place in Pennsylvania. I had my own bed. I had my own bathroom. I slept better than I had in … forever.

Chuck claimed a couch on the front porch for his spot.

"It was a perfect day," Anne said when I asked her to look back on that time. "Everyone wanted to go to sleep, but nobody wanted to miss hanging out. We stayed up all day. Chuck was going on about that sandwich—the prosciutto, the capicola, the mozzarella—and how long it had marinated. I'm surprised he didn't get sick. We were all living in the moment. Nobody took any photos. Not one photo. We just listened to music and had a barbeque. Chuck said, 'Anne, this is paradise. I gotta bring my family here.'"

A shout-out to all the people who host bands, comedians, actors, or any type of creative vagabond. Your hospitality enables so many things to happen and helps in ways I don't have time to describe in these pages. (Because Chuck wants this to be more about him.)

July 29, the last day of that leg of the tour, Chuck wanted to quit so he could stay in town to see Garbage. We listened to Garbage almost the entire way to Pittsburgh as penance for not allowing him to quit. No way we'd make our first no-show that night as Nicole Naab and Nicholas Schmitt had turned over every rock to find enough support to bring us to Pittsburgh. Their enthusiasm proved enough to restore my own. That night we had one of the coolest crowds, great sound, and the band gave it our all. Aside from Cris's amp buzzing loudly, the set felt like our best show yet.

After "Tractor," I asked, "Show of hands. How many of you have seen Chuck live before?"

He countered, "How many have seen me dead?"

An eerie quiet, save a few uncomfortable chuckles, permeated the club. I felt butterflies in my stomach, unsure how to respond. You won't often hear me get nervous onstage, but this felt weird.

I decided to push my luck. "You're a lot less crabby that way."

And just like that, Chuck laughed, and we all relaxed.

On my deathbed when I'll picture the time I toured with Chuck, one of the memories I'll see is Joshua dancing and thrashing around during "Relocation" that night. I remember him glancing at me to confirm we were still locked in. We grinned, sweated, yelled, and jumped—doing exactly what we wanted to be doing at that moment.

All the BS of dealing with Chuck, all the self-doubt about my worthiness to the tour, all the money lost, all the time away from my family, and anything else you've read me bitching about all disappeared that night.

We headed home after the show, heads held high.

CHAPTER FOURTEEN

08/2017-09/2017:
Mosleyhead, Live Tonight,
(not) SOLD OUT!

I had texted John, the tour's next run's bassist, a few times with no response during the last couple days. As we drove home, he got back to me. *My car broke down, so I can't make the trip with you guys.*

This news came a week before we embarked on a thirty-day, twenty-five show run, along with a three-day recording session with Matt Wallace.

Chuck took the news in stride. "I got a guy."

We booked two practices at Joshua's house to break in Randy, an old friend and bassist with one hell of a resume. He has spent time in several Cleveland hardcore and metal bands.

The practice gave me a lot of anxiety. After crushing several great shows, our performance felt like a letdown. Chuck also planned to leave Cris behind on this run, as their relationship had strained to an uncomfortable level.

He told me, "He doesn't listen. He plays whatever he wants. You don't hear him like I do. He just goes off, and it distracts me."

I understood, and I had heard some of that, but Chuck's guitar sound typically gobbled up Cris's guitar playing, especially when the distortion came on.

"I get it." Even as I started playing Devils' advocate, Chuck shook his head. "But we're recording in just a few days, and he knows the songs. He really shines playing leads and solos, and his parts will stand out more on a clean recording than us live."

Chuck had other gripes, and we talked about making a change several times leading up to the run. In the end, Cris came along, for better or worse.

The day before we took off, I got a voice mail. "Hey, Doug. This is Heather calling with [name redacted] Rent-A-Car. I was just giving you a call to confirm a reservation for a minivan tomorrow, um. Also want to get some information, um, from your driver's license, um, to go over the length of the rental …"

When I returned her call, she informed me they had cancelled the rental due to me needing it longer than thirty days—I needed it thirty-one.

I panicked. I couldn't breathe. The only reason we found an alternative mode of transportation was that my wife handles things like this in stride. She got a company to agree to stretch a rental past a month. Now, in the end, they totally lied and screwed us over (I'm looking at you, Steve at the downtown Cleveland branch, you jerk.), but we had a way to get from point A to points B-GG.

We left the night before our first show and drove straight to Huntsville, Alabama, arriving around noon. As we sat waiting, Chuck felt something fall from his back pocket. He had squatted right in front of a sewer drain. Whatever had fallen out, slipped inside.

"Oh, shit! My phone."

We all jumped at his outburst.

"Fuck. It fell down there."

He checked his pockets again. "Maybe my cigarettes too."

We used my phone to shine a light down but couldn't see anything.

He said, "Cris, you're small. I'll bet you could fit down there."

In the end, we found his phone still in the car and his cigarettes still in his pocket. Most likely he heard a pebble or something falling.

A monsoon assured we'd have a weird first night. Randy and Chuck weren't on the same page yet. Randy brought along a bigger amp than we'd previously used, so his low end, even at the lowest setting, overpowered us all.

Cris laid on the stage during "Relocation," another visual protest at his growing unhappiness. Chuck shot me glances a few times as Cris's guitar playing sounded totally counter to the rest of us. "Faster Disco" included some off-the-wall guitar. Cris had never hidden his dislike for the song, but now he had crossed a line in Chuck's mind.

"I'm going to bus him home."

"From here? Tonight?"

"Would you rather put up with this all tour?"

"Let's talk to him. Give him until LA. When we record, let's see how it goes."

"And if it's terrible?"

"We mute those tracks, and you do them yourself or get someone else."

He agreed.

Cris got upset that Chuck harped on how many beers Cris could drink. Randy also got put off by this, especially since Chuck always had a beer or a shot in his hand. Chuck claimed he had nursed two beers for the last four or so hours. He said he made it appear like he drank a lot.

We left straight from the show for New Orleans. Chuck was antsy to meet his grandson for the first time.

I drove until the street began waving and the streetlights left trails behind them. We slept a couple of hours at a rest stop before Chuck took over. I woke up as the sun crept over the trees. Chuck and I spoke in hushed tones. I tried to joke a bit, having argued about our breakneck pace the day before.

He said, "We're getting pulled over."

I looked at the speedometer, now falling under ninety as he prepared to merge to the side.

The cops, Alabama Drug Task Force officers, asked Chuck to get out and led him to the rear of the car.

We were screwed. We couldn't afford a speeding ticket, and Chuck had enough legal problems that anything could get used against him as an infraction to his probation and would prevent further travel.

After ten minutes of grilling Chuck, the officer approached my window. "Why did the driver take so long to pull over?"

"I don't know. I was sleeping, and—"

The officer's face reddened. "You weren't sleeping when you passed me!"

"I just woke up. We've been driving all night. I don't really know what's going on. I had just opened my eyes and asked a question, but I wasn't really awake."

He proceeded to ask where we were headed, where we had been, and other stuff, but, honestly, I was too nervous and exhausted to remember much of anything.

The officer gave up on getting info from me and retreated to his vehicle.

After another few minutes, mostly filled with Cris and Randy rightfully making fun of how out of it I had sounded talking to the officer, Chuck returned to the car. "He's letting us go."

"Really?"

"He didn't care about speeding at all. He wanted to bust us with drugs."

Cris leaned forward. "Even if we wanted drugs, we couldn't afford any."

I added, "Probably saw your dreads as we drove by and thought his day was made."

Chuck agreed. "He asked me if I wanted to roll the dice. I asked him what he meant, and he said he could call in the dogs to sniff the car. He said he was sure they'd find something. I told him, go ahead; we have nothing to hide. He asked me again, 'So, you wanna roll the dice?' I told him no. He said, 'Good answer. Now get out of my state.'"

The cop car followed us to the Mississippi border.

Shortly after we entered Mississippi, a Pantera song came on the radio, and we all said that none of us were big fans of the band. I mean, yeah, I blasted *Vulgar Display of Power*, and I did wait in line at a midnight release event for *The Great Southern Trendkill*, but I haven't listened to them in years. Though, one time, Phil Anselmo gave a shout-out to Neurosis in front of a packed Ozzfest crowd as I was walking next to a member of the band. He ducked behind me as the crowd applauded. People told me how awesome my band was and gave me high-fives for the rest of the day. Unofficial member of Neurosis for a day … fool for a lifetime.

As we poked a bit of fun at Pantera, the skies opened up and unleashed a rainstorm from Hell.

Randy said, "We're down in Pantera country for sure. They probably sent this storm for disparaging their name."

In New Orleans, Chuck met his newborn grandson, Wolfgang, and I could see the instant recognition and love in their eyes.

I sat with Wolfgang in my lap on a second-story balcony overlooking the French Quarter. When he fell asleep in my arms, I didn't ever want to move. As much as I'll miss Chuck, I'm that much more heartbroken for his family—especially Wolfgang, who won't ever get to really know his grandfather.

I Facebook-streamed Chuck cooking us gumbo, and it turned out black rather than the reddish brown he typically shoots for. I don't know what that means, but I do know I wolfed down three bowls of it, giving my shrimp to others.

The New Orleans show marked the next time we overloaded a sound system and the first time a fight broke out during our set. One moment, things hummed along, and the next, I noticed people rushing to the door *en masse*. I had a clear shot of the fight through a glass door and noticed fists being thrown. By the end of the song, we played to a nearly empty room, aside from a gal who had a small part on the *Walking Dead* and a bassist named Alex who had played in a couple bands I love—Agents of Oblivion and Deadboy and the Elephantmen.

After the show, we stayed up late and crashed at Todd's house. He's a musician from Cleveland who goes way back with Randy. When we showed up at his place at 4 a.m., he was still out and about. I texted him that we had arrived.

He responded, *Just go in.*

He failed to mention his gal and two ginormous dogs were there, and they had no idea we were coming.

We followed a massive storm and some of the blackest clouds I'd ever seen west to Texas.

We stopped at a rest stop, and Randy said, "Man, we gotta stop talking shit about Pantera."

The promoter didn't attend our concert in Beaumont. In fact, when we arrived at the club, we were convinced the whole city was a movie prop from a dystopian post-apocalypse flick. No one walked around. No cars drove on the road. Eerie, man.

Cris said, "I keep waiting for zombies to come at us from all directions."

That night I fought dehydration and another kidney stone. The pain got so bad I couldn't think straight.

The club had no monitors, so we sounded rough. Randy was still learning the songs, and Chuck and Cris battled to get their guitars heard. During "Song 2," I approached the bar and noticed a guy sitting at the back of the club and covering his ears. Chuck's guitar, with his distortion and delay, thundered through the club and bounced off the rear wall right at this guy.

After the show, Randy complained about the constant raising of volume. "I want to superglue the volume nobs on Chuck's pedals."

I said, "It's not even a distortion pedal anymore. It's more like dick-stortion, 'cause only a dick would ever need it to be that loud."

In Houston, Randy got stuck being the *de facto* sound guy. The monitors conked out during soundcheck, so we spent hours rerouting stuff until we got them on. Then, as soon as we started playing, the main monitor cut out. Anytime Chuck stepped a certain way, his guitar shorted out. Then the PA system cut off, effectively silencing us. We had to wait until it rebooted before we continued. This happened a few times.

The show's promoter, Herman Garcia, let us crash at his place. I ended up on the tile floor surrounded by cats.

With no proper way to communicate what we had experienced during our thirty-hour drive from Houston to Los Angeles, I'll touch on a few bullet points, and then, if you feel inclined, you can try a drive of that length yourself, okay?

All you need is three other dudes, only one other of whom can drive, and you're all set.

It was 5 a.m. on Monday, and our recording session—1,600 miles away in Los Angeles—started at 11 a.m. on Tuesday.

Chuck drove first, which meant an hour-long hunt for a coffee shop that sold what he needed. Houston is massive. It took us ages to reach the northwest side of the city coming from the southeast.

As we left town, we heard reports of a hurricane headed our way. Herman evacuated and later told us he saved his cats by floating them on top of his neighbor's surfboard.

An hour or so outside of Houston, Chuck needed more coffee. We found a rest stop in Columbus, Texas. I went inside to use the restroom and found Chuck standing by himself, giggling. He stopped me before I could pass.

He pointed at a decoration for sale high up on the wall.

He giggled. "Check it out."

Wall decorations—mostly crosses—covered the long hallway wall leading to the restrooms. They were various sizes, shapes, colors, and even boasted a wide range of ethnic styles—Native American to Celtic to Eastern European in design. What had Chuck giggling—and I mean, full-on, doubled-over, eyes-glistening-with-tears type laughing—was a round Native American decoration featuring two wolves howling at the moon, their cries escaping as foggy breath.

He managed one word between giggles. "Wolfpack."

"Oh, Jesus." I retrieved my phone. "Hold still."

Chuck reached for the decoration, so happy and proud to have found it. He howled in the gas station as he stared at the wolves. This helped rejuvenate his desire to start Wolfpack Productions and to add his juvenile drawing to our merch. We did some research and found another company had already claimed the name—as was Wolfpact, Woofpack, and a dozen other variations we searched. Eventually we settled on Woofpact. com. You could've seen the infamous drawing on that website before it became defunct, and you'll notice our logo on the documentary about Chuck.

After passing San Antonio, the speed limit along Rt 10 stayed at 80mph the rest of the way through Texas. Now, I'm no speed demon, but that section of the drive got my blood pumping. How big *is* Texas? Well, as the sun fell behind the horizon, we still hadn't reached New Mexico.

I ate a ramen cup cooked in the sun for a couple minutes. The guys got Mexican food at the gas station—one of the few times Chuck had nothing but positive things to say about tacos. He said something to the effect of, "They didn't speak any English, so I knew it would be good."

Whatever Randy got, he didn't expect. The food ended up being much smaller than his stomach grumbled for, so, before long, he felt hungry again.

The Pantera jokes continued as a massive storm belted us for endless hours. We wondered if it would rain every day on that run. In truth, we didn't see another drop for three weeks after that night.

As we reached El Paso, Chuck grumbled about needing espresso and that he could drive for a bit. We passed an exit that advertised Starbuck's on the sign.

"Oh great. There goes our last chance at decent coffee. Now I'll be driving with nothing, and my stomach is already upset."

I rolled my eyes. "Dude, we're in the thick of the city. Let's get past it, and we'll find a Starbuck's right off an exit rather than driving around city streets, catching every light."

Chuck took a turn with rolling his eyes. "But it was on the sign."

"But did you see a Starbuck's sign off the exit? No. Which means we'd be backtracking to that sign we saw before the exit, which wasn't all that close."

Chuck, now angry—like, legit angry—did his impression of me. "Kids, we can't stop 'cause we might take a full minute, and then our schedule will be blown."

We all laughed, even though we were ready to be anywhere but in a car with each other. Chuck's funny, have I mentioned that before?

Another fifteen minutes or so later, we pulled off the highway, and Chuck got his Starbuck's. Chuck took over driving and blasted Garbage while I tried to sleep. I woke up due to a vocal alarm from Randy. We had stopped for gas. I peered out the window and watched a military-armored woman swiftly pass our car, inches away. Her rifle stayed aimed ahead, though she peeked in our windows.

I sat up. "What the hell?"

I noticed a few other armed people advancing from every direction.

"Shit," Randy said. "They're searching for illegal immigrants."

Sure enough, they swept the area, obviously focused on a specific target. We heard some of their chatter and more coming from walkie-talkies, but we left before getting involved in whatever they wanted to accomplish. Not long after, we entered a checkpoint on the highway, but they merely waved us through without asking any questions, like the checkpoint into California from Nevada.

We rolled across Arizona through the night.

"Is that the Mississippi?"

I traveled the desert, listening to Baroness, Mushroomhead, Faith No More, and Russian Circles before Chuck woke enough to return Iggy Pop, Portishead, Sinéad, and Cake back into regular rotation.

The wind blew so strong in Desert Hot Springs, California that I photographed Randy, Chuck, and Cris leaning forward into the breeze and being held up.

We turned north, Chuck driving now that we had entered "his town." After hitting traffic and stopping at Guitar Center for strings, we pulled under an archway and into the parking lot.

Randy asked, "Did that say Sound City?"

I nodded. "Ayup."

"Like, *the* Sound City Studio?"

"It is. We're not recording in the main studio, but Matt is set up here in the complex though."

Randy blinked. "Dude, do you guys realize how many people have recorded here? Fleetwood Mac, Tom Petty, Kyuss, Queens of the Stone Age—fucking, I think Pat Benatar …"

"Grateful Dead too," Cris added.

Yeah, so you can understand why four music nerds got a little geeked out, right?

Matt met us at the door, and I did my best not to gush. I mean, I gushed. But in a reserved way.

Thirty hour drive, Randy had only had four shows to learn the songs, Chuck still didn't have lyrics for parts of songs, Matt had never heard us or had any idea what Chuck was going for, our equipment was, for the most part, busted, secondhand stuff bound together with tape and prayer, and Chuck wanted to cram in as many songs as we could in two and a half days.

Everyone handles nerves in their own way. Me? I ramble and tell horrible/cheesy jokes. Matt took my babbling in stride and even did me a solid by laughing along to a few dull zingers. Within a couple hours, we settled in and got to work.

The studio isn't a big area, so no space goes unused. Gold, platinum, and other awarded records line the hallway toward the vocal booth and bathroom.

Good luck getting cocky in your performance when passing a plaque commemorating Matt Wallace and Maroon 5 selling 10,000,000 records.

As I stared in disbelief over that astounding, almost incomprehensible number, I accidentally kicked something. I had just enough athleticism and adrenaline to catch another plaque before it tipped and hit the floor. It had been propped on another ten or so plaques, and they were next to another row of ten or so more wall decorations.

I flipped through them: Faith No More gold-awarded cassette tape and vinyl, Chantal Kreviazuk's double-platinum award, *The Crow: City of Angels* soundtrack, and on and on and on.

The longer we stayed in the studio, the more the gravity of the situation hit home. Matt Wallace has been responsible for so much music that I love and even more that I didn't have much exposure to. For example, he produced a record by R5. You might not know them by name, but their singer is the star of a Disney program my kids watched religiously at the time. During my brief stint in broadcasting, I had probably spun three-dozen songs or more off records Matt had his fingerprint on. Spin Doctors, 3 Doors Down, Deftones, The Replacements, Train, O.A.R., Imperial Teen, Poe, H2O, Green Apple Quick

Step, Bowling for Soup, Dog's Eye View, R.E.M.—and that's the tip of the iceberg.

I told Randy, "Dude, I'm seriously trying to just breathe and comprehend where I am."

"Totally."

Randy says "totally" a lot, and now I say it too. It rubbed off on me. Totally.

My conga got set up in an isolation booth, while Chuck, Randy, and Cris chose amps in the main room. We could see each other through a glass window. Matt's desk, along with rack upon rack of pre-amps, equalizers, and various effects stood in the main room with the guys, to my right.

With the clock running, we had to get rolling. Chuck wanted to try "Bella Donna" first, as it's the song we felt most comfortable playing. We ran through chunks of it a couple times, and Matt checked levels. I wore my headphones over both ears, making it tough to hear myself as I played along. I adopted a one-ear-on/one-ear-off technique throughout most of the session; though, a few times, I forgot to remove it—now, for the rest of my life, I'll know where and when it goofed me up.

We did four full runs through of "Bella Donna."

Chuck mistakenly flubbed the line, *She sat on your doorstep*—instead saying, *She shat on your doorstep*.

He took our howling laughter in stride.

Chuck's voice sounded warm and ready from take number one. Typically, he needed hours to get in the flow and build his confidence. Not around Matt. He trusted Matt. He knew whatever happened, Matt would help him sound good, so he attacked the microphone.

Chuck noodled a bit on the guitar. "I've got an idea for an intro." He tried it a few times. "Fuck it." He stared off into space, and the studio fell quiet for several moments.

Was he angry and frustrated already?

Cris asked, "Are you sleeping?"

Chuck snapped to attention, and we continued.

Blaming the multiple cups of coffee flowing through my veins doesn't truthfully explain my playing. I got nervous, flustered even. *Dammit, Jim. I'm a medical device salesman, not a percussionist.*

One of the toughest parts of playing "Bella Donna" live is that Chuck starts it off so slowly. He speeds up as he goes, but it can drag, making the pocket hard to find. Not that day. Chuck's mix of nerves, exhaustion, and excitement had him speeding along.

I motioned for him to slow it down, the opposite of what I typically did live.

He shook his head. "No, I'm on. It's good."

I shrugged my shoulders. "It's faster than we typically play, but I like it this way."

Matt asked for a moment to review what we had recorded. Chuck fell asleep on a couch almost instantly.

Matt had us do a punch-in during the outro, and then *boom*—the basic tracks for our first song were done.

"Blue Heart" came next. We started up right away. I flubbed in two parts, and even when on, I played loose, suddenly unsure of myself.

I missed the rim for a hit, screaming, "Fuck!" even knowing we'd probably repeat the song several times to smooth out things.

Nope.

Everyone else sounded awesome on that first take and that became the basic tracks. Matt had to move and correct my performance, and I'll beat myself up about it until the day I die. That song means so much to me. I know they've added a full drum kit, so, in the end, you might not hear a damn thing I play on that song, but I'll always hear it.

I said, "Chuck, we played that one fast as well."

He shook his head again. "Maybe a tiny bit, but I don't think it was bad."

"It was a lot faster than we play live, certainly enough that if it had been a show, you'd stop and start over. I'm not saying it's bad. I just know you're always worried about finding the right pocket and groove."

I liked "Blue Heart" with a bit of life, but I wanted another crack at it.

He asked, "It's good. Right, Matt?"

As if answering himself, Chuck started playing the guitar for "Mr. Smith."

Someone, I think it was Cris, said, "Chuck, relax or you'll stroke out."

We ran through the song, and it sounded awesome right until the last note rang out. Something upset Randy, and he said, "Dammit."

We giggled at the goofy expression on the tail end of recording such a tense, melancholy song. Call us immature, but we laughed every time we listened and heard him say "Dammit." And, for the record, I'm typing this sentence at 10:51 a.m. on Jan 25, 2018—five months after recording—and I giggled when I heard "Dammit" at the end of the unmixed demo Matt sent us.

After that point, we all said it ad nauseum, trying to mimic how Randy had said it—frustrated, disappointed.

If it were any other song, I'd fight for his outburst to stay in the recording. Heck, maybe Dug would approve.

Two takes later, the song had more or less been recorded.

Matt turned toward us. "Randy, hit your D."

Randy did.

Cris caught on. "It's out of tune. Do we need to do the song again?"

Matt said, "No. We'll just have Randy come in on that outro."

Randy tuned.

Matt said something like, "Ready to be a genius?"

He had these little sayings or suggestions or phrases that helped put things into perspective. He has a knack for calming you down or focusing your attention or deflating your ego in a positive way that creates a great atmosphere for work.

We called it a night after a good ten or eleven hours.

The following day, I woke up feeling like I had slept in a concrete mixing truck that had rotated all night. The extreme highs and lows of the last week, coupled with the long drive and the stress of recording, had my temples throbbing.

Randy, Cris, and Chuck worked on "Song 2," a mellow tune I had never played on. Chuck didn't ask me not to, but I thought it sounded so full and powerful without percussion the first time I heard it. His lyrics, his guitar playing, and his voice carry the song without distraction.

I sat with Matt, eyes closed and listened as they played. The song ends with two or three minutes of spacey, echoing guitars that, no lie, I could listen to for hours and hours without getting enough.

When we played "Song 2" live, it typically got positioned in the middle of our set, a good time for me to grab the guys a beer. Just as hearing "Chip Away" each night the year before, "Song 2" became that moment that made it all worthwhile. When that song hits, the ending has so much life and so many layers.

Matt clicked his mouse a few times, I think labeling or arranging tracks. "Have you ever thought of singing that first verse higher?"

Chuck tried a few versions of the first line. *"A simple—"* Cough. *"A simple look into—"* He cleared his throat. Cough. *"A simple look into your eyes."*

Matt said, "Higher."

"A simple." Chuck nodded. "Maybe."

Matt raised his hands in surrender. "I'm just your consultant, so you can tell me I'm on crack or whatever."

"No. I like it. I'm just still recovering from the drive and worried about my voice holding up."

"Steveland" came next. Chuck still hadn't decided about when he wanted us to join in. He played the song solo a couple times, and we tried various points of entry. When Chuck had finished his guitar and singing track, his phone rang and, he went outside. We continued recording, and Matt cued us to when to start.

I recorded my conga in one take. I thought we were still figuring things out, so I didn't pay attention to when I did the three or four different fills that I played live. Not that it really mattered. Nothing I did could affect the structure of the song, as it all followed along with whatever tempo Chuck set.

I don't remember if we ever practiced or played the song with Randy before recording. If we had, it had been when we bombarded him with all the rest of the songs from our set along with another five to ten songs we never played. While recording, Randy winged it, but it became obvious he wasn't sure of himself.

Matt had him record separately. "Someone call out the notes."

Cris stood by Randy as the song played and informed Randy of the changes and what to play.

The studio version stretched, I want to say to ten minutes or more, with the last seven consisting of an outro repeated over and over. Chuck added a dozen vocal overdubs. Cris played xylophone and some extra guitar tracks. I didn't push for my backing vocals, as Chuck filled in the space and more, giving Matt plenty to choose from.

We listened to the playback.

I bobbed my head. "For a song we've only played live a couple times and that had so many question marks, this sounds pretty damn good."

Chuck asked, "Do you have a keyboard?"

Matt did.

"Can you get, like, a Hammond organ sound?"

Matt could.

Chuck added another layer that, like the rug in *Big Lebowski*, really tied it all together.

"Relocation," for me, represented the elephant in the room. A fifteen to twenty-minute song so raw and demanding that I didn't see how we could properly tackle it.

Chuck, however, pushed to try it.

Cris, Randy, and I all expressed concerns.

I pointed out, "Chuck, you don't even have lyrics for parts of the song yet."

"I'll finish them after I hear how long I'm singing."

"How will we know when the changes are coming?"

"Just follow me like we do it live."

He had a point. Chuck had cues in his head, but, as far as communicating them onstage, eh, we had to guess.

Chuck plays and sings the first verse by himself. He's joined by Cris and Randy for the second and third verses. I come in during a buildup without a set number of bars to speed up along with. *"Just watch me,"* he would tell us.

As I started with my conga, we fell off.

Randy stopped playing. "I can't hear. I couldn't hear Doug."

Cris and Chuck were also thrown off.

Matt suggested, "Want to play to a click track?"

Chuck shrugged. "Worth a shot."

We started again but didn't get far before Randy stopped us again. He shook his head. "No. No."

Chuck looked annoyed. "Why did you stop?"

"There was no coming back from that."

Matt must've agreed, because he said, "Eh, let's try it again without the click."

I caught myself coughing, tapping my feet, scratching my head and performing any number of other nervous ticks. I shuffled my feet and stretched out my arms. I wiped sweat from my forehead.

Chuck started the song.

When he reached the end of the third verse, I began my pattern. I realized quickly that my headphones had slipped over my ear on both sides, making the mix hard to follow.

The song speeds up, and speeds up, and speeds up as Chuck repeats, "On and on and on and on."

Unable to hear properly, my only chance at staying in time was to watch Chuck's fingers as he played. Of course, somehow—and this is classic Chuck and not his fault at all—he leaned to his left. A light in my room reflecting off the glass wall blocked my view of his fingers. If he moved an inch in either direction, no problem, but his sense of space and place proved the perfect disaster.

So, I guessed. I listened, and I watched, trying to time my pattern with the rise and fall of his elbow.

As the song reached the proper speed, Chuck nodded his head—the signal for us to transfer into the next part of the song, a nebulous bridge with no set time, no set lyrics, and very little idea how it went. And if I felt that way, I can't imagine how Randy saw it.

Chuck thundered forward, his fingers a blur and his vocals a mumbling mess. He nodded again, which I took as the signal to transition into the song's final section. I caught myself quick enough not to derail the song, but I knew my conga strikes fell off-time for that measure, if they had even stayed on previously.

As I recovered, we switched into the next part. The tempo remained fast and furious as Chuck sang, *"I would die for you,"* over and over. Each time, the line bended into the next line, so it becomes more like, *"I would die for, you I would die, for you I would, die for you, I,"* and it gets even more mixed up from there.

I missed a hit with my right hand, and I scolded myself. *Don't be the reason we have to redo this song.*

Chuck wanted the song to stretch as long as we could take it in the studio. At some point, way earlier than I expected, the guys stopped. Dammit, we screwed up. I thought it had sounded good, all things considered. My adrenaline pumped, and, though I had those two goof ups, the song sounded huge.

Frustrated, I caught my breath and hoped I hadn't caused us to end prematurely.

I peered through the glass, trying to read Chuck's expression. The dude was smiling. Randy appeared relieved. Cris … well, Cris always looks like he's ready for a nap.

Matt said, "This song has a great vibe."

I asked, "So, we're on the right track?"

Chuck said, "That was it."

My eyes widened. "Like, *it*, it?"

He shrugged. "Yeah. I thought it sounded great."

"I goofed up in two spots," I admitted, hoping the wrath of God wasn't unleashed upon me.

Matt asked, "Where?"

I explained, and he isolated my track.

I returned to the booth and overdubbed one part. If memory serves, Matt copied and pasted the missed hit into place near the end.

At some point Cris suggested a change or overdub or something.

Chuck considered Cris's idea and said, "I might have to admit, you have a better ear."

Cris responded, "Just less damage."

For lunch, Matt recommended a Mexican joint a few blocks away.

Randy ordered two burritos.

Matt asked, "You sure you want two?"

Randy said, "Yeah, man. I'm extra hungry, and if there's anything left, I'll just have it for dinner."

The lady at the counter stopped working for a moment. "Two?"

Randy nodded. "Yeah, please."

We took the food to the studio, and Randy's eyes ballooned. He looked at the silver-wrapped food in front of him. "What is this?"

"Your burritos, dude," I said, instantly hoping he'd not want the second one. (I'm fat, you see.)

"I, shit, really?"

Matt laughed. "I tried asking if you really wanted two."

Randy cocked his head to one side, apparently recollecting just a couple minutes ago. "Dude, and the lady even said something."

We all nodded.

He shook his head. "I was thinking they would be small, like at that gas station in Texas. I finished those in, like, three bites, and I didn't want to be starving all day."

He couldn't even finish the first one, and I'll bet he's still working on that second one.

I asked, "What other songs do we need to do?"

Cris said, "That's all six."

We counted them out loud.

Randy nodded. "That's all the ones I know of."

Matt swiveled in his chair. "We can get started on vocal tracks."

"Hey, Chuck." I decided to relinquish my insistence on focusing on two or three songs and polishing them up and instead wanted to ride the wave of fast-paced work we had accomplished. "What about that one other tune? The one Cris and I just play on the chorus?"

"'Nirvana?'"

"No, the slow one."

He noodled a bit.

"Yeah, that one. We should try it."

"Really?" He slung his guitar over his shoulder. "I'm not sure if I want you guys to play all the way through or just in certain parts."

I said, "You don't need us during the verses. I think it sounds cool, sparse like that, but it has a powerful drive when we kick in."

He performed the song by himself in one take. He only had the first line of lyrics written, so the rest he ad-libbed bits and strewn pieces together.

As he played I fell in love with the song. I glanced at Cris and pointed at the monitor, trying to indicate how much I enjoyed the song.

He furrowed his brow, confused.

I mouthed, *I dig this.*

He shook his head and, I think, mouthed, *No, it sucks.*

Typical Cris humor, but, by that point, I had heard him say something negative about every song we played.

We set up to add our two musical cents to the song.

Chuck said, "Maybe don't play on the first chorus."

We ran through it, but Randy and/or Cris played during the first chorus, so I joined in. We all agreed it sounded better with us all coming in anyway.

Matt asked, "What are you calling this one, then?"

Chuck spitballed a couple titles, but went ahead with "William Wallace's Nephew, Matt."

Chuck explained, "Cement had 'King Arthur,' and VUA had 'King Arthur's Cousin, Ted', so this is like an extension of that."

We finished after a take or two. Seven songs, or at least the bones of them. We had a few hours to add the muscle, and fat, and organs, and teeth.

Cris passed out on the couch. Chuck paced, talking on the phone. Randy messed around with Chuck's guitar and effects. He strummed "Dazed and Confused" by Led Zeppelin with the reverse delay activated, and it sounded cool.

Randy had seemed tense all morning. I tried to put myself in his shoes. He had jumped on last second to tour, play, and now record seven songs he didn't know with a band he had met a week previous, and his job as bassist required him to hold us all together. Not only that, but Chuck hadn't gone easy on Randy since we'd left. Even though they'd known each other a long time, friendship only goes so far when you're getting called out over and over and told you're messing up.

Anyway, I guessed he felt stressed over the whole thing, and I didn't want Randy stewing on something to make this session a negative experience. I sang along to his playing. I'm so glad you can't hear how bad I sounded singing Robert Plant vocals.

Randy grinned. "Man, it's still stuck in my head."

We had heard a live version of it playing at the club in Houston. Randy and I had stopped during our frustrating stage set up that night to enjoy the song.

He had heard something new in that live version. He wanted to work it out as he played around. He lightened up a bit and relaxed. Whatever had him upset was forgotten, for at least a moment or three.

Matt sat in front of his monitors, cleaning up "Blue Heart." "So what's the plan with this solo?"

I shrugged.

Chuck had played the riff he had in his head, and it fit better than I expected it would, but a few bars before and after the solo remained a simple groove with nothing to grasp onto.

Matt listened to Randy play and said, "That might sound cool coming in and out of the solo."

The two discussed it a bit, messing with settings on the pedal, and then Randy gave it a go. One of the challenges was to get a handle on when the sound would ride up to take the lead and when to pull it back before it interfered with Chuck's solo.

For a few takes, either Randy started too early or too late, causing too much to happen at the same time.

"Start tiptoeing in with the reverse delay," Matt said, keeping an eye on the monitor as Randy played. "Build the energy ... A couple more bars ... And you're out."

Randy stopped, and we listened as the effect-laden guitar faded at just the right time.

"Damn, that sounds cool," I said, looking to see if Chuck had come back inside. "Just don't let him know I said so. I've been trying to get him to omit these extra sections since I first heard the song."

Matt and Randy discussed the part further, talking about options for changing the layers and length of the delay.

We woke up Cris to see if he wanted to take a crack at it. To his credit, the kid went from comatose to nailing a tricky effects overdub in a matter of seconds. He stayed awake and worked on a few other songs. I don't know which tracks will be used on the final mix, but I do know Randy completed "Blue Heart" with one final Jimmy Page-inspired idea.

We knew the last day of recording was going to be hectic. We had a show to play that night, so we only had a few hours to get all the overdubs and final vocal tracks done.

Cris had campaigned hard to play drums on the songs, and he had suggested several other percussion layers, which might've worked, but dammit, I wanted him to back off.

In my notes I wrote, *Cris wants to play over all of my conga, and it's annoying as fuck*, but I meant it in as nice a way as possible. I wanted to be involved in these songs as much as I'd wanted anything outside my marriage and kids ... and chicken wings.

He and I played tambourine, maracas, and a few other hand-held instruments on "Bella Donna," "Steveland," and "Blue Heart." Then, with the addition of Randy, we added handclaps too.

At one point, I had a fleeting idea about a different tambourine sound, and Matt indulged me. I missed my opening mark but did it through the rest of the song.

I exited the booth. "I missed my cue and—"

Matt interrupted, "Oh, guys. There goes the Grammy!"

The perfect comment coming from such a good place was exactly what I needed to hear. I thought, *Man, I should've messed up the first take and had him put me in my place so I could've relaxed on day one.*

Chuck added Hammond B-3 organ to "William Wallace."

Matt played "Mr. Smith" for us, isolating various tracks to get a vibe for what we had recorded.

Randy said, "Man, you guys need some consistency."

Chuck gave him a sideways glance. "You mean in our playing?"

Randy pointed at the various colored waves on the screen. "Yeah. You guys should be strumming the same thing."

Chuck gave a sage "*hmmm*," his code for *I don't believe you, but just in case you're right, I won't commit to an answer yet.*

Cris stood. "I swear to God I played the same thing you do."

Chuck shook his head, listening. "You're not playing the same rhythm."

We listened, and the first chorus fell off at a few points.

Cris grinned. "Well, maybe …"

Matt ended up slicing and dicing from the second chorus, and it sounded great.

Chuck entered the vocal booth. Watching him and Matt operate, I got a glimpse at greatness. They had their own shorthand language. Here were two professionals and friends who hadn't worked together in thirty years, and yet, you wouldn't know a moment had passed since the *Introduce Yourself* sessions.

Say what you want about Chuck and Faith No More separating, but I wondered what magic Matt and Chuck might've culled from each other if they had continued to record together. If Cement or VUA had done a session with Mr. Wallace, forget about it.

At one point, Chuck struggled for a second time on a line, and I giggled.

Randy asked, "What's so funny?"

"Dude, every time Chuck goofs up something more than once, Matt says, 'Come on, Dawg' and, like, Chuck knocks the next take out of the park."

Chuck feared Matt calling him out or expressing doubts about his talent. Matt kept the perfect balance of urgency and playfulness in his voice, literally the only way Chuck would stay focused and confident. I've never seen anything like it. These guys were born to work with each other. The pair had total respect and trust in each other.

Matt opened a channel to the vocal booth. "*Daaaaawwg?*" The word came out elongated and inflected up and down, communicating a full sentence in a simple word.

Randy laughed with me that time. From then on, we had a new catchphrase anytime one of us made a mistake or took too long, or we said it simply to get a chuckle.

"William Wallace" proved extra labor intensive for Matt, as not only did Chuck not play to a click track but our overdubs during the chorus were, let's say, free floating over the top, since we were learning it on the fly.

Randy and I stepped outside while Matt shuffled our slop into respectability. Across the parking lot, a film crew set up inside Sound City Studio for a video shoot with a high-profile hip-hop artist, but I don't think we ever found out his name. We knew enough with the amount of security watching us and judging by the expensive cars that had arrived that we weren't welcome to intrude.

Randy and I walked around the building a few times.

Randy said, "Dude, I can't believe we are here."

I agreed. "I've been working up to this for years, imagining it in my head, and I am still blown away by the fact this is all coming together."

"Everyone I talk to doesn't believe me when I explain what I'm doing. Two weeks ago, I was just working at the tattoo shop with no idea what was coming."

"This is one of those moments that I'll look back on for the rest of my life and realize more and more how huge it impacted me."

"Totally."

"Totally."

We walked inside to listen to more of Chuck's vocals. Shortly after, we packed the van. Chuck ran out of steam, though we felt like we had accomplished tons more than what we had hoped. The songs weren't perfect, the music sounded sparse, and two of the songs still lacked completed lyrics, but hot damn, we had some tunes to feel proud of, and we knew the extra practice would help all of us onstage.

Matt played us a few old Faith No More tracks from the first two albums and one bit of audio that Chuck never wanted to see the light of day.

I mentioned to Matt how I wanted Chuck to rename "Song 2" the "Seagull Song" after the birds had sang with us in Portland, Maine and due to the unreleased Faith No More song, hoping maybe he'd let us hear it, but no such luck.

As quickly as it had begun, our session with Matt freaking Wallace ended.

I thanked Matt before we pulled away, but I'll never be able to repay him for helping us the way he did.

Chuck wrote a batch of songs about loss and self-doubt, reflecting on his life, describing how badly beaten and torn up he felt inside and how after all these years he still didn't have the answers he sought, recounting the turmoil and isolation he struggled with every day.

I connect with the songs more and more each time I hear them. I thought Chuck had found an outlet to properly communicate his feelings to hopefully put them into perspective for himself. I hoped he could listen and share, and the music would act as a therapy to graduate to the next stage of his life, not unlike the stages of grief one follows.

He proved he could tour as a solo musician. He proved he could still sing and write emotional lyrics. He proved that he belonged alongside the well-respected musicians and songwriters we all adore. And he proved he could do it in his own voice and style, something I even had the audacity to question. Sure, "Relocation's fifteen minutes would never be heard on rock radio, and "Steveland" could possibly ruffle feathers due to an unlicensed use of a line from someone else's song, but Chuck bared his soul unlike any other time. His spirit shined on full display, and he felt the results, for good or ill.

I wish he stuck around to soak up the feedback, love, hate, interest, curiosity, aid, and guidance people could've offered after hearing it.

CHAPTER FIFTEEN

Go East, Mosbey Boys
8/17/17 to 9/2/17

The glow of a successful recording session followed us onto the stage at the Viper Room that night, though it didn't stop the bickering. Cris and Chuck struggled to see who could get louder; Randy tried to hear where we were in the songs, and my fingers continued to crack as I smashed the conga as hard as I could.

We opened with "Living Sound Delay," and, by the three-minute song's end, Cris had zoned out, causing Chuck to abandon his singing and stage banter so he could signal Cris to stop playing at the same time as the rest of us.

During the song's choruses, I engaged a vocal effects pedal programmed with a delay to stretch Chuck's vocals and give the tune a little psychedelic vibe, so Chuck yelling, "CRIS! CRIIIS! CRI-CRI-CRI-CRIS! CRIIIIS!" echoed around the club as part of the song.

Playing Los Angeles meant Chuck was home, so he put extra pressure on himself to look and sound great.

Los Angeles, as I told you before, is almost as exotic and foreign a place as NYC, London, Paris, Moscow—hell, Mars, really. It's so vastly different than the reality I know in Cleveland that visiting feels like a vivid dream. Sure, everyone famous lives and works in Los Angeles, but it truly hits home when you run into one of your favorite musicians, like Rob Kleiner from Tub Ring, walking through the smoky club.

Author Ian Thomas Malone also drove from out of town and arrived early enough to chat, which felt super cool. The downside of hob-knobbing with celebrities is that I couldn't afford the ten-dollar cans of Pabst, and I was thirsty.

Downtown Brown, the band Chuck had toured with in 2014, opened the show. Neil, the band's vocalist and driving force, is a character. He relocated from Detroit to Los Angeles. He's hustling, doing all the things you're supposed to do as a band looking to spread the word. All the things we weren't doing.

Jonny Sculls had organized the show. His band, Pvsher, played also, showcasing the flashy side of rock. The guy has a hell of a voice. At the risk of being accused of brownnosing, he's a handsome guy with style. Pvsher kind of remind me of Thirty Seconds to Mars with dashes of Filter, Black Veil Brides, God Lives Underwater, Stabbing Westward, and maybe, Pitchshifter.

Jonny and his wife, Lacey—who had been the singer in such bands as Pigface, Lords of Acid, Nocturne, and Halo (and even did a stint on VH1's *Rock of Love with Bret Michaels*)—couldn't have treated us better nor been more supportive of Chuck, encouraging him to return down the line. Jonny's father attended the show, and we all shared stories of how we had first heard Chuck, and he told me how Chuck's music had impacted Jonny as a kid. I'll say it again, interacting with genuine people on the road is what makes it worth living in a van.

In Cleveland, we have few options to get noticed by labels, management, or the press, so it's easy to resent Los Angeles bands or Nashville dudes or NYC groups, as that's where all the big wigs operate, but man, it also demands that each band or musician maintains themselves at the top of their game and develops a character and identity and finds a way to generate a buzz in a town full of competition and jaded eyes and ears. Most musicians in the Cleveland area seem to favor T-shirts, scowls, and a blue-collar delivery, making the Los Angeles approach even more different. Neither is bad or wrong, it just stood out as interesting to me. One of the biggest bands from my town is Mushroomhead, who clearly developed an image and unique identity.

We stayed with Michele Norkon, Chuck's high-school friend who we had crashed with the previous summer. I opened her fridge and saw a can of Tecate beer.

I laughed. "That's the same kind of beer they had backstage at the show Chuck did with Faith No More."

She said, "That's one of the cans you guys brought back from the Troubadour. I don't drink beer."

I recalled my last trip backstage when I grabbed three beers. "I still have my can at home too."

In Oakland, we had the good fortune of playing with the second singer who donned a cape onstage. Chuck and I argued that night over a trip into mid-California to visit his sister and other family—one day later and he could've gone to a family reunion they had scheduled. I didn't want to block him from seeing relatives, but I needed help driving, as it added seven hours onto a six-hour trip. If he had mentioned this a few weeks earlier, or, better yet, as I had booked the shows, I gladly would've given us an open date. He thought I refused solely because my wife happened to have business in Oakland and I wanted to hang out with her. You can't tear yourself apart thinking about what-ifs, but this ended up being his last chance to see his sister before he passed away.

Reno, the following night, proved as interesting as the time Fred Savage visited there in the movie, *The Wizard*. We watched as a dozen cops stormed a strip pub across the street and dragged out people after a big brawl over cover charges.

At the show that night, Chuck reunited with an old friend, Joe Pop O Pies. He wrote lyrics, which Chuck had "borrowed" (with a few tweaks) for the Faith No More song, "Spirit." They caught up as the rest of us waited in the car. We didn't have a place to stay, and we had a long drive to our next show, so we left right away.

Have you ever driven through Oregon? Do yourself a favor and try it. As the guys slept, I circumnavigated mountains, drove over rivers, and had a hard time staying on the road, because I wanted to soak it all in. I saw charred trees and bare patches of ground along the snaking road. Living in Ohio, I had always heard about forest fires out west, but, until I saw the aftereffects, the immense power and threat of the fires didn't compute. Mile after mile of devastation stretched around us. Some areas showed signs of regrowth, having survived a fire years before, while other areas looked so fresh from the flame that the ashes still smoked.

When we stopped for gas, someone pointed out that the sky should appear cloudless. Giant clouds of smoke from massive fires had blocked the sun. I felt chills even while sweating under the sweltering heat of the day.

Someone told Chuck to ask his phone, "What does the fox say?"

When he heard the computer answer and make a goofy noise, Chuck couldn't stop laughing … or asking, over and over and over. He loved showing people that trick.

Madras, Oregon had become the center of the universe for a few August days in 2017 during the eclipse.

We played two nights in a row on a stage built outside. We had nowhere to stay, but our buddy Ian set up a tent for us. The event happened in a dirt field with a food truck providing our only source of nourishment, and damn the food tasted good.

When we pulled onto the plowed field after sitting in traffic with millions of others pouring into the city, a woman sang by herself onstage with a guitar. I listened, watching her perform with jerky motions and a foot-tapping I couldn't find logic in.

When she finished, I approached her and the sound guy. "Good stuff. I only saw the last couple of tunes, but I enjoyed it."

"Thanks." She grinned, but her glance communicated frustration. "But I did terrible."

"Sounded good out there." I pointed to the open area in front of the stage.

She added more about being disappointed in herself.

I asked, "Are you playing again tomorrow, like we are?"

She nodded.

I turned to the sound guy. "What time do you have us scheduled to play today and tomorrow?"

He glanced at a sheet of paper. "Uh, well, one of the bands haven't shown up, and they're supposed to play, like, now, so I dunno how that'll change things. Another band was here, but they went into town, so I'm not sure when they'll make it back."

I asked, "So, you don't have anyone to play for the next hour or so?"

He nodded.

I pointed toward our van and looked at the woman. "Look, if I grab my conga and join you, would you get back up and try again?"

She studied me, perhaps searching for a sign if my words were genuine. "I would. Yeah."

"Then let's do it. I'll be right back."

I jogged past the beer tent where Chuck had already made himself comfortable. I grabbed my conga. Cris followed me with his guitar, and we became the backing band for the woman, before we even knew her name. As we played, I watched her feet, still moving in a pattern that didn't make sense to me, as far as keeping time went. We played some originals and some covers for about forty minutes until we all needed to find some shade.

They call the area *the high desert*, and it's no joke. Having lived on beer and pizza for a week, I felt dehydrated when we had arrived, but the extreme heat and no shade had me feeling like a hot dog on a griddle.

"Great job," I said. "Do you feel better now?"

"Yes, thanks. I'm Lauri."

"I was trying to follow your feet for the tempo, but—"

"Oh, I'm not moving them along to a tempo. They're squirming because I'm nervous up there."

That made more sense.

Lauri admitted we were the first musicians she had played onstage with before.

I did a double take. "Really?"

"You guys are some of the first musicians I've played along with, period. I just recently picked up the guitar again after not playing for years."

Cris said, "You sounded good."

Ian pointed toward a smoldering mountain. "We played last night, and a line of fire stretched from way over there to all the way over here."

Half-joking, I asked, "But we're safe, right?"

"Well …" He trailed off.

Playing that night under a billion stars helped put the importance and beauty of our tour into perspective. Most of the crowd had retreated to their sleeping bags by the time we played. The following morning, I spoke with so many people buzzing about how great we had sounded from their tents that I couldn't help but smile. Sleeping on the hard dirt with no pillows or blankets proved too uncomfortable. When I retreated to our van, I found it full of the other guys who had already succumbed. The desert heat dropped and left us shivering.

I had zero expectations of enjoying the eclipse beyond saying, "Hey, I saw the eclipse," but, as the sky grew dark and the moment arrived, my jaw dropped. What an amazing sight.

Afterward, we were all dazed—even more so than usual.

Randy said, "Wow, man. That was life changing."

Those are big words, but yeah, I felt something—maybe a reaffirmation of how small I matter in the scheme of things or maybe how everything shares a connection all over the far reaches of space or maybe I saw something super neat.

Ian grinned. Cris had wide eyes. Even Chuck, Mr. I'm So Cool and I've Seen Everything and Done Everything, spoke about the moment in high regard.

"That made the trip worth it," I said.

"Yeah?" Ian asked.

I nodded. "Yeah, it's really easy to look at a balance sheet and see a negative sign and get bogged down, but, if we had said *no* to these shows, I would never have experienced that."

"Cool, man. Glad you did."

Damien, the event's organizer, had a piano player hit the stage as soon as the eclipse ended. His style, coming from a black-metal/doom-metal background, made for a perfect companion to the atmosphere.

That night, Damien joined us onstage. He had spent the entire weekend walking around with an endless joint and had offered it to me over a dozen times, each time forgetting that I had told him I don't smoke. He crossed the stage midsong and stuck the joint in my mouth. To be clear, smoking weed is legal in Oregon, so, when I inhaled, I didn't break any laws. Kids, don't always follow your dad's example, but remember to always be a good guest.

After our set, Damien, who had toured with the band Vital Remains, called everyone onstage, and we jammed for over three hours. I spent time on my conga, behind the drums, and on the microphone as various musicians came and went.

Chuck cooked amazing omelets the following morning. Though exhausted, he remained in good spirits, joking and enjoying the road. If he had stuck around, I'd have asked him to include some of his recipes in this book—or better yet, in his own cookbook. Then again, every time he made something, he always had secrets he didn't want to divulge.

We had back-to-back dates close together in Portland, Oregon and Vancouver, Washington. Months earlier, Chuck had received a message from Jonathan Beck asking if Chuck could help his twenty-year-old son get in to either of those shows. Both clubs only did twenty-one-and-over gigs. I messaged on behalf of Chuck and asked them to come early to hang out before a show. We had no power to demand anything from anyone. I thought, if they arrived as we set up, maybe we could sneak them in for soundcheck or I'd get Chuck to serenade Jonathan's son with a song out on the street.

They offered to let us stay in their home. We took them up on their offer. Since we had an off night and two shows within driving distance, they got more than they bargained for, as we basically moved in for three days.

We spent our off day driving, but we also had to complete a half-dozen or so interviews, which then fell on me to transcribe and get to Chuck's publicist, Tracy at TAG Publicity. When we arrived at the house, we gathered in the backyard in a covered canopy. Inside, they had couches and a gas firepit.

Jonathan said, "My son, Gage, told his bandmates about this, but we promise we won't let everyone know you guys are here, so you can just relax."

I laughed, knowing not many people would actually care if we were around, but I appreciated the sentiment. Hell, with how some of the crowds had been, a little positive reinforcement was much needed.

I leaned forward. "What does Gage play?"

"Keyboard."

Randy and I exchanged a glance.

I said, "We just recorded a new song, and Chuck added a keyboard part. Why not have Gage come with us to play."

Randy nodded. "The club would *have* to let him in if he was part of the band, under twenty-one or not."

Chuck joined us in the back patio.

"So ..." Randy began. "Dude's gonna play keys with us tomorrow on 'William Wallace'"

"Who?"

"Gage, their son." I said.

Chuck lit a cigarette. "Can he play?"

Jonathan described Gage and his band, but Chuck was already onboard.

He nodded. "We'll run through it tomorrow."

That night, I slept in a room covered in *Big Lebowski* décor and a cat on my chest.

Jonathan told us, "You're here, you're part of our family. Make yourselves comfortable."

And we did.

Cris retreated further from us, even posting cryptic Facebook posts about his unhappiness. Chuck and I didn't know how to take them. I mean, we were sitting with him, hanging out and laughing, as he posted about how miserable he felt.

I highlight this and Chuck's moods here and there, but keep in mind these things don't go away. They build, day to day, show to show, long drive to long drive, like Augustus caught in the chocolate tube in Willy Wonka—the pressure builds and discomfort spreads.

Chuck took it as another sign that we needed to find another guitarist for the next run. Not to fire Cris but to give him a chance to soul search and see if he even wanted to tour. And either way, I would understand. We weren't making money. We weren't getting attention. We weren't selling merch. We didn't have a new CD to push. We weren't eating or sleeping properly. It was insane to keep things status quo. Yet, we did.

The following day, we set up in the garage and played a few songs with Gage. As we played, I heard a knocking noise that kept throwing me off.

"Is there a dryer running?"

"It might be, but it's upstairs," Jonathan told me.

We started the next song, and I heard it again. "Sounds like it's coming from our car." I walked out to determine where the noise emanated.

Across the street, two young girls had set up boxes. They kneeled on the sidewalk, playing hand drums along to our songs. I cheered them on so excited someone had heard my percussion and had wanted to try it themselves. Eventually they came over, and we talked about drums. Doesn't get any cooler.

Gage played "William Wallace" with us that night in Portland. He picked up the notes and the groove easily enough, and Chuck, having recorded the song a few days earlier, had enough lines bouncing around his head to give it actual lyrics.

A few people who had seen us at the eclipse shows also turned up to watch us again, so we must've been doing something right, right?

When we "rushed" Chuck from the club that night—although the club had already closed and only the owner and a few of his buddies remained—our fearless leader had forgotten his dinner, and he got pissed.

I didn't have any patience to weather his crabby complaints. "I have enough to deal with. Be a man and eat your food like a big boy when we all do or stash it in the car or something."

He decided we had talked enough, and I don't know if we shared a word until the following night aside from completing more interviews.

Ashley Beck remembers sitting around the fire, watching me attempt to get the guys to answer questions for an interview in which we discussed five albums we brought with us on the road.

She said, "Every time you'd ask Chuck about [insert band name here], his first response was always, 'What about 'em?' We were all laughing so hard."

Doug: "Portishead."
Chuck: "What about 'em?"
Doug: "Tell me about their album, *Third*."
Chuck: "What about it?"
Doug: "What do you like about it?"
Chuck: It's good."

Doug: *Sigh*

Chuck, shrugging: "I dunno. Beth Gibbons. What else needs to be said?"

Doug: "Stellar material. This interview will get a lot of clicks."

The following night in Vancouver, Washington, one of the bartenders opened a closet for us with some PA gear, and we pieced it together. When we finished setting up, some drunk guy, who I still don't know if he had any affiliation with the club or not, started barking orders at us.

He'd say, "Guitar, stage left!" but Cris hadn't even plugged in yet.

The guy barked again. "Stage left. C'mon!" He threw up his hands. "Whatever. Bass. Give me bass!"

Randy played two notes, and the guy yelled again. "No! No! You need to adjust—"

This continued for several minutes until I blew up at the guy. I don't remember what I said, but I remember gearing up to jump off stage at him and wondering how many people there would prevent me from lashing out.

Through all the drama and disappointment on the road, Cris, Chuck, and Randy remained *my guys*, and no one could get away with yelling at them. The guy backed down, thankfully, and we went ahead with the show, but my blood boiled the entire night. I never got in a groove. I stayed onstage after the show, embarrassed to face anyone, until Randy talked me off the ledge. Apparently, people had enjoyed the gig.

Randy digs a band called Thee Oh Sees. I had never heard them before that tour leg. He got us hooked on their song, "I Come From the Mountain," which, after each verse line, the band sings, *"OOU-OOU."*

We added the *OOU-OOU* to our conversations.

For example: I'd be talking to Jonathan in the kitchen, and Randy walk between us to go to the garage, and he'd say, "Mind if I pass Thr*OOUGH-OOU*?"

Jonathan would respond, "But if you leave, I'll be bl*OOUE-OOU*!"

Hours on end turned into days of baiting each other into new words that fit the scheme. And no, I'm not exaggerating. This is one hundred percent tr*OOUE-OOU*!

Good luck trying to avoid doing this now.

Our three-day stint at the Beck's house came to a tearful end the following day as we shoved off for Boise, but Chuck had planted a seed before we left. He asked me to stop the car as we pulled from the driveway.

He called out the window, "John! Give her that baby!"

Apparently, Jonathan and Chuck had engaged in a late-night discussion about relationships. Jonathan, who had dated Amber for a long time, had asked Chuck, of all people, for relationship advice. Jonathan had two grown children from a previous marriage, which brought a certain amount of reasonable hesitation.

I asked Jonathan about their interactions, and he told me, "When Chuck and I were alone going to Portland to get his licorice roots for tea and again in the mornings by the fire drinking coffee before everyone got up, we discussed Pip and Ashley, along with the joys and hazards of relationships. I told him that Ashley wanted to get married and have a baby, but I felt too old for a baby and too scared of Ashley realizing someday that she 'had settled' to get married. Chuck told me a bit why he had chosen not to marry but that he regrets being afraid and told me not to live fearfully and that Ashley obviously is committed to me. As far as becoming a dad again, he complimented me on Gage and Ivy, suggesting I was an okay father, and that if he was ten years younger, he thinks he might've wanted another kid. Kids keep you 'young', 'give you a purpose and focus.'"

Sure enough, later that day as we drove to Boise, we got word that a proposal had occurred—the future in-laws had agreed, and wedding plans had commenced.

Boise. We played after three Pantera-type metal bands at a free event. We needed energy. We needed a loud crowd. We needed to sell merch. Chuck needed to mess with everybody.

While Randy, Cris, and I finished setting up, Chuck disappeared. The three of us jammed songs by Queens of the Stone Age, The Doors, and "What's in My Head" by Fuzz—our official warmup song on that run. The crowd cheered us on, so we kept going, not that we had much choice. When Chuck did arrive, he started with "Sinéad," instantly killing the buzz.

Randy told me later, "As Chuck started playing, a guy in front, who played guitar in one of the openers, said, 'Man, I was digging these guys until the singer started.'"

By the end of the song, half the crowd had evacuated for the smoking area out back. Realizing this, Chuck did the opposite of what common sense dictated and played more mellow tunes. I'm all for messing with a crowd, but …

A drunk gal up front screamed, "Play something that rocks!"

Chuck immediately started the mellowest tune he could—"Mr. Smith."

"Love is God—"

She yelled, "Boo!"

All we could do at that point was crack up and go along for the ride. We played a decent set and won back the crowd with a distorted, noisy last few songs.

Someone in a Polkadot Cadaver shirt had brought Chuck a twelve-pack of beer that he had brewed, but security wouldn't let him give us the bottles. As low on funds as we found ourselves, free beer would've helped us along nicely.

At 3 a.m., we cracked open beers and discussed staying up all night. At 3:15 a.m., I fell asleep. At 7 a.m., Chuck got me out of bed, trying not to wake up our generous host. (Thanks, Levi!) He led the charge to get rolling, as we needed to reach a studio in Salt Lake City as early as possible. Of course, as soon as he started driving, he took us on a thirty-minute detour to find coffee. He then drove from 8:15 a.m. to 10 a.m., stopping three times for potty breaks, smoke breaks, and I think the third time he did it strictly to piss me off. It worked. About ten miles outside of Twin Falls, Idaho, I took over driving.

Randy and Cris had hit the free beers pretty hard the previous night, so, when they started complaining about the drive, I'd had enough. Neither of them could drive, so all they had to do was sleep or play on their phone or do whatever until show time. I felt every part of the babysitter, the father, the boss—and I wanted none of it.

We arrived at Joe Haze's studio outside of Salt Lake City.

Chuck set up in the live room by himself. He wanted to get a version of the Sinéad tune down. He felt supremely confident that not only would we get Sinéad done, but we'd get to "Take This Bottle" as well.

Joe and his crew were super friendly and supportive, making it that much tougher to grumble about exhaustion or annoyances. The view from outside the studio was breathtaking. Coming from Cleveland, I don't see mountains too often, let alone majestic peaks and storybook views like that. I took several photos for reference material for a mystery/suspense novel I had written.

The first hour or two blew by in a blur of Chuck's typical distracted delays with minimal progress. He got into a groove and, spread over several takes, recorded some somber, evocative vocal parts and guitar that sounded so Mosley.

He took a quick break, pulling me outside to talk. "So, what do you think?"

"Sounds good. I think you can add some layers to the solo and really beef it up to reach the shock level you want."

He nodded. "And for 'Take This Bottle' … What was it you wanted to do with the arrangement?"

I had always wanted to fill out our version of the song so it stood on its own, outside of the medley we played. It fit Chuck so well lyrically and stylistically, and I thought if he gave it a chance, we could make it something special.

I got so caught off-guard by his willingness to try my idea that I had a hard time remembering what I had proposed over a year ago. "Verse, chorus, I sing second verse—unless you want to give it a try?"

"No. I won't remember the words."

"We could write them down but whatever. We go into the second chorus, but, instead of fading out to end, we add a half verse where you sing the first line again, and then I'd like to go into a short solo before coming back to a doubled chorus to end it. You could also end it with a noisy, downtrodden solo instead. On their version, they add the *'Take it away'* part. So I could sing that, or we could get a few people to make it a chorus-type ending. It's too bad Michele didn't have business here too."

"So, second chorus, then first verse again?"

"No. Just a half a verse. You say—"

"Half verse?"

"Yeah. So, you say—"

Joe or one of his staff poked out their head. "You guys ready?"

I assumed Chuck would revert to the short version or spend too much time trying to remember that we wouldn't get anything done, but he nailed it within a few takes.

We set up my conga to play along in lieu of a click track, but it didn't work, so we abandoned it.

There is a take where, right as I came in, Chuck said, "Doug, don't play."

I had forgotten about it until after Chuck passed. Joe Haze sent me all the rough tracks isolated. I listened along with my wife. As the song started, I waited for my cue and used my desk as a conga.

When pre-recorded Chuck said, "Doug, don't play," I froze.

My wife and I shot each other looks of disbelief before laughing and crying.

By the time we played, drank and left the club that night, all of us had transformed into zombies. We faced a long drive to Denver. We would discover late that night—or early in the morning, depending on your point of view—Chuck had left his book bag at the club in Salt Lake City.

He was livid. "You guys have one job. I asked you if you double-checked everything."

In my eyes, Chuck had always been the guardian of his bag. It was his space, his property, and I never touched it. Before he got in the car, I remember asking him if he had all his stuff, but he was too tired to be bothered by then.

He bitched and moaned between naps and never stopped complaining about it. Ever. He included it in our conversations right till tour's end. The guy had lost, broken, lent out tons of my stuff and always had an excuse, but the one time ... Damn you, Chuck.

Anyway, the next morning, I awoke in a parking lot in Wyoming, listening to Cris and Randy talking to some weirdo in a rusted box truck.

They got back in the car, both giggling.

Randy said, "Dude, that guy was just trying to sell us snowboards ... in Wyoming. In the middle of nowhere. In August."

"Is that the Mississippi?"

Cris added, "He asked what we were doing on the road, and, as soon as we told him we were on tour, he asked us what drugs we wanted. Told us we could look at stuff in the back of the truck. Yeah ... no."

In Denver, we shared a bill with Stephen Shareaux, with Drew Fortier playing guitar for him.

At some point, Christopher Duvall, who we had met the previous summer, handed me his phone. "Check out who just commented on my post about this show."

Bill Gould wrote he and Chuck had played at Herman's Hideaway thirty years earlier, adding a story about bed linen procurement from a nearby motel. He also included a photo depicting Jim Martin wearing nothing but a towel and standing outside a motel in an alley.

I glanced up from my phone and realized I stood in almost the exact spot the photographer had snapped their shot. I peered down the narrow alley between the motel and the club. "Aside from a paint job, this place hasn't changed in decades."

Drew, being the busy guy that he is, had to hop a plane that night to get to his next event. Before he left, he joined us on "Tractor." It was the last time he and Chuck played together.

The following day, we had off. I spent a chunk of time unloading and cleaning the car. What a disaster. After that, I caught up with my accounting for the tour, walked to the bank and worked on transcribing interviews, collecting reviews, and booking shows for our next run.

My wife called, angry, saying, "You need to be more present, even when you're not around."

I'm sure she's right. I have a terrible time multitasking. If Don Rickles were here, he'd have some barb about how I have a hard time single-tasking.

I went to see *Spider-Man: Homecoming* by myself. (Thanks for the ticket, Christopher.)

Upon leaving the theater, I found myself outside this shopping mall area, strolling around with no one in sight. I felt so disconnected from it all. Just as Chuck had felt like an outsider at punk shows, I felt like an outsider to this mall culture and from the guys in the band, maybe even to the music industry as a whole. Promoters, bands, clubs, and others used to tell Chuck and me that we were too nice to survive the business. Maybe we didn't belong.

I peered at the sky, some odd notion of how ridiculous the scene played out, and said, "I don't belong here."

I didn't know where I meant. Alone? At the mall with real people? On the road away from my family? At a bar playing Chuck's songs for strangers? None of those options?

Chuck always said, "The road is for savages," and he was right. The road is for savages, wild dogs, and vagabond spirits searching for the next high. A crowd, a drink, a drug, a girl, a guitar solo, or maybe all of them presented the ultimate prize to attain, and yet I found contentment with tang-flavored water and a free movie.

Have you ever seen *Rat Pack* with Ray Liotta? I was Joe Mantegna as Dean Martin, sitting by myself in a hotel room watching TV as the party raged downstairs. Now listen, I'm not saying I didn't have fun. I had the time of my life. But I shouldered the burdens myself, and that weighed heavily on me. Especially knowing what my wife had to sacrifice and what our parents endured back home to keep things maintained. I am a savage. I am a road dog. And say what you want; Joe Mantegna and Dean Martin are cool.

I wanted to call my wife to explain how lost I got while also needing to stay here, that I had developed an addiction to the road while still regarding it with fear, that I wanted to pull this jalopy into the fast lane and open her up yet I knew the realistic dangers of running out of gas, that I represented a part of something so beyond money and laundry and taxes and square meals but that I desired all four of those things. Instead, I paced the parking lot and thought, *What a mess I am—an outsider to normalcy and to artistry and to creative writing and to myself. Where do I belong?*

The glaring red Target sign watched me, judging.

"I don't belong here." I sipped my water. "I don't belong here ... *'Cause I'm a creep.*"

I giggled, Radiohead song now firmly stuck in my head, and drove to the motel.

Chuck called from a bar and asked me to meet him, but it was my day off.

We shoved off from Denver the following morning, headed east. We pulled up to the club in Wichita, Kansas and saw six guys in cowboy hats standing out front.

"Uh …" Randy asked. "Are we sure this is the right place?"

I searched for a parking spot. "Get ready, boys. This might be a rough one."

Luckily, Wichita proved me totally incorrect. The club, the promoter, the crowd, and the other bands were all super cool and excited.

I met a guy named Echo, a staunchly pro-Wichita dude. As he told me about the city, a stumbling-drunk guy approached us, knocking over a huge ashtray and garbage can in the process. He pointed at us. "You damn liberals. You're the problem."

Echo said, "I'm actually—"

The man interrupted. "Global warming!" as if that proved his point.

I live for these types of situations, so, of course, I invited the guy to keep talking, and I urged him on a bit. Now, this passage is not to be political, at all. I am not taking sides here, just some friendly conversation to see what an extremely drunk and upset person will say or do.

I said, "So, the liberals are causing global warming?"

"No!" he yelled. "You caused the hurricane!"

This took place a day or two after Hurricane Harvey had unleashed on Houston.

"How did I do that?"

He stumbled backward but stayed on his feet. "Global warming. If we had global warming, there wouldn't have been a cold front to turn back the hurricane. That's what caused most of the damage."

Eventually, he knocked over the ashtray again and called us several slurs—security led him out.

After we put the kids to bed that night, Chuck took me outside of our hotel room to chat. He admitted he felt drained and stressed and unhappy with a lot of things. We cleared the air of any tension between us. In fact, we both admitted to having a good run together despite how much time we had spent in close quarters. He mentioned our 2018 shows, which we had started booking.

I told him, "It's good to see you excited about something. I can see this tour working, if you commit and fly straight. Let people see and hear how good you can be on a consistent basis."

He nodded, though he stopped short of any promises to fly straight.

Someone who had attended our show took us to an intersection of streets named Mosley and Douglas. We took a few photos. Chuck got a hold of some cardboard and wrote, *Will Rap Over Hard Rock for Food*—a nod to the VUA album. He sat on the ground behind a building downtown, and we snapped more photos.

In Oklahoma City, we played with Zander Shloss, a well-known punk who has turned solo in recent years. He approached Cris, eyeing him up and down. "What are you? A roadie?"

Cris said, "No. I play guitar with Chuck."

Zandar's eyebrows rose. "Okay, I guess I'm just old-school. We dress up for shows."

The other opener had a rockabilly, bluegrass, punk feel, and we all dug them. The washboard player got a little tipsy at one point and fell off the front of the stage.

As they played, I asked Cris, "Are you seeing what I'm seeing?"

He shook his head.

"The cello player looks a lot like Fairuza Balk."

Randy agreed. We both thought it was odd that he had, within the last day or so, told us a story about how Fairuza Balk and he exchanged music back in the day. Maybe you don't find it an odd occurrence but ask yourself when was the last time she got mentioned in a conversation, and then ask yourself when was the last time you saw someone who looked like her, because neither happens often.

The bluegrass punk band invited us to their house for a late-night jam. I played washboard for the first time ever.

Cris kept saying head-scratching stuff, like, "Man, Wichita isn't so bad."

I'd say, "Dude, Wichita was last night. We're in Oklahoma City."

Cris would nod. "Oh, yeah. What state are we in?"

I'd clench my jaw. "Confusion."

Five minutes later: "Do you guys always jam like this in Kansas?"

"Kansas?" the singer of the band yelled. "Do you not see the red dirt?"

Cris glanced around, in the pitch-blackness of 2 a.m. "Nope."

This happened every day, all day.

A big deal? No. But I think what drove me nuts was how much time and effort I had put into booking, promoting, arranging, investing, designing, practicing, and peacekeeping for the tour to happen, and to have him brush it off, hurt. Not in a personal or deeply harmful way, but man, he made himself an easy target for my exhausted emotions and breaking pride.

Pulling into a gas station north of Dallas, we saw the aftereffects of Hurricane Harvey first hand. Gas lines stretched onto the highway ramp, prices had risen, and an unsettling lady who desired to discuss the apocalypse and our Lord and Savior,

Jesus, approached us. It didn't take her long to realize she had struck up a conversation with the wrong group.

Cris, Randy, and I humped around Deep Ellum that afternoon, though the scorching temperatures threatened to melt me. Chuck, who had grown up in LA, had no issues with the heat. Fucking guy wore long pants, a long-sleeve shirt, thick boots, and I don't think he even sweated.

My buddy from high school, Evan, came to the show. I'm glad he did, because, well, no one else showed up. In fact, two of the openers couldn't make it due to the storms. That night, we played "Nirvana," a new song Chuck had wanted to try. The song had as many temporary titles as it did set lyrics. This was the only time it got performed outside of practice. I recorded some of it during soundcheck.

The club, a dump of a place located in the darkest corner of town, screwed us out of money. Their talent buyer and manager, who played in some sort of boy band, made promises about paying us back. Surprisingly, we never heard from them again. Class acts.

The road to Memphis felt like Hell at the end. Chuck drove the last leg, and I fell asleep. When he woke me up, crossing the bridge into the city, I felt my insides churning, like the morning I got the kidney stone.

Within twenty minutes, my whole body writhed in pain. I couldn't even think straight. I had a hard time reading the GPS off my phone to direct Chuck to the club. When we arrived, the discomfort grew so sharp that I took off to find cranberry juice. I laid down in someone's grass instead.

I looked up nearby hospitals.

Everyone at the Hi-Tone had a blast, but I couldn't even complete a sentence. The band we played with, HEELS, put on a funny, intense live show, but I watched from the back, laying down. Even though the temperature had risen to a gazillion degrees, I felt cold. I'm almost never cold. I recall very little of our set aside from sweating through the chills.

Now, here's why Chuck is your hero and my hero and the everyman's hero. Sure, he wrote good songs, and he possessed a unique voice, and blah, blah, blah, but the way he earned all his ace-in-the-hole medals was by talking to everyone. *Everyone*.

That night, a guy had set up a portable BBQ pit in front of the club and had been cooking for hours. The smell alone could drive a man insane.

After the show, Chuck pulled me aside. "Can I get, like, twenty bucks?" He led me outside. "I talked to the barbeque guy earlier. He said whatever he has left at the end of the night he'd give to us, super cheap."

I handed him twenty. I sniffed the air. "Do you need more?"

That night, we feasted like kings. Except Cris, who passed out in the van on the way to the house. Someone had given him banana pudding, which he had stepped in and tracked all over the back of the van. And that wasn't the worst of it.

The following day, we played Atlanta. It represented a turning point in the tour and the last day that Chuck and I shared as close friends. Strap in, everyone. From here things get dark and uncomfortable.

CHAPTER SIXTEEN
Every Rose Has It's ...
Crappy Days
9/2/17-9/12/17

We had had to switch clubs last second after Star Bar mistakenly double booked us and never caught the issue until days before our show. This, coupled with Dallas stiffing us and getting shorted on another recent show, began a trend of crappy circumstances that followed us to the end. On the flipside, you can say we had benefited from incredible luck considering the situation and that Chuck-fans had proven so generous with their couches, maybe we deserved a cold dose of reality.

Chuck asked me to borrow the van to run some errands. In the past, this would've caused me great anxiety, but he had remained so positive, helpful, strong even. And I knew we all needed a break away from the grind.

My kids picked out a toy for me to bring on each tour leg. This time, it happened to be a Matchbox DeLorean, painted blue and white, which my brother had gotten as a kid. I found a place to take photos with it each day. In Atlanta, I saw a young boy outside the club playing with his own cars. I joined him.

Watching my bandmates struggle to get motivated each day

left me wondering if I should've kept this run to three weeks. If I had, we'd be turning north for home that day rather than facing another couple thousand miles and several more shows. I feel like I'm painting an awful picture. Playing and recording with Chuck still felt surreal, but day-to-day operations drag you down no matter what.

During the first song, Chuck barked at Randy about keeping up and at Cris about turning down. Michael Burgess, who took a ton of photos from the show, captured a moment of Randy yelling back at Chuck. He looks pissed and frustrated, doing exactly what we all felt.

We had wanted to play "Come Around" for Donn, who had driven all the way from Toledo for the show. That song had fallen off the setlist for the most part as Randy hadn't had time to learn it. We started and stopped a few times before abandoning the song, with an apology to Donn.

Randy approached me between songs. "Man, what's going on?"

"Do you think he's using?"

His eyes widened. "Do you?"

I shrugged. "This doesn't feel like he's too drunk. His timing is off."

Timing issues typically telegraphed Chuck's sobriety or lack thereof.

Randy glanced at Chuck. "We gotta talk to him."

I promised, "I will."

After the show, I cleared the stage and loaded the truck. Chuck held court outside, once again leading everyone to the smoking area rather than to the merch booth.

"Hey, Chuck." I shut the van door. "Walk with me."

He and I headed across the parking lot. He reflected about the moments he liked from the show.

I cut him off. "You'll never convince me that you weren't on something tonight."

There, I fucking said it. Cards on the table.

"What?" He genuinely looked caught off guard.

"Dude, you were all over the map. We couldn't even finish songs. Randy and I spent the whole set giving each other questioning glances—"

He shook his head. "No. Randy couldn't hear, and he was throwing me off, like he's starting to do every night. You know that."

"I don't know. Tonight felt different. Your guitar playing actually stayed on, but your vocals, they came in at random times."

"He was off. I'm telling you. I couldn't hear. And Cris, I don't even know what he was playing."

"What about 'Relocation?' You skipped entire lines. You came in early on—"

"No, I didn't. How could I? It's the same length every time. Eight, then eight, then eight."

"You came in to the second part halfway through the phrase."

He shook his head, his eyes steel.

I continued. "Then you started the *I would die for you* out of nowhere, and it definitely wasn't eight, eight, eight."

"I wasn't off, and I'm not on anything."

"You didn't leave and buy anything?"

He shook his head.

"You're not on any drugs?"

"No. I've been clean since January, and you're really starting to piss me off."

"Are you drunk?"

He gave his stock "I've had, like, one beer and a shot, well, two beers, and one jack, and one car bomb ... and Donn bought me one" type of response.

We discussed a bit more, but I had no proof aside from what I'd seen and heard. He sulked off, and I sat by myself on the curb.

Down the strip from where we had played, a drinking/art party had wrapped up, and I heard ladies giggling and planning their night. Across the parking lot and a bit down the hill, bass thumped from a packed dance club. The traffic had backed up all the way down the street. I craved to know that feeling of a crowd attending one of our concerts and getting that excited.

We stayed at Michael's house in the mountains outside the city. I forced myself to crash out, as we had another long drive the following morning. I heard Michael and Chuck talking on the back deck. When I awoke, I heard them talking as breakfast sizzled and steamed on the stove.

The hard part about monitoring Chuck was the guy had mastered being a user and could manipulate almost any situation to appear that everyone else had dropped the ball while he remained a rock. That's why, on the following day, I second-guessed myself.

After sleeping a good chunk of the ride to North Charleston, Chuck stayed distant but said, aside from feeling tired, he remained in good spirits. He and I snuck off and had a few conversations about the status of things, and he reiterated his commitment to staying clean, though our lighthearted joking and typical shorthand fell flat.

Then one of the openers blew us away.

If you get a chance to see a female duo called Hey! Alligator, do it. They sing dirty and humorous lyrics over Casio hip-hop beats. They perform under alter egos; they play horns; they wear costumes; they dance all over the club, and they mix in prerecorded skits between songs. What else do you need?

Never had I seen Chuck get so animated during a show. Sure, he enjoyed and loved bands we played with or saw together, but he wasn't the giddy-fanboy type, and yet, there he knelt on the floor when the girls demanded everyone in the club to do so. He took photos of their set. He giggled. He hopped around when commanded.

He asked them to join us onstage during "William Wallace," though only one of them did. He also asked them to accompany us on a future tour. He gave them all our current dates and told them, "We'll put you on any of these shows you want."

Chuck and I closed out the bar with the owner that night, sharing war stories. I relaxed. I wanted Atlanta to be a random blip on the radar, a mistake.

That night, we stayed with the promoter, Cleveland native, Nathan Petro.

Over some pizza and beers (and his wife had made, like, a cheeseburger casserole or something that melted in my mouth), Nathan told Chuck something to the effect of, "You taught me an important lesson a long time ago about asking for what I want."

Chuck asked, "How?"

"I went to the Faith No More show at the Agora, back in '97. I saw you talking to some people. I asked you for a backstage pass, and you actually handed me one. When I told my friend and girlfriend, they asked me to go back up to you. I asked for another one, and you gave it to me. Ever since then, I've never been afraid to ask for what I wanted, because I knew I might actually get it."

I laughed. "Small world."

Nathan gave me a questioning glance.

"I was the guy he was talking to," I confessed. "After he gave you those tickets, I asked him what they were and then if I could have one. You got the last two."

The following morning, Chuck and I were out back, and again the discussion of the future arose. Chuck wanted change. I encouraged it, realizing that if he continued doing the same thing, he might get depressed and slip into bad habits. Hell, I thought he *had*.

We drove across South Carolina and into Asheville, North Carolina for an off night. At the bar, we ran into a gal recently transplanted from Long Island. She had seen us at Mr. Beery's. Chuck borrowed a guitar, and Cris ran to our car to grab his.

They got up during an open mic session and performed "Song Two."

When they finished, Chuck mumbled, thanking the crowd. He glanced at me, and I tried to communicate that he should announce our free show the following night. Via some miracle, he understood what I tried to say.

He stood by the mic. "Oh, and, uh, tomorrow, we're playing a free show at—"

A girl sitting up front looked at the other people at her table and said, "Nobody cares. Nobody cares."

I laughed, even though it came at the expense of my bandmates.

Outside the bar, a guy stood near us, wobbling. He glanced at the concert poster inches from his face. Glanced at Chuck. Glanced at the poster. Back at Chuck. "That you?"

"Yeah."

He looked at the poster again. "You do Bad Brains covers or something?"

Cris said, "No, he was in the band."

The dude wobbled. "You were in Bad Brains?"

Chuck puffed his cigarette. "Yeah."

"As what?"

"Singer."

The guy eyed the poster. "So, you sang for Faith No More too?"

"Yeah."

"Whoa!" The guy's eyes went wide. "You were in a band with Mike Patton?"

We all fell silent.

The guy's cheeks reddened as he realized why Chuck and Mike being in the same band at the same time wouldn't make much sense.

I fought back the laughter as long as I could before exploding. I stumbled away, bellowing, trying to keep my balance but failing.

The guy looked mortified. "Oh, man. I am *so* sorry. I didn't … I'm gonna buy you a shot."

He retreated quickly as we all enjoyed the moment.

A moment later, a random guy approached Randy, Cris, and me. He wanted to know if we could tell him about the hotspots around town.

"We're not from here either," we told him.

Within minutes, his boasting about owning the largest stash of the best cocaine this side of the Mississippi had us giggling. Why? Because we pictured Chuck asking if we were crossing the Mississippi again. But his approach also sobered me up. Call me naïve. I know people do drugs, and I know people sell drugs, but, like, isn't selling to random people in a strange city a really unsafe idea? How do you not end up in jail, like, every single night?

My friends, Sarah and TJ Dutton, had moved from Ohio to Asheville a year prior. They offered to put us up.

Chuck claimed their front porch as his territory and made it clear he wanted to be left alone. The only person he talked to was Sarah who, after I told her about Chuck wanting to meet his birthmother, approached him with her recent success of finding both her birth parents and discovering she had half-siblings as well. She gave him some info and a few contacts who had helped her.

The skies opened up and dumped on us as we loaded in the club the next night, the first drops of rain in three weeks.

Chuck found a piano in the basement of the club, so he spent a few hours twinkling away and drinking. I still felt like he wanted distance, but I needed him to be involved to help me and the tour during its last week. I sat with him a while but got angry that he wouldn't engage me in conversation.

Later, I learned he had called the first agency Sarah had given him the number for, and they had agreed to send a packet of info on how to proceed. Suddenly, his fantasy of a reunion had taken a big step toward reality, and he got shaken by a mix of excitement and dread. I wish I had known. I wish I hadn't assumed …

Onstage, we struggled through our typical push-and-pull battle with Chuck. Our first song, "Living Sound Delay," came to a messy out-of-whack ending. Chuck got miffed as he unexpectedly decided to stretch the song longer, but we followed his previous instructions.

Sarah told me, "You guys stopped, but Chuck kept going. When you tried to tell Chuck you were going off his head-bob cue, he said, 'There's not only physical cues, but you have to feel the song as well. You have to get inside my head.' You responded, 'That's the last place I want to be.' During another song—one of the new ones—Chuck started and stopped a couple of times.

He apologized for not remembering the words, as it was a brand-new song. You said, 'That's never stopped you before.'"

A couple Chuck had met from Holland at the bar the night before did, in fact, attend. I'm not sure if they liked us, but they came.

Chuck kept saying he felt exhausted, but he also refused to sleep. He stayed up all night, even feeding and walking the Dutton's cow as the sun rose.

Sarah told me, "When he fed Maggie, he was totally drunk. He was bent over, too close to her. I told him, 'Keep your face away. Babies hit their mother's utters to let them know they want more.' Maggie punched Chuck with her nose. He was, like, three inches from her nose. If she had hit him full force, he probably would've gotten a black eye."

To help Chuck get out of his funk and to ward off the cold we constantly passed back and forth, Sarah gave Chuck a bottle of "fire cider." It's some insane concoction of spices and vinegar and devilry, meant to burn your soul alive or something. I still have one of those bottles in my fridge. The last time I took a sip, my chest hair fizzled off.

We drove across the state to Wilmington. Chuck and I did an interview before the show, but the other guys disappeared. Then, right before we played, Chuck disappeared. I could see him from the stage, standing outside and smoking. He peered at me through the window, grinning when he saw my frustration. I beckoned him in with urgency, as the sound guy wanted to check his stuff.

Chuck came in, all snotty attitude, and peered into the crowd. "I don't even see the sound guy. He's not even ready for me yet."

"He was ready ten minutes ago. He must've gotten frustrated and is on to the next thing."

Chuck located the soundman, standing right in front of us.

"See?" Chuck said. "Looks like everything's fine, Captain Xaggerate."

After the show, Chuck had his party pants on and refused to leave, even though the club had closed. Only a couple, who also needed to leave, remained. The gal had already dropped and smashed a bottle outside, and I think she had vomited too. Chuck was livid that we forced him to go.

"Chuck, the promoter left an hour ago. I don't want to get to his place too late."

"Then you go."

"How will you get there?"

"I'll find my way."

To his credit he (almost) always did.

I pulled over the car. "Go ahead."

"Here?"

"Yeah, it's a ten-minute walk back to town."

He thought about it a moment before telling me to keep driving. He was pissed.

The following morning, Chuck pulled me aside, again, to have our daily update. He had grown tired of the drama. He wanted to make sure that after our November 3 show, we would break for the year and regroup in 2018. He told me he had decided to change the band lineup, and he really wanted to change our Faith No More medley.

Due to a miscommunication, we had a fluke off-day after Wilmington, so we returned to Asheville to stay with Sarah and TJ again. We had the Hey! Alligator disc spinning the whole drive. We soon knew all the words and had incorporated them into our conversation.

When we got close to the city, Chuck asked that we drop him off downtown, so he could drink alone. We picked up Sarah and headed downtown ourselves. We saw Chuck sitting at a bar called The Ugly Monk.

I suggested, "Let's go somewhere else."

Sarah later told me a story. "We were at the bar, early in the night. You and I were talking, and Chuck came in and saw us. I could tell he was upset, angry. He stared right at you. I got scared. I mean, I didn't know Chuck at all. The first two nights, he had stayed on the porch, isolating himself and sleeping a lot through the day. I didn't talk to him much before then. He said to me, 'Yeah, your boy here wants to handle me too much. I don't like to be handled.' You had just told me about all the in-band drama and your recent confrontations. I thought maybe you guys were gonna fight. I mean, he looked like he would deck you. I had no idea what would happen. Would I have to get in-between Chuck and Doug? Then his expression went to mush. 'But I love him so much. None of this would've happened without him.' As quickly as the tension rose, it faded. Then it was a lovefest the rest of the night."

Though I remained blissfully unaware of that exchange, I still had drama to confront.

Cris appeared extra down. He hadn't said more than a couple words during the last few days. When he mentioned that he felt certain his time with Chuck would end after this run, I said, "Hey man, walk with me."

Maybe that's my catch phrase?

I led him down the street and tried to present the situation as openly and honestly as I could. How Chuck felt. How I felt.

I admitted, "Whatever is going on with you and Sophie, I can't help there. I don't know the situation, nor do I really want to. Good luck with all of that. But, if you want to continue, I'll go to bat for you."

He said he appreciated the gesture, but he wasn't sure anything I said would make any difference. I remember thinking, *You're probably right, but …*

Yeah, I got frustrated, and I disliked dealing with extra BS, but Cris stuck with us all summer. He recorded with us. He put in the hours. Maybe, if he and Chuck had some time away, they'd want to reconnect.

I thought all along that Cris needed his own project. His mind roared in a constant state of new riffs and new lyrics and new vocal patterns—none of which would ever get used playing for Chuck. Maybe he'd have the winter to start a band and then be itching for the road by spring.

Randy had this habit of observing someone doing something and then pointing it out. Like, "Okay, I see you, jay walker, walking across the street, giving zero fucks. Okay!"

It's one of my favorite things in life. So, just like I said "totally" all the time, I started in with the "okay" bit.

Okay, bass player, I see you standing over there offstage, acting like you can't hear anything. Okay, waitress, I see you not laughing at my bad joke about the soup. Okay, reader of this book, I see you wondering what all this *okay* nonsense is about.

Throughout all the nights we spent at the Dutton's house, I slept in a tent in the backyard. That morning, I awoke to singing and guitar playing. Cris and Randy serenaded me with a freestyle song about … well, I don't remember, but they had coffee.

We headed farther west, inland, as a hurricane traversed the east coast and dumped on Charleston, a city we had visited a couple days earlier. The second near miss of the summer.

We arrived in Chattanooga and friend/promoter, Shannon, showed us the posters for the night, featuring awesome artwork from Holly Doucette of Chuck's face, based on a photo from

Andy Watson. Amazingly, Chuck "didn't hate it." He actually let his guard down and admitted he liked it later on.

The door guy at the club had tied a balloon onto a sewer grate to celebrate the *It* remake that got released, I think, the day previous.

The club had a back-porch area, so I sat there and talked to as many random people as I could. One guy, a shifty kid, really, claimed he had fled the hurricane currently crushing Florida. The longer we talked to him, the shadier his story became. Apparently, he had a trunk full of guns locked in safes. He had a military background and big-time connections in law enforcement and the CIA. He also claimed to have "high-end drugs." He told us he could get all the good stuff—powders, pills or whatever we wanted. I like meeting new people, but I decided to try and avoid him the rest of the night.

In Knoxville, we played the Open Chord. Hey! Alligator opened for us again. This time, we knew all the words, and Cris even wore one of the girl's shiny silver outfits.

William S. Tribell, who produced a radio program in Tennessee, came to interview us—sort of a Hunter S. Thompson-type, free-spirited punk journalist. Corralling Chuck for interviews is hard enough. With William, it was like chasing two Mosleys. We tried to do the interview in his car parked around the back of the building, but distractions followed us everywhere.

Cris borrowed an amp from the club worth as much as all our gear combined. He stood on it and jumped off. Before I got too angry, Chuck stumbled backward and knocked it over. It still worked when we left.

Eric Saule, one of my favorite people on the planet, and his equally as awesome wife, Susan, attended the show, as they happened to work nearby. I wanted it to be the best night and impress them. Instead, our set reflected pure chaos, though perhaps still entertaining.

We ended with one of the Hey! Alligator members joining us on "William Wallace" again. This time, she stood next to me, so I got to hear her trombone. I remember thinking how I needed to tell my parents that I had performed with a trombone player. Maybe they'd change their minds about me acting like a responsible husband and father by touring, because a horn player was a real, legit musician.

We went out after the show with Brant, who offered to let us stay at his place. William and his gal came along, so we could finish the interview, and Sarah Dutton joined the party, having surprised us by driving from Asheville.

By the time the bar kicked us out, William had interviewed anyone who would talk. Chuck would only reply with strings of swears and giggles. To cap off the interview, William had asked a fire truck questions. Seriously, he talked to the fire truck parked on the street and held out his recorder for the truck's replies. He has audio proof.

We didn't get to Brant's house until close to 4 a.m., and Chuck talked super loud. I think my third time saying, "Keep it down!" was when Chuck got miffed.

He glared at me as we stood on the front porch. "Who cares how loud I am?"

"Dude, it's late. I just don't want to piss off Brant's neighbors."

Chuck scanned the area, other homes clearly surrounding us. "What neighbors? What neighbors?"

"Chuck, people are in every direction."

Still searching for signs of life, he said, "Where? No one's on that porch, or … um, let's see … Nope, no one over there—"

"Because it's four in the morning. They're sleeping."

"Well, if they're asleep, then they're asleep."

The following morning, we left the area but not before seeing a house with confederate flags blocking every window. Ugh.

In Nashville, our club got changed last second after another double-booking snafu. We played in the shadows of the Titans stadium. We knew they had lost, because we sat in traffic for over an hour to drive a few blocks as tens of thousands of fans walked to their cars, looking downtrodden.

Chuck and I ducked out for dinner. We sat at the restaurant rather than bringing takeout to the club, and we had a conversation about how beat down he felt. Chuck paid for the food—a first.

I asked, "What's up?"

"I don't want to go home. I mean, I want to go home, but I'm not ready."

Within forty-eight hours, he would be in Cleveland, dealing with reality.

Their landlord had stopped paying the mortgage for fourteen months, so the bank had foreclosed on their place. They didn't even know until the bank had listed the house for auction. They had searched for a new apartment to move and had had all sorts of issues in the meantime. Their neighbor downstairs stole their mail, including Chuck's royalty checks. Their now ex-landlord (or someone) cut their cable cord a few times. The utility companies planned to shut off their gas and water and electric. The cops constantly got called for violence downstairs. One night, someone busted in the downstairs door. More of the typical non-stop insanity that permeated every aspect of Chuck's life.

He also told me, "We're going to drop off Cris in Akron at his mom's house."

"So, that's it?"

"I don't know, but I think so. At least for the next run."

"He and I talked a bit in Asheville. I can't tell if he wants to continue or not. I think he likes the idea of the road, but he needs to be creating. His mind goes a million miles an hour, and he needs an outlet for all his riffs."

"Well, the main thing is that Erica and her boyfriend are evacuating the hurricane with Wolfgang, and it looks like they're coming to our place."

Hurricane Irma decimated the Florida Keys the day prior, and Chuck's daughter lived in Pensacola, Florida. Chuck was so angry that his daughter had waited until the last second to head north.

"You're going to have five adults and a baby in a two-bedroom, one-bath duplex?"

He nodded.

Add all the people and the situation, not to mention we were coming home empty-handed again, and you get a glimpse into his reality. The shows were his freedom. He didn't care if we made a penny. He just didn't want to deal.

Randy told us he needed to sit out the next run to catch up on bills.

"Okay, I see you, Mr. Tattoo Man, sticking a needle in my arm and leaving a mark. Okay!"

When I dropped him, Cris, and Chuck off, we had played twenty-five shows in thirty nights, driven over eleven thousand miles, recorded seven songs with Matt Wallace in two and a half days, recorded two covers with Joe Haze in about five hours, gone through twenty-three states, saw a second couple get engaged, and witnessed the eclipse.

Break time?

Before reading this next section, I must warn you that my daughter accidentally erased the notes I took during this run of dates, and my hard drive died with all my video and photos, so I have less quotes and specific oddball moments than previous chapters. In a way, it fits the exhaustion and anxiety I experienced during this period. I felt scatterbrained, scared, and spent all my energy holding things together, for better or worse. To anyone involved in booking, promoting, playing, allowing us to crash, and/or feeding us who feels left out of the narrative, my apologies. I'm torn up about it, and we (Alex, Dallas, and I) appreciate all that you did.

A week or so before leaving for the fall run, Chuck and I went to Detroit to see Dead Cross, a band featuring Mike Patton. We crashed a fan meetup at a bar down the street, and I enjoyed the double and triple takes people gave Chuck when they noticed him.

We ran into Trey Spruance, the guitarist for Secret Chiefs 3, who opened the show. I noticed Trey and Chuck getting along well and envisioned them producing some wonderfully weird stuff.

Chuck touched base with Mike about the songs we had recorded to see if Patton's label, Ipecac, would be interested in releasing it. Afterward, Chuck had a lot of positive things to say. He had always liked Mike, but obviously they had a weird relationship dynamic.

"Typically, when we see each other, it's back stage for just a few seconds. This was, like, the first time we ever just shot the shit, man to man."

My third and final chance to get a photo with Chuck and Mike, my favorite two singers, came and went.

Chuck gave me a blow-by-blow of how their conversation played out, but I didn't witness the exchange, so I can't verify what they had said.

(Per Chuck):

Chuck: "So, we did this record with Matt Wallace, and I'd love to get it to you when it's mixed, but I'm not sure it fits your style or the other stuff on your label."

Mike: "Hey man, your style is my style."

I told Chuck he did good.

He then misquoted one of his favorite lines from *The Godfather Part II*. "See? I can handle things. I'm smart, not like everybody says. I'm not dumb. And I demand respect."

He used that one a lot.

On the way home, Chuck told me, "The first time I met Mike Patton was at Roddy's house. He was sleeping on a couch. When he woke up, I was there. He seemed scared, or nervous."

"Do you blame him? I've known you twenty years, and I still get nervous."

Chuck had more details, but we stayed up late, so you get the short version.

Drew Fortier helped us find a guitarist for the seventeen-shows-in-eighteen-nights run we had from September to mid-October. Dallas hailed from New York and painted houses. Meanwhile, I reached out to Alex Bergeron, Jr. again, who we had tried to recruit earlier in the summer and had met in New Orleans.

The two guys traveled to Cleveland for a couple days of practice. I love these guys. They saved our bacon and tolerated so much BS. We did most of the practicing ourselves, Chuck suddenly growing distant. Where had the excited, refreshed songwriter from May and June gone?

Our first practice happened at Chuck's house, but the chaos proved too much to accomplish anything. Cats and dogs ran around barking and fighting; Chuck paced around on the phone for long stretches.

Alex said, "Chuck didn't want to be there."

Dallas added, "Chuck was glassy-eyed and cleaning the litter box. He told me, 'It may seem like I'm messed up, but this is how I always am.'"

Chuck told me he hadn't yet recovered from our long run, and he dreaded more shows. He wanted a break. He had a lot on his mind, and he needed time to sit back and think.

Flies buzzed around us as we limped through the songs.

I told the guys we would relocate to my house for the rest of the week. Chuck came super late to one practice, late to another, and I think we canceled the final practice altogether. When he did show, he reminded me of Mosley circa 2016—scatterbrained, distracted, crabby, and forgetful.

Alex and Dallas brought an ardent positivity, so the new songs sounded fresh—what a joy to play the set without picking apart each song. We tried a few different Faith No More tunes and worked on a newer medley.

We played "Why Do You Bother?" without Chuck, and it sounded cool. We pitched it to him, and I think we ran through it a couple times but never got past that. He didn't want to add more full-length songs.

Alex noticed, "Chuck wouldn't commit to anything."

We pitched "R n' R," and he agreed but only to the first small chunk for the medley. Bye-bye, "The Crab Song."

We pitched "As the Worm Turns," and he agreed, mostly because he knew the lyrics fairly well, and it was short. Gone went "Faster Disco."

Chuck had us add "We Care a Lot," which surprised the hell out of me, as he had always been so dead set against it.

"But I won't do the verses," he told us. "You'll never get me to do those."

I mentioned we didn't ask him to do any of it. The medley sounded awkward; at least, I felt it did. The songs didn't have the natural progression and transitions the old medley sported. We spent a good chunk of an afternoon hitting our heads against a brick wall, trying to make it feel organic.

Chuck wouldn't cave, suddenly dead set on these three snippets of songs working.

Dallas said, "Chuck seemed like a classic case of self-sabotage."

Alex added, "Like he felt unworthy."

My brother, Craig, stopped by practice and had a chance to hear us flame out, over and over.

Chuck asked Craig, "Can you tape us, so we can hear how it sounds?"

We started and stopped and started and stopped, each trying in our own way to push and prod three song snippets into a cohesive medley.

Chuck suggested to change the ending of "R n' R" in the hopes to smoothly transition into "We Care a Lot." We tried the last few parts several times. When we transitioned, Chuck fell silent and waited, expecting Dallas to start the next song.

Chuck said, "That was a little short."

I pointed out, "Well, you were supposed to say, 'We care a lot,' at the end."

"Oh, right. I forgot."

I teased, "So, you were late."

Chuck said, "I was never."

I tried to continue, but Chuck's face lit up in a grin.

As I thought about his last statement, I started laughing.

My brother chuckled. "I was never!"

I suggested, "There's your album title, right there."

We fell apart a half-dozen more times.

I used humor to hide my aggravation. "Maybe we're better off if you don't tape this."

Chuck and my brother are kindred spirits. Though Chuck and I have twenty years together, Chuck wanted feedback from Craig instead.

At practice, we discussed how the first few notes of "Relocation" sounded similar to Hole's "Doll Parts." We added a bit of that song to our set before playing "Relocation." We didn't practice or plan it that way, but sometimes Chuck launched into it. None of us had the lyrics memorized, so we often ad-libbed a line here and there.

Chuck made it hard to get comfortable or have any fun during practice. I feared he'd chase away the band before we left town.

Alex decided to follow Chuck's everything-will-be-fine attitude.

Dallas had some reservations. "Part of me wondered what the fuck was about to happen, but I'm not a runner."

The first show, in Virginia, had a lot of issues, but Chuck told us, "It was okay if there were bumps in the road," because he didn't expect a turnout.

His reassurances proved hollow; during soundcheck, Dallas hit a major instead of a minor. "Chuck shot me a look. It made me so fucking nervous, to the point I couldn't even eat before we played."

Chuck's timing fell off, and he barked rudely at Alex onstage. I got worried Alex might get disheartened enough to walk off. Hell, I might've. But he took it all in stride.

I got in Chuck's face to defend the new guys.

Chuck shook his head. "No, I'm the only one who can make mistakes. We all know I'm going to make mistakes. That's why everyone else up there must play perfect."

After the show, Alex took the high road. "If there's things you notice or want played differently, just let me know."

I know Chuck respected the gesture.

Dallas and Alex acted like professionals. They helped set up, load in, work the merch booth, drive, and they are cool guys to hang out with. When touring with Chuck, he has no interest in sightseeing or doing much aside from sitting in the hotel room. Alex, Dallas, and I took side trips, like visiting Jay and Silent Bob's Secret Stash comic shop in Jersey.

We played another six- or seven-band bill at Dingbatz, and not once did they complain about our set time. We set up and got loud without bitching. We played on Long Island at a club with no stage or sound system, and they took it in stride, even as we got blasted with feedback the entire time we played.

We slept on tile floors. Dallas found out the hard way that he had accidentally brought a kids-sized sleeping bag. We ate awful. Alex cut himself while trying to pry open some food.

Alex admitted that cut was "deep, too. I hid that from ya'll. It should've been stitched. I borrowed electrical tape from Dallas and used that."

Chuck's temperament sucked, when he came around at all. I quickly understood this run wouldn't mimic any of the others. Even when our sets started well, we'd hit a moment that derailed us. It got hard to joke onstage when Chuck and I weren't joking off it.

He ditched us every day until we played at Ralph's in Worcester, Massachusetts—a unique venue with a lot of character. Mathew Grant and Michael Yarish streamed the set on Facebook live. Chuck smiled, and his laid-back attitude returned, not fully, but I didn't find it necessary to watch my every word around him. It translated to a fun show. The first on the run that had all four of us grinning.

I left my pillow at Dallas' friend's house, ugh.

Dallas said, "You laughed and talked in your sleep. Your head popped up, and you laughed and talked, so I said something about a potato. You said, 'There wasn't any potato.' And then fell back asleep."

In Lewiston, Maine, the owner of Little Joe's Bar treated us like kings. Ken had seen us in Portland earlier in the year and asked us to play his place. We stayed at his house, and it allowed us to bond together as a band.

The following morning, we drove to Derek Deidrickson's place in Massachusetts and spent a few hours in a treehouse in his front yard to film clips for a pilot TV show based on small houses. First, they interviewed Chuck, who started off nervous as always. After that, they had Alex, Dallas, and I pose for a few shots. Then Dallas, Chuck, and I got into the treehouse and played three songs. We played in close quarters with no electricity for amps or effects, stripping the tunes to their core. Alex didn't come up, but I don't recall why. Might have come down to a space issue in the treehouse. When Derek had first asked us to play, the band only comprised of Chuck and me.

We did one take, playing "Blue Heart," "Mr. Smith," and "Bella Donna." You can find the pilot on YouTube.

Providence, Rhode Island proved wild enough that our set wasn't the weirdest thing happening. The sound guy zipped around the club on roller-skates; a guy stood right in front of Dallas the whole set, yelling and trying to get on the microphone. Chuck asked guys from the two openers to join us during "Relocation," but they came up a few songs into our set and jammed along with all the tunes. We sounded like a noisy mess, but Chuck thrived in the chaos.

Alex said, "Rhode Island was our most memorable show."

Dallas agreed. "Rhode Island was my favorite."

We ended with "Relocation."

Alex recalled that song worked great live because it "droned on and on and hypnotized the crowd."

After the show, we went with the promoter, Jason Nadeau, to his band's practice space for a few hours of rock karaoke. I sat back and enjoyed songs ranging from Agents of Oblivion to Katy Perry to Megadeth.

I tried to keep a positive face on things between me and Chuck, but the other guys could sense something was amiss. They both asked me separately if Chuck was mad at them or unhappy with their playing. I assured them any anger or stress he exhibited was aimed toward me, so they didn't have any additional worries about it. I avoided discussing his possible drug use, but the signs presented themselves again as his attitude and performance became erratic. That night, we *all* wondered.

After our show in Syracuse, Dallas got Chuck's guitar repaired. It had been cutting in and out for a few nights, and it felt like it happened more frequently that night.

"Is that the Mississippi?"

Playing the Mohawk in Buffalo meant a lot to me. I had lived in the area as a kid, and I always wanted to revisit, having done something with my life … or at least as a conga player. Preshow, Alex and I shuffled to the Anchor Bar for wings while Dallas and Chuck played pool.

As we snapped photos of each other, sauce in beards, Alex said, "On this run, I've had a Long Island iced tea on Long Island and buffalo wings in Buffalo."

After that, we meandered through downtown before meeting Chuck and Bob Coldicutt, who had helped us get the show … and we ate more wings.

At the second restaurant, Chuck asked for a ramekin full of wing sauce.

I asked, "What in the world is a ramkadin?"

A ramekin, he explained, got used for preparing and serving certain dishes.

Bob suggested, "You mean like a to-go cup?"

Chuck shook his head but then sort of agreed.

I said, "Dude, you just made up that word."

Alex said, "You realize you're busting the balls of the only guy at this table who was a professional chef?"

Chuck said, "Well, Bob wasn't really bustin' my balls."

Message received, Chuck.

During our set, Chuck thanked "Cleveland," making the oldest rock-stage mistake/cliché possible. To make amends, I threw on my Jim Kelly jersey and won the crowd back.

I thought we sounded strong in Buffalo, noisy yet controlled. Alex and Dallas grew comfortable with the material and with the chaos onstage. Chuck's guitar, however, kept cutting in and out, even after the repairs the day before.

We played a free show at the Phantasy in Lakewood, Ohio. Michele, the owner, and Chuck both had stories from Faith No More playing there way back when. I told Michele that Mike Bordin had asked me if the club still existed when I had met him.

Joshua Nelson's band played before us, and he joined us onstage for "Relocation" and "William Wallace." Having never heard the second tune, he added some cool stuff on the fly.

During our set, I saw a familiar face approaching from the back of the club.

"Okay, I see you, Randy! Coming and showing your support, while trying to get me drunk. Okay!"

During "Song 2," I left the stage and found my parents, who witnessed their first real Mosleyhead show. I know they would rather watch me working a real job and being a better dad and a better husband and making money, but they still showed support.

My mom said, "Doug, now I get it."

Around this time, Chuck added two bars to the first verse in "William Wallace"—not that he told us in advance or that he remembered them each night. It certainly kept us on our toes.

Chuck's guitar died as we started our set. It had lasted about 140 shows and had endured admirably until the end. Chuck borrowed a guitar from Joshua that night.

Update: October 25, 2019

I talked to Pip recently. She laughed when recalling this night at The Phantasy in Cleveland. She and Chuck had posted up by the merch booth to handle sales. I had thought it odd, as to get Chuck to sell shirts was an almost impossible task, but, as per usual, there was a reason. We had printed two different batches of shirts for our last run. The fronts on both had the same image, but the back, on half of them, had part of the obscene logo I mentioned earlier in the book. Chuck had demanded I print the howling wolf with penis on the shirts. I had relented, but only on half of the shirts. Chuck, wanting to sell more with the wolf, was at the booth with Pip, only offering that version. The couple got such a kick out of their maneuver that they giggled the whole time. You can talk about official marriages, common law this, or signed document that, but, as far as I'm concerned, laughter had sealed their marriage and their love for each other.

Dallas, Chuck, and my brother went to buy a guitar the next morning before we skipped town, heading north for Detroit. A group of familiar faces from the shows we had played in Ypsilanti earlier in the summer greeted us in front of the club. My brother also surprised us by driving from Cleveland. Though we had some sound issues, we steamrolled along, and we had keyboardist Lisa Hart join us for a few songs.

We certainly aimed for more of a friends-hanging-out-at-a-party-and-jamming vibe, and the Detroit show totally worked in that way. We had friends, fans, club staff, and relatives all hanging out, getting to meet each other and adding to our set. People knew our songs outside of the Faith No More material. They understood our humor beyond the goofy stuff we said. They appreciated the effort. They supported Chuck's comeback. I want to think it was because we remained brutally honest and genuinely appreciative of anyone who took interest in us, even if they attended to witness a Mosley train wreck.

I fell asleep that night to the sound of my brother and Chuck talking, and I woke up to them still talking the following morning. They're kindred spirits of mischief.

We raced to Madison, Wisconsin, arriving in time to set up and soundcheck. We played first, so we only had a quick set and no room on the back-lined stage. The sound, club, and crowd treated us great.

The last time we had visited Madison, only our second show on the road, Chuck was in a bad way. No one had come to the show, aside from Kurt Baron and his gal. So, to see them at the club and to play a great set felt like redemption.

After our early set, Chuck told me, "I wonder where we would be if we'd had Dallas and Alex with us all year."

I nodded. "I've been impressed with all the people we got to work with this year, but, yeah, having a stable lineup would've been cool. Maybe next year we try to keep this going?"

"What about Chile and Brazil?"

Two promoters had started organizing shows in South America, but they only wanted to fly two, or at most, three of us. They planned to hire local musicians to fill out the band, saving them thousands in flight cost.

I said, "Again, you could leave me, hire a drummer down there and do something closer to VUA."

He shook his head.

That night, Dallas "met a jaded comedian who bought me a beer."

We passed over the Mississippi River, but Chuck didn't bat an eyelash.

We played Ellefson Coffee in Jackson, Minnesota—the last band to have that honor before major changes happened to the Megadeth bass player's coffee shop.

In South Dakota, we played a great club, Bigg's—though more crowd had gathered to watch the pool tournament than us. The sound blasted, massive. Did anyone record it?

After the show, I spent some time thanking the sound guys for caring to make the monitors and house sound flawless.

One of the engineers said, "Good job. I had a tempo monitor on you. Even during all that chaos, you had some really long stretches when you stayed right on."

Being a walk-on to the squad, feeling things out as I went along, it felt great to have someone compliment me.

A guy told me, "Man, Chuck is so cool. We gave him a ride to the store, so he bought us cigarettes."

A few minutes later, Chuck waved me over. "Hey, a couple people drove me to the store, so I bought them cigarettes. Can I borrow like twenty bucks?"

We played a private party in Iowa. Seeing Chuck interact with young kids and toddlers and play a show while watching kids dance to his music put things into perspective. I remembered why we had set up this tour; I remembered Chuck was a kid himself and that even as he grinned ear to ear, Chuck felt alone, disconnected, and not good enough.

At some point, Alex got a hold of a dozen or so stink bombs. Occasionally, you'd hear plastic crack and a little giggle from Alex. Then, if you didn't move fast enough, you'd get caught in the cloud of stench.

We limped into St. Louis, our only off night on the run. As I checked into the hotel, the guys witnessed a robbery outside.

Chuck decided to stay at the hotel as we explored. He claimed an old friend had asked to meet up, but yeah, looking back, I should've noticed the red flag. When we left, he sat outside the hotel. When we returned, a few hours later, he still held court in the exact same spot. I tried talking to him, but he shut down anything meaningful.

He fed me the usual, "My back hurts. I'm exhausted. There's so much going on at home."

The four of us exited the elevator, and I heard a noise. I turned and saw Alex dashing for the door. Damn stink bombs.

Chuck pulled me aside to talk the next day in Louisville, my eleventh wedding anniversary.

He said, "Someone asked me to play a solo show in Jersey. If you can't afford to or don't want to come, I can catch the bus. I want to play a stripped-down set, play the songs we stopped doing, like "Sophie," "Nameless," and I'll do "Song 2" and maybe "Mr. Smith."

"We've been going nonstop for months, and that's coming off your rehab and all the house stuff. I'd understand if you didn't want me around."

"It's not that." He took a drag on his smoke. "They can only pay so much, and I know you're stressed with money and want to be home with the family. The Dog Fashion Disco show will be our last of the year. This would be different. Just me."

I said, "It'll be awesome to hit the road with a new album to promote."

"Fuck, yeah."

Chuck and I had recently partnered with a new booking agent who wanted us to go out on a lengthy tour of the US through January and February, our longest run yet.

I said, "Being in Fargo and Minneapolis in January could be a disaster. Not sure a minivan will handle the snow."

He brushed it off. "We'll make it work."

When we'd agreed to keep touring in 2017, I'd only had one request. "Be honest with me." I didn't want him sneaking around and hiding his addictions behind my back. I didn't want him depressed or unhappy or overworked without some warning. I didn't want him to leave and reform VUA or replace me with a drummer without a chance to prove myself.

I had become an addict myself—addicted to the road, the stage, the songs, and even to taking risks, though much more modest than Chuck's. I felt panicked. Was this it? Chuck was headed to LA in a few days to take a drummer to the studio to beef up the solo disc, covering up and possibly erasing some of my contributions and changing its spirit and vibe.

I admitted, "I know I pushed for a full kit or for some programmed drums on a couple songs, but I'm crushed it's not me going."

"We're not erasing you. The drums will follow your lead. Sometimes they'll be loud, and sometimes they'll just keep the beat. You won't be gone. Your stuff will blend together. You'll see when you hear it."

His words comforted me, but not for long.

He said, "I want to bring Tim and Jason from VUA for the Dog Fashion Disco show."

"Do you want me to play?"

"Yes. It's still us, but I think it would sound awesome with full drums and Tim. It won't be for the whole set. We'll build and get louder as we go, like we always do. Only this time, we'll take it through the roof and leave everyone there with wide eyes, going *Whoa!* when we end with 'Relocation.' Drew and Dallas might come in. Joshua will play bass on some songs and Randy on others while Joshua plays keys. Alex can come, but I know it's a long haul from Louisiana. I reached out to Cris to play."

I raised an eyebrow.

Chuck saw my expression. "Yeah, why not?"

"I figured you guys would reconnect. I just didn't expect it would be so fast. That's a lot of dudes to get onstage. You know we only have, like, a thirty minute set, right?"

"We'll play a couple songs and leave enough room for 'Relocation' at the end."

When we reached Toledo for our last headlining show of the year, I had an inkling this might prove the end for me as part of Chuck's band. I had given all I had and felt damn proud of what we had accomplished, even as I struggled with how many opportunities we had squandered. I decided that if he fell off the wagon again, he needed to return to rehab and rethink if the road represented the best place for him.

I spent three to four hours a day talking on the phone, writing emails and sending messages about booking international tour dates that I knew I might not play.

When we took the stage, I decided nothing could phase me. I wouldn't care if Chuck disappeared and forced us to play the "Epic" intro for ten minutes. I wouldn't get miffed if Chuck didn't follow the setlist or forgot words or restarted a song ten times or blamed me or Alex or Dallas for mistakes we didn't make. I stood at my conga and hit it with as much conviction and power as I could, and I fucking smiled, man. Twenty-seven people were in the crowd. So what? I knew almost all of them and knew we were blessed to have them with us for this possible finale.

Chuck counted them from the stage before we started "Living Sound Delay."

"Twenty-five, twenty-six, twenty-seven. That's like twenty-eight more than yesterday." He rechecked his math. "Well, maybe twenty-four more."

We played the song, and Chuck extended the outro before sliding us into "Blue Heart."

He said, "Thanks for sticking around. That's the last time I'm going to say that."

His droning guitar solo cut right through everything. It sounded massive, chaotic, and beautiful. I can't think of another musician, especially one claiming to be such a crappy guitarist, who could communicate so much with feedback and distortion and delay without playing notes. Go give "Come Around" a listen and focus on the feedback guitar—haunting, depressed, anxious, angry, punk.

I watched Donn, standing by a pole and singing along to a tune Chuck hadn't released yet. He had seen us seven times throughout the last two years, though this marked the first time we had played his town.

As the guitar notes faded, Chuck said, "Sorry. I messed up a couple lines."

I said, "It's official. Donn knows these songs better than you."

"So we'll move on then. Let's see if I can remember these ones," he said and strummed shakily into "Bella Donna" for the last time.

We had played it at every Chuck show, save one or two. It was the first song we had clicked on, the first one I had created the drumbeat for, the only new thing we had to play for most of the runs—and look, it's a great tune. We had recorded it with Indoria and again for his solo album. When we played it live, I extended the outro until Chuck could flip pedals and take a sip of beer and gear up to launch into "Death March," often the highpoint of our set from a fan's point of view.

As we reached the second time "Bella Donna" breaks into complete silence, Chuck reached to sip his beer. He said, "Thanks ... *and* sorry. This is the first bar I've been to that sold Olde English, since I was, like, sixteen."

I said, "Chuck has a new CD coming out that, I think, will be titled, *Thanks ... And Sorry.*"

I kept thinking, *This is it, this is it,* but I wasn't sad. Unlike Paris, exactly a year before, October 15, I didn't sob. I didn't guzzle whiskey. I found a peace, a satisfaction, and, if this was it, fine. My ear-to-ear grin got wider, somehow ... I dunno, just go with it, okay?

"Tractor" thundered, and I hit the conga harder, knuckles aching and threatening to bleed more. Chuck held a calm intensity. He controlled his voice and hit the transitions, making the quieter moments serene and the loud moments a tornado.

I walked offstage while they played "Song 2," finding a couch side stage to sit and listen.

Dammit, I hope his album gets released before you read this, so you can listen along or at least know the songs I'm mentioning.

He sang, *"Don't ask me to dance or look at the moon, 'cause this is all too much, and it's all too soon ... "*

I stood side stage to watch the last time he would play this beautiful song. It ends with reverb and delay—a mellow, psychedelic tune. A cross between Pink Floyd and Mogwai and ... Mosley.

Chuck wore a Mosleyhead shirt onstage. When I busted him for wearing the shirt of the headlining band—himself—he admitted it was the first time he had ever worn one of his own shirts.

We took off after the show. Within a couple days, Alex had gone home, and I had dropped off Dallas. Chuck flew to LA to attend a Livewire event with Thom, visit family and friends, and work on the solo record.

Instead, I guess he did heroin and slept a lot.

I received calls from people in LA, telling me they noticed the same signs of drug use that I saw. They were worried too. Then he lied and got caught up in his own words.

He got pissed at me when I made a comment about how messed up his Facebook live video came across from the awards event.

"Dude, you don't know what you're talking about," he said after I had expressed my worries.

"I want to tell Pip and your sponsor and—"

"This is between me and Pip. It's not any of her business right now. I already decided I'll tell her what's going on as soon as I get back."

I wanted to mention that if he wasn't doing anything, as he had told me, he had nothing to tell her.

Chuck spent a day in Matt Wallace's studio with an old drummer buddy to record some of the new songs. He called me several times that day with updates. He really liked how it sounded, especially as the drummer had almost zero practice.

Now that the day had arrived when my parts would get buried or maybe even thrown to the curb altogether, I felt panicked. I paced around the house, mind racing. I knew why it was happening, and I had agreed, but I still hated it.

Chuck reassured me every time. "Dude, your stuff is good. Just some songs need a little extra kick. They need to be filled out to hopefully attract radio or a movie soundtrack or label with more crossover potential."

Hearing him quote me to me was odd, but it certainly wasn't the first time he had used my own arguments to prove his point.

"And I agree. I just wish it was me."

"You're still there, and not all of the songs will have these drums."

You don't have to believe me when I tell you that I'm glad the percussion got added. You don't have to feel bad for me, as I witnessed some amazing songs that I had helped create get recorded. You don't need to demand that a version with only conga should get released. But, if you do any of those things, I'll support you.

Before Chuck came home, he admitted to buying drugs, but he told me that instead of using, he threw the stuff away.

I told him, "If you're still using—"

"I'm not."

I thought about our opening slot at the Agora, only days away. "I don't think I should play. It just seems to be encouraging you to keep getting away with it."

"Just … just play. Let's do this, one last time."

CHAPTER EIGHTEEN

11/03/2017; One Last Time

Our last show happened at the Agora in Cleveland on the same day that Primitive Race released *Soul Pretender*, their CD with Chuck. Tom Petty had died the previous day. Reports hadn't confirmed yet, but rumors spread that drugs had been involved, making him the third celebrity-status musician taken during our tour.

Cris, who had called me for directions, never showed. Randy got caught up at work. Drew couldn't make it.

Walking around the club reminded me of the final scene in *Big Fish* when the dad and his son recognize all the people from the stories he'd told through the years. I felt like I knew everyone, and they all knew that, no matter how things went, this show meant a lot to me.

I was worried Chuck would get too messed up to play. I was worried people would think I looked like an asshole playing conga while Jason's drums masked everything I did. I was worried I would kick over my conga and yell at Chuck for so many different things. I was worried that one practice hadn't been enough. I was worried that Dog Fashion Disco would regret putting us on the bill. I was worried the sound guys would cut us off midsong if we played too long. Hell, Chuck *wanted* them to.

I said, "If we fall behind, just cut 'Relocation' and play something shorter."

"No." He shook his head vehemently. "Even if we get to twenty-five minutes on the dot, I'll start playing it. Let them turn us off."

Along with the time constraints and the typical technical and Mosley delays, Chuck, Dallas, Joshua, and I took the stage for "LSD" and "Blue Heart."

Tim and Jason joined us for the first half of "Tractor" and into "As the Worm Turns," and then we finished "Tractor." Chuck started to play "Punk Rock Movie," but he couldn't remember enough words to finish it.

I felt silly up there, but now that the show had started, I didn't want to walk off. Chuck sounded erratic; though I think it stemmed from nerves rather than drugs or alcohol. He had forgotten, as usual, all the cues and signals we had plotted at practice, so Tim and Jason flew blind. I tried to guide them along, a train barreling forward with only one side still clinging to the tracks.

We ended with a sloppy, meandering version of "Relocation." The last show, the last song, the last goodbye proved as chaotic as every moment in Chuck's life. As much as it breaks my heart, we didn't cause the *Whoa!* Chuck had desired.

When the band stopped, Chuck got furious and urged us on—faster and faster. "I didn't tell anyone to stop!"

We limped along a couple more minutes before exiting the stage for Dog Fashion Disco.

After the show, I told Chuck, "Hey, man. I'm proud of you and all that we did these last two years. You should be proud of yourself. I know you have a lot going on, but I'm looking forward to what's next, whether I'm involved or not."

The last time I saw Chuck alive occurred at the same place we had met, twenty years earlier.

We spoke a couple times on the phone during the next five days.

I thought about the show Chuck had mentioned in Jersey. He could go and make a couple bucks. If we made a weekend out of it, maybe we could sell some of the extra tour merch and give him something to stay focused on. I didn't know if he wanted me to go along, but I thought it might be good for both me and him. Get back to what we had started—no pressure, no hectic schedule, no car rentals, just a fun weekend of shows.

I texted him at 10:39 a.m. on November 9. *Earlier in the year we had an offer to play outside of Philly…if you want I could try to book a fri/sat/sun in December including philly and That jersey show just for you. If you want, I could drive and play on a couple of tunes…it would be stripped down, stripped down…play the mellow stuff. If not, no biggie.*

I went about my day, working on this book and following up on various emails regarding booking. The winter run was shaping up, with promoters confirming new dates each day. We weren't sure who would fill out the band, but Dallas had mentioned he had interest, if he could afford to miss work. We also had a tentative idea about a spring run across Europe, so I wanted to see if Andy could join us again there. Joe Haze had our cover songs, but we needed to finish a few last touches. Chuck's solo record sat in the hands of Matt Wallace, who only needed the go-ahead to start mixing.

I spoke on the phone with Adrian Harte who had flown from Europe to interview the members of Faith No More and others for his book about the band, *Small Victories: The True Story of Faith No More*. He had sent Chuck questions months and months earlier while Chuck spent time in rehab. He still hadn't answered them. I suggested Adrian should call Chuck while stateside to get the interview done.

My phone rang in the early evening, not sure exactly what time, but I remember the sun had set.

Chuck's sponsor, Kristen, asked, "Are you sitting down?"

I wasn't.

"Chuck is dead."

CHAPTER NINETEEN
In Chuck's Own Words

April 20, 2012

I think I'm in fucking heaven. Last October I was arrested for felony possession of heroin. This outcome comes as no surprise to anyone. I've been a mess most of my life. So, where did it all go wrong?

A long time ago, actually, on a beach far, far away...

I started smoking weed at 11, via my fourteen-year-old mentor Frankie; surfer, skater, Zeppelin and Sabbath fan extraordinaire. In my world, he was the coolest. He knew Tony Alva, was a big fan of surfers; Larry Bertleman and Gerry Lopez, and we drooled over the latest "Jeff Ho" surfboards. His mom and my parents were old friends, so we grew up together. He taught me how to skate, "surf-style", how to roll joints, and how to play, "Stairway To Heaven" on guitar.

I had been studying classical piano since the age of three and a half. By twelve, I was taking private lessons and studying, Theory and Composition. It was during one of these lessons that I heard a song on the music store's stereo that changed my life. The space-aged rock song opened my brain to a sound I'd never heard or felt before.

Experiencing a visceral rush, I asked, "What is that?"

"Hang on to Yourself" by Ziggy Stardust and the Spiders From Mars blasted and I couldn't take my ears off the music.

"I wanna play that," I said, and switched to guitar lessons that day.

My skill level and understanding of theory had me learning at USC with college kids. My mother harbored dreams of me becoming a classical concert pianist, but when I coupled the discovery of David Bowie with Frankie's ample weed stash, a new obsession with, you guessed it, sex, drugs, and rock 'n roll took over.

Which led to more sex…

Which led to more music…

Which led to more drugs…

Bringing us back to present day, minus a few details that we'll get to later. Sitting in my cell, in a residential treatment facility in Youngstown, Ohio. Unlike my last incarceration, this one I volunteered to stay separated from my family, friends, dealers, my band, and everyone else who does or doesn't matter in my, "Vida Loca" for at least a month.

I hope my visit ends up being longer 'cause it's what I need. Not to mention that if I hadn't found a place within three days, the city of Cleveland promised to make good on their invitation to spend time at that respite, otherwise known as county jail. At that point, I would've run out of options until they could do me the esteemed favor of locating a city funded, "ahem" retreat to house me.

I'm *not* built for jail. I'm claustrophobic, I enjoy living on my own schedule, and to my professionally trained tongue the food tastes unpalatable. I wonder if I would starve or go mad first.

I'm surrounded by four all too close walls. I'm told when I can eat, shit, and socialize. Half of my days are spent in group therapy sessions, talking about God-awful things, and the other half are spent alone thinking worse. My guitar, bike, and Pip's camera, have once again found their way back to the pawn shop, so we can fend off bill-hounds, but I told you I'm feeling like I'm in heaven.

Why?

Well, two reasons.

One: 'Cause I'm finally where I need to be, getting clean from heroin, the last in a long list of drugs that has physically enslaved me, causing me to do things I would've never done otherwise. Things I'm very ashamed of.

Two: I am still alive after surviving at least twenty bona fide experiences that realistically could have ended with me dead. Some were actually fun, but you probably don't want to let your kids read about them.

Sitting here reflecting on the past, I figure I might as well explain where I came from so you can grasp the tricky, winding trails I traversed to earn my current seat at rock bottom. A good place to start explaining my history is just before it began.

My dad, Charles Henry Mosley Jr. came from a family with a lot of brothers and sisters. He and his siblings were raised by their mother, Juanita, in Dallas, Texas. Part black, part American Indian, and Jewish, my dad faced bigotry and mistrust from every side. He came up to California at age nine, joining a gang in east L.A. shortly after arriving.

One day, when he was only thirteen, rival gang members chased my father across unfriendly turf. He and a fellow member of his own gang hustled across a bridge, which provided their only chance at escape. Falling behind, the rival gang opened fire at my fleeing father, hitting his friend several times. Jolting with fear, my dad leapt off the bridge, breaking his leg in the shallow waters below.

While healing, he met Mr. Kenyuki who ran a dojo and offered self-defense lessons. So, you could say my dad literally jumped himself out of a gang and into the mentorship of a black belt in Judo. As my father allowed the teachings of Zen, balance, and self-defense to guide him, he started focusing on work, growing up, and on helping others.

A brief stint as a truck driver, working around the movie studios at Culver City, couldn't provide enough to get by, so he joined the armed forces. My father found himself in the galley cooking; pretty much all a Negro could do at that time.

Around 1960, he started working as a bus driver for a Jewish Children's Home. His ability to handle the kids led to him taking care of them in every aspect around the clock. The only problem was that, since he didn't have a degree in the field, people much younger than him who were doing much less work were making more money.

But, I'm getting ahead of myself. Chuck Mosley Jr. isn't my dad.

Well, my birth dad, anyway. I was adopted.

California law prevented me from retaining any identifiable info, but I learned that my birth mother was seventeen when she birthed me. She was Jewish. Her family owned a music store in the San Fernando Valley. It was 1959. She met a musician, who coincidently shared my adopted father's Black and Indian heritages. You've heard the tale a hundred times; white girl meets black boy, they fall in love, she gets knocked up, her parents find out, separate their daughter from the boy, who may or may not even know about the baby's existence, and then convince her to give the baby up for adoption to hide their shame.

Just like the Police song, I was, "Born in the 50's." December 26th 1959, shows on my birth certificate, though if you read the internet you'll find a few other dates mentioned. I arrived at Queen of the Angels hospital in Silverlake, an East Hollywood section of L.A. right next to Echo Park. Yeah, that Echo Park.

The last five days of the '50's, my first five on the planet, were spent without a family at the Children's Home Society.

Meanwhile, Chuck Jr. met Marian at a dance.

Marian Hambro was 39, divorced, Jewish, and a mother of two girls, Loraine and Shirley. Charles Mosley Jr. had earlier fallen in love with a woman and they had had a child, a girl named Nicholet. Sadly, his love died of cancer. Chuck Jr., being on his own, felt forced to place his daughter Nicky in the care of another family that he knew. He later reunited with Nicky, admitted to her that he was, in fact, her father, and then started weaving her back into his life.

Chuck and Marian fell in love and got married just like the Brady Bunch with three girls between them. I guess they decided the only thing missing was a boy! Voila ...

Word has it they came to the Children's Home Society and the nurses and attendants all thought that I was Chuck and Marian's natural son because of my uncanny resemblance to Chuck Jr. They led the pair to me; Chuck and Marian fell in love again, and boom: Happy family!

One of my father's jobs was being a bodyguard to a longtime friend, Paul Robeson, which once landed him at Charlie Chaplin's house for dinner. Even more astounding was the ill-effects on my father's career due to Mr. Robeson being blacklisted as a communist during the Red Scare. Chuck Jr.'s ties with equal rights groups, various other civil rights groups, and his relationship with Mr. Robeson led my father to being followed by the F.B.I. for years. This killed several job opportunities, and he was even called, "un-American and subversive" by then L.A. mayor Sam Yorty in the Herald Examiner.

When I wasn't in school and Nicky couldn't watch me, my dad took me to work with him at the Children's Home. It was pretty cool. There were lots of kids, a swimming pool, and tons of stuff to play with. My dad took us kids on all sorts of outings, to the beach, camping, and even to Disneyland.

I tagged along as if I was one of the orphans myself. Some of the other kids resented me because I didn't actually live there and because I had a home to go to ...but the girls were always nice.

They all wanted to look after me. I'll admit that being handled, kissed, hugged, and fussed about by a bunch of beautiful, black and white, Jewish, hippie girls may have contributed to my taste, love, and libido for the opposite sex. As the great James (Jim) Martin once said, "You were raised by woman as a woman!"

I had a few stepsisters too. They were stepsisters to one of my sisters, but I won't be saying which one. I guess they were really step-stepsisters then. Ellen was one of them and she was my age. I guess it's fair to say we liked each other growing up. By the time we were seven or eight, the older siblings started pushing, no urging, us together like a couple of human Barbie and Ken dolls. Part entertainment, part curiosity, and part '60's teenage perversion, but we were not related by blood and we never ever went all the way.

Meanwhile, hanging out with my sister and steps was fun in the summer and consisted of hanging at sis' little place on Venice Blvd, watching people drink beers and smoke cigarettes. They taught each other the latest dance steps to the current

Motown hits, and then we would pack up and go to the beach to hang, swim, and I'd watch them looking good while flirting with all the beach dudes.

My summers were a slight break from my constant barrage of school, homework, judo, and piano lessons that lasted until all my neighborhood friends went in for dinner, or in some cases, for the night. I was always kept pretty busy.

When I turned seven, I learned to ride a bike and fucking loved the freedom, the danger that it provided. I was really into Evil Knievel, so as soon as I got on two wheels, I focused on learning to wheelie and stuff. We had an empty lot around the corner, where we put up jumps with makeshift ramps. We started jumping over milk-crates, then shopping carts, and before long we were daring each other to jump over cars and shit. We took shovels and rakes and made a full-fledged dirt track in the lot, complete with mud pits, berms, whoopty-doo's, jumps, giant holes, the works.

Word spread and kids starting coming from other hoods to help us out. We started having huge races there. We had so many people we were organized, but unofficial and unsanctioned. No one ever really got hurt and it went on for a couple of years until the city came and bulldozed the lot and fenced it all up. After that someone built an apartment complex there.

It was too late, I was hooked. No bulldozer was going to stop me. I started going to official tracks and racing BMX all over southern California. There was a course at Palms Park in West L.A. that became my home track.

The bikes back then weren't really built for the shit we were doing, so we started tearing them apart in metal shop or at the local body shop. We'd be chopping off part of the seat pole and bottom bars and replace them with aluminum parts and raise the ground clearance. We made our bikes lighter, but also stronger, by installing fatter aluminum rims with MX nobbies. It was evolution through necessity: The Halcyon days. This was like '71, '72, '73, when BMX bikes were only put together in specialty shops.

My elementary school had been predominantly white, but at age eleven, I started at Louis Pastor Jr. High, which was all black with a sprinkling of whites and Latinos. Now remember I was involved in Judo, piano, BMX, skating, surfing, body surfing, hanging with the g's, gymnastics, and, oh yeah, I was smoking weed.

This is when things started getting a little weird. I bought my first weed from some gangsta buddies of mine (No, I won't be mentioning the names of their gang.) that I used to BMX with. I didn't get high the first few times, but the third or fourth time, when I was over at Frankie's one Friday night, things clicked.

He asked me, "Have you smoked weed yet?"

I affirmed, not mentioning that I hadn't actually felt the effects of the herb.

On Friday nights, growing up, my parents and I would go down to Venice to eat dinner at this one seafood place right on the beach. Afterward we'd stroll along the boardwalk. One of those nights, I think I was like seven or eight, we were passing Venice Pier and my nose caught a whiff of something that was definitely not cigs, a pipe, or a cigar. It was the infamous weed. I knew instantly from the descriptions rendered to me by my elder hippie brethren from the neighborhood.

Not only did I know what it was, but I also knew that one day in the not too distant future, I'd be smoking it. You see, I felt I was predestined to warp my brain and turn my mind inside out. In elementary school we would make each other pass out by way of hyperventilation. Judo taught me to fall without consequence from different circumstances. My favorite of these was falling from dizzying heights. At eight years old I was jumping off the roof at my house, by eleven I was leaping from second story buildings. With all my activities I kept upping the stakes, so I was getting high naturally…

Anyways, back to Frankie's that fateful Friday night, no sooner had I confirmed his question when a bag of weed magically appeared between his thumb and his forefinger. He looked devilish as he let the bowl slip and roll down as he held onto the tip of the bag.

I was like, "whoa!"

He blasted "Paranoid" by Black Sabbath and proceeded to roll us a joint. We got very high and went skating in his parking garage on my brand new "Bahne" fiberglass skateboard with Cadillac wheels.

All of a sudden, I sucked again.

I was bailing left and right and so was Frankie, but at the same time, no matter how much pain we were in we were laughing our asses off. Sore and banged up, we decided to switch to tennis. That went much better.

Needless to say, I loved it. I got some weed from Frankie and brought it home to share with my step-cousin-in-law. It worked for her, too. We sat around and laughed and laughed and… I realized I was a smoking pro. Well, I was ok smoking weed and riding my bike, surfing, and swimming, but for some reason I could never skate well while high.

Anyways, at this point someone came into my life, via a rising cult, that changed everything.

Synanon was founded in 1958 by an alcoholic named Chuck Dederich who, with a group of friends, sat in a circle in a hotel and came to terms with their disease. Alanon was the model/basis of the following – an aggressive form of taking it out and just putting it down. Alcoholism can kill you, so there was some medical assistance with that but it grew from there into a nationwide entity with posts outside of the U.S. There were locations in L.A., San Diego, N.Y., Detroit, San Francisco, and Puerto Rico among others with the home base being Santa Monica located in a giant old brick building located at the end of the Pico Blvd right on the beach. A Drug and Alcohol free society within society. An alternative lifestyle where drugs, alcohol, and physical violence were strictly forbidden. The Aforementioned circle of Alcoholics in a room evolved into what was called the Synanon Game where former drug and alcohol users would converse in a circle, let out their frustrations with life and each other at the top of their lungs when inspired with no boundaries on language. They took in junkies, dope addicts, and alcoholics on a regular basis, cured them, put them to work within their community and let them live there as long as they wanted. Word got out, as it always does, and pretty soon they were attracting outsiders that came down weekly to play the "game" and just hang out. This included everyone from regular working stiffs to rich and famous celebrities and even my folks. My sister and brother in law had discovered its existence and started hanging around as well and eventually asked to come live there and help look after the children of the residents, and they accepted.

The game survived on donations from outsiders and insiders who brought their savings/fortunes with them and later found ways to make money legitimately.

I started hanging out on weekends, when time permitted. There was a game on Saturday for kids. We were called notions. We hung out, played "the game", completed various jobs, ate, swam in the pool, worked out in the gym, and the best part for me … is that they owned the stretch of beach that spanned the width of the building. There were a couple of surfboards, including the first "Jeff Ho" I ever saw from the Zephyr shop, located right around the corner. I'd already been skating and surfing for a while now, with Frankie, but I mostly body surfed cause I didn't have my own board. Now though, it was like I had my own board 'cause I could use it anytime a la my weekend involvement. Oh, incidentally, this is where my new romance with pot was cut short, Synanon being a drug-free environment and all. I complied for the couple of years that I hung out.

Anyway, I found something else, or should I say, someone else (Sorry, Hon), and I was hooked. I started going down to the beach early first on the weekends then sneaking down during the week working on my shred before school when the water was glass-smooth. Sometimes I'd beat the other surfers, sometimes they'd beat me down there. One morning I raced to the beach and noticed only two guys out there to share the waves with. By the time I'd got the board, found some wax, came down to the water, one of the guys passed me on his way out of the water. Even better.

I stripped down to my first pair of the cooler, longer shorts I'd ever owned (Remember, this was '72 and nuthuggers were all the rave back then.) I had no wetsuit and there was no way I was ever gonna be seen by another surfer or local wearing nuthuggin hot pants bathing suits. Never!

I padded out to catch my first set of the day. Waves crested a little bigger than usual that day, probably due to a storm off of Mexico or something, but they represented the biggest set I'd attempted up till that point.

While nervous, I realized, 'Oh well. If I kooked out, at least there's only one dude watchin.'

I got out there and only had to wait a second for the next set. They were breakin' to the north about six to eight feet. I padded, got up, took off. One of my best runs to date. Remember, I was only 12 and only just started surfing. I remember catching a glimpse of the remaining, lone surfer in my peripheral. I felt so stoked, padding back over thinking he had to see that I'm cool when I heard, "nice."

Wait. That voice was not coming from a dude. I glanced over and froze, when, much to my surprise and now pleasure, I realized the surfer was a girl. She was beautiful. Curly black hair about down to her shoulders, what seemed to be olive skin, as dark or darker than mine, full lips and translucent green eyes, I was already in love. I knew I had to say something or I'd blow my chance.

I clumsily said, "I'm just glad I didn't come out for nothing."
She said, "Well, I'll take that as a compliment."

All of a sudden I felt really young. I'd never really heard that phrase before, took a minute to get it, didn't know what to say next. I realized she might be a lot older than me, although I couldn't gage her age.

She asked, "You from around here?"
"Mmm hmm"
"What's your name?"
"Chuck"
"Hey Chuck, I'm Zooey but you can call me Zoe!" She grinned. "Where do you live?"

She was forward and casual. This eased my tension.

"I live down on Venice and LaCienega, but I hang down here a bunch on the weekends." I pointed to the building that housed Synanon.

"Yea, my mom's been hangin' round there too, during the week." Then, boom: "You wanna come over? I live just around the corner."

I was like, 'Whoa, this was all too good to be true!'

She told me I could change and shower there if I wanted to. I was losing my mind. Bobbing around on my board, just caught a great wave, and this beautiful, possibly much older girl is talking to *me*. 'Inviting me over her house? To shower?'

My brain was about to explode. I really couldn't take much more of this, but I said, "Hell, yes!"

She said she had been about to come out but did wanna catch one more wave before we left. By now, I'm on autopilot.

I was like, "Nah, I gotta get to school anyway before I'm too late." Tryin to sound cool. So I dropped the board off, explaining to her that, "I just leave it here" without actually telling her that it wasn't mine. I guess cause she had complimented me on my taste in surfboards, while showing me that she also had a Zephyr/Jeff Ho board. This was the first in a row of uncanny similarities between us that just made me like her more and more as each minute went by.

Walking back to her house and she said, "I know you're part black 'cause of your hair and your lips and you're a little dark but what are you mixed with?"

She was so straight out, it caught me off guard. I told her my mom was a white Jew and my Dad was Black and American Indian.

She yelled, "I knew it!"

Startled, I jumped backward.

"Those high cheekbones." She then explained that her Grandma was Lakota Sioux and her Grandpa was a former slave, this was her dad's parents. Her mom was Dutch and Italian. I guess this explained her exotic features. I told her I didn't know or wasn't sure what tribe I was from on the African side or Indian. She said I was probably Blackfoot. She talked about the indignation of the slaves and the Indians as I drowned in her eyes. Before I knew it we were at her house, which was actually an apartment, which oddly enough, was later owned by Synanon to house their sprawling growing population.

She showed me in to her bathroom and told me to jump in the shower and she'd get me a towel. Right before I jumped in the shower, the door flew open, exposing me in all my 12-year-old glory to her. Her wetsuit was unzipped from the neck down and she'd pulled her arms free, leaving the suit hanging around her waist and exposing her topside.

I freaked.

She looked me up and down, smiled, threw the towel on my shoulder and closed the door. It should have been exciting, but I was horrified. This is embarrassing, but, fuck it, I had no hair down there yet.

As I washed off my shame, re-envisioning what I had seen, she poked her head in and told me to just leave the shower on 'cause she was gonna jump in right after.

I said, "ok."

As soon as I heard the door shut, I padded dry and threw on my pants as quickly as possible, so as not to get caught with them down…again. When I exited the bathroom, she looked me in the eyes.

She must've sensed my embarrassment, because, she said, "It's no big deal. I like you. I think you're cute."

I wasn't sure if she meant me being naked or hairless or her letting me see her breasts. Then she pointed to her room, told me to wait in there.

She put her hands on my cheeks and kissed me on the lips. "Cutie pie."

I floated down a short hall, following a waft of incense to the open door into another world. Green and blue Christmas lights hung randomly and meshed in giant fishnets on the walls to my left and right with fake crabs hanging in the netting, posed like they're crawling around. Nightstands on either side of her bed held lamps that lit up the wall above her bed. On the wall above the head of her bed hung four posters, situated in a diamond formation. At the top David Bowie, to the left Jimi, to the right the Stooges, at the bottom Led Zeppelin!

'This was meant to be! What a Rock God shrine at the altar of wonderland.'

Only I felt like Alice. Ziggy was playing on her turntable.

I thought, 'She's too cool.'

Then I got this sinking feeling. There's no way she'd like me like that. Maybe as a little buddy or something. She's gotta be like fifteen, at least. It turns out she was just way beyond her years, mentally and physically.

She returned, dressed this time in a frilly kind of white blouse and jeans. "How old are you?"

I said, "About twelve and three quarters.'

I lied. I was just barely twelve. She looked surprised. I wilted.

She said, "I'm 13. I thought you were older than me."

"Oh...that's cool."

For a second I felt like a used car and she was the buyer.

Her eyes went wide. "Shit, I'm getting' late for school, too. Wanna hang out later or tomorrow?"

I said, "Yeah."

She scribbled her number on notebook paper, followed by, "Call me later!" But she wrote a heart instead of a period below the exclamation point. How uncool, but I loved it.

I was so happy I forgot to ask her what school she attended. She kissed me one more time before I ran out the door and all the way to the bus, which I caught just in time to get to school as the tardy bell rang. I had had my first kiss almost two years earlier with Darla, one of my neighbors, but this was different.

I called Zoey as soon as I got home from school. We talked for two hours until my folks got home, and then again, after I was done practicing, we spoke until nine p.m. when my parents made me hang up. We had so much in common. We both loved Bowie, Zeppelin, The Jackson 5, surfing, bikes, guitars, and skating. Sometimes sharing so many passions can work against a relationship, but we bonded so tightly. I became protective of our thing, like a two person private club. It was perfect. I prefer social interactions with small groups of two or three. We were our own secret.

Early that Saturday we went surfin' together. Then we went back to her house, listened to music, and jammed on guitar until I had to go to Synanon. I asked if she wanted to check it out and she agreed. I think, mainly to appease me, but she might've had her own reasons for tagging along. To her credit, she tried it, but it wasn't her cup of tea.

I think her mom had issues with drugs, so Zoe grew up knowing what she didn't want to be like. She had messed with weed a little, but rejected it for the natural high that comes with surfin' and a lot of the same stuff I liked to do.

After that we fell into a pattern for seven or eight months. We were one, inseparable. Then one day she called me crying. Turns out her mom got a job in the valley and they were moving in three days. I helped her pack, and we hung out as much as possible, until she moved.

She promised to call when she got settled.

Now, as I mentioned earlier, the FBI had been harassing my father for many years due to his involvement with civil rights sit ins, peace marches, and vocalizing for change through various other demonstrations. It had died down around sixty-eight, but through no fault of my own, we started getting strange phone calls, breathing, hang-ups, and weird questions. My folks thought it was starting up again, so they quickly changed our number and left it unlisted.

I was pissed, mortified, crushed. I never got Zoe's number because it wasn't set up by the time they moved. I didn't even know what city they moved to in the valley. She fell completely off my radar. Just as abruptly as our relationship had started, it ended.

I recoiled mentally, physically, and socially. I was always very shy reserved kept people at a distance. Zoey had pulled me out of my shell, but the more I realized it was over, the more I started to revert back to my old ways. I stopped hanging at Synanon every Saturday, and I started smoking weed again. I didn't want to miss her anymore. I started getting more reckless and trying more stuff.

My heart broke. For the first time.

Chuck also gave me another chunk that we started to transcribe, but he needed the notebook back before we got much.

In (I think) 1975 I went to see Pink Floyd at the LA Sports Arena. Trippin' my brains out on some window pain. The music augmented, demented by the acid was awesome while it lasted. Before I knew what was happening a sense of fear took over, followed by chaos, followed by mayhem, followed by running, falling, watching, people being beaten with Billy clubs in what turned out to be a full on LAPD instigated riot. Made it out, unscathed, but totally buzz killed, confused at all the hate and aggression. It was really ugly. They recreated the scene in the movie "The Wall" so closely from what I remembered that at first I thought it was footage from the concert I was at.

My parents saw the event on the news, knew I was there, and forbade me to go to any more concerts for a while, although I meticulously, resourcefully snuck out to Yes, Peter Frampton and Led Zeppelin at The Forum. But for the most part, I was only allowed to hang out with my Jewish friends from the Valley. My folks thought they were nice kids and I'd be safe from trouble. So we started hangin' out, cruising, Van Nuys Blvd and going to the smaller clubs in the Valley.

This is when things started to change for me. Growin' up my influences were the Rolling Stones, the Beatles, The Who, The Kinks, Motown, R & B, Jackson 5. Then Jimi, Black Sabbath, Zeppelin, and David Bowie when I was eleven-twelve. Roxy music and especially David Bowie really spoke to me in a very personal way. Alienation, his lyrics, being a loner and different from all my friends, being mixed, being adopted, not feeling like anyone else in my world, I don't know I just locked on to everything every word, the music.

Hangin' out in the valley, we stumbled in our search for new thrills onto some smaller clubs where bands with cool, silly, different, new names were playing. Of course we had to check it out. A placed called the Sugar Shack is where I first encountered a band called the Runaways. Hot girls playin' hot rock, angry and tough and sexy. Needless to say I was in love. Plus there was more. I first saw the Dickies at some club in the Valley and I was totally blown away. Not since I saw David Bowie and Iggy Pop when I was thirteen and fourteen respectively had anything changed my whole perception of music and the world. I'd heard and read about the Ramones and punk rock in "Circus," "Cream," and the few English mags I could get my hands on. But that was to change, pretty much overnight. As far as my parents were concerned (God bless both their souls) I was out with my valley friends every night. Wednesdays and Saturdays I'd usually end up in the valley, 'cause I still hung out with my Jewish friends cause they were my friends. They were still always game for checkin' out somethin' new as there were always new bands to check out and we all loved the Runaways, plus there were three or four girls in our little gang whom we all liked and we were always switching around, making out with each other 'til we settled on the one we liked the most, then basically hang with that person. We'd go on double, triple dates and stuff, but music became a drug for me. I needed more and more. I went to Hamilton High in West L.A., which was boring, average, combination of friends from my predominately white Shenandoah Elementary School and my mostly black and Latino Pasteo Jr. High. There at Hamilton were only six of us who appreciated the allure and danger of newness, freshness, refreshness, of punk rock. Jeff C., Jeff N., Keith McCune all loved music and mind altering situations, Emily and Michelle were Ramones fans morphed into everything punk rock and me who loved everything from the Jackson 5 to the Ramones to Genesis to Lynyrd Skynyrd to whatever but now it was all about punk shows, 'cause there were so many bands. There was cool, different artsy psychotic types of new music popping up every day, not to mention ones we'd heard and read about coming from England, New York, Cleveland and other places around the country and world. Plus they were the cheapest shows. It was the halcyon days of new music. It took all our money and scamming to check it all out and be a part of as much as possible. Keith worked in a record store so he brought home Sex Pistols' *Nevermind the Bollocks*, the day it came out. On our first listening we laughed and threw it out the window, championing our local bands and true punk rock heroes. But upon reflecting and reminiscing the tunes, the hard rock, not perfect, but driving and rawness norms and the world you've grown accustomed to accepting as the dejected record lay on the corner of Franklin and Beachwood at the foot of the Hollywood Hills we decided we fucking loved it with a capital F. We retrieved it from the street and played it over and over the rest of that day of drinking and drugging and some debauchery with a couple of girls from the neighborhood. Keith's parents were divorced, like a lot of kids near school, but his mom lived in Hollywood, which was our respite for and from clubbin' and partying since all the good shows were in Hollywood. I could get permission to spend the night at his dad's, stock up on money and partyables and end up in Hollywood, somehow make our way back to school by morning or vice versa. At this time, I was still doin' Judo, still BMX racing, I was on the volleyball team, I still made it to the beach some weekday mornings and weekends all day, and I worked at my mom's bookkeeping job as a file clerk. Needless to say burning the candle at both ends. By seventeen, I'd been playing piano for 14 years and guitar for five. I've never been that good on guitar, but on keyboards, well it was second nature and I was very good classically speaking and I was writing/creating stuff all the time. So I decided it was time to be a part of what I truly loved, music and the burgeoning punk rock scene. My Rock fantasies never much really involved me playing piano in the mirror in my room, but putting shampoo in my hair, pulling it down over my shoulders, and singing David Bowie songs into the comb. But I had to work with what I had. At that time, it wasn't a voice. The first person I ever jammed with was Rory Johnson, my buddy from Pasteur Jr. High. We were both big fans of Stevie Wonder so that's the sound we were creating. Rory played bass, but we could never find the rest of a band, so… that kind faded after a while. I wanted to play in a band like the Dickies, 'cause they had keyboards and great melodies, played super fast, or like the Damned, one of my all-time favs, 'cause they were punk rock, super melodic, kind of gothy, with lots of room for keyboards. But my musical connections were limited, so I was asked to join this metal band! Can't remember their name, but they were pretty, kind of well-known in the valley and had a bunch of groupies from Hollywood who loved to be naked all the time. Yes, I partook. The first time, I remember being in a bathroom snorting some cannebanol [sic], which was kind of like PCP with less chemical, more hallucinogenic and these girls came in changing and primping. At one point they were all topless or naked and one came up to me took the remaining line I had left and proceeded to start performing oral sex on me. She then thanked me for the line, before finishing getting dressed and primped. I said, "You're welcome" then went outside and played heavy metal to a house and yard and pool full of half-naked, fully naked, and fucked-up crazy mix of metal heads, rockers, and bikers. Most of them didn't like me very much, the guys anyway, with my funky suit on and my newly bald head. Being at the beach all the time I pretty much stopped combing my hair all the time and was diggin' and trying to cultivate the Hendrix-into-Marley look 'til I was reported for ditching school and my parents shaved my head as punishment. I cried at first. Then as the climate of the times dictated, I started to like it. It started to grow on me, no pun intended. So anyway, these guys didn't like me, but they used me for a while. I saw many things I didn't like about bands and stuff in that short time, certain types anyway. Became friends with a bunch of bikers. I think I was their only black friend. I'm only half black so I was "ok" 'cause I was half white. I saw guys guzzle a bottle of tequila and drop dead.

That last word looks more like "dean" in his handwriting, but I have no idea what "dean" could mean, unless its code for a drug or something? Either way, that was about it from Chuck and his work on the book. He relayed many stories to me over the years, along with many more in interviews and while talking to people at shows.

One other chunk I want to include is from 2016. Early that year, guys from the Faith No More camp reached out to discuss the rerelease of *We Care a Lot*. As the release and show announcements got closer, Monica at Speakeasy via Tim Moss asked Chuck to offer a few quick statements about the album that the band could use in a press release. Instead, as Chuck was known to do, he handed in a sloppy, meandering page-long paragraph. I've included it below with only a few edits so you could get a small taste of Chuck's writing style, similar to how he spoke.

hey tim, ok....so me and billy were in our first band together, The Animated, he left to attend berkley, started playing with mike and roddy and john, i think as faith no man, billy, roddy and mike broke off on there own and called it faith no more... came down to l.a. a couple times when they didnt have a singer, billy asked me to do it i think because he loved irony, and i wasn't a singer, never rehearsed, just played, i yelled and ranted to the beat...was fun, but different style then i was used to...then they got courtney, then they got rid of her with three shows pending....in s.f., i went up, we actually rehearsed, it was different for me, i was part of the l.a. punk scene, there was always a thing between l.a. and s.f. scenes, so it was all new to me up there, i was nervous cause it was a full house, didnt know anyone, except my girlfriend, but was really exiting, there music wasn't like anyone else, and they played hard and i appreciated that, but i wasnt a singer, so i mostly rapped or ranted to the beat, david bowie was my idol, so when there was a melody, i tried to croon like him, but being so nervous and not a singer, it was hard for me to stay in tune, but i managed, somewhat....then, i was in the band and there were more and more shows then we were going to record and that made me really nervous, a couple demos at first, i was good at yelling but couldn't do that the whole time, then going to record we care a lot, i had to call on my david bowie spirit, and finally took hold of the singing thing and managed to stay in tune, rap was new and i really was into it but i was no good at it, so i did it anyway, to their monster beats, and thought of bowie for the melodies, the studio was in a barn north of s.f. and we stayed there and recorded for a week. matt wallace was really encouraging, and gave me confidence, he knew i was nervous and apprehensive, so he just kept recording more and more tracks, he was a genius and saw something in me and just layered me and put it together and made me sound good, i always remember the smell of frankincense at shows and at the studio, together with this new music, i always felt like i was part of something new and different than anything else out there at the time, and it made me feel privileged to be a part of it.....the eeriness of the music, especially, "why do you bother", which has always been my favorite...psychedelic scary music, it all felt very new and special, it was all very exciting to me, although i tried to act like i was used to it, but it was alot of fun, and nervous at the same time, wondering if i was capable.......i have to feed the dogs and meet the gf, lemme know if you need more, ill be back shortly?

CHAPTER TWENTY

November 9, 2017
Onward, Blue Heart

After I finished the phone conversation I never wanted to receive, I sat in silence surrounded by a thousand pieces to a jigsaw puzzle that Chuck had left behind. Each piece represented an unanswered question or an unfinished goal, and I didn't even know what the puzzle needed to look like when completed.

I contacted family and friends and spread the word. I worked with Pip and a longtime friend of theirs, Natalie, to create a formal announcement of Chuck's passing. When it posted during the evening of November 10, social media exploded with an outpouring of grief, loss, remorse, anger, and confusion. I rode the wave and tried to communicate with anyone and everyone, old friends and strangers alike. I learned so many new things about Chuck in seventy-two hours; however, in a daze, I couldn't comprehend anything aside from the genuine, positive, heartbreaking effect Chuck had on so many around the world.

A few days after his death, I met with Pip, Natalie, and Mary Jo to help arrange a memorial for him. I didn't know how to help, so I tried to offer comedic relief and wine when appropriate.

Pip's brother, Ian, flew in from California, offering a hundred helping hands and an equal number of shoulders to cry on. He even bought a book for me to read with my kids during the difficult time.

My gut instinct said to race ahead to finish Chuck's various projects so we could grieve with new music, his last gift to us all, but various obstacles slowed my roll. I learned that Chuck had spent the last couple months of his life waging a smear campaign about me to anyone who would listen. It turns out that as soon as I had accused him of falling off the wagon in August, he had told people nasty things about me. He told close friends not to trust me. He told business associates I was on a power trip. He let other musicians know he considered moving on without me, if they wanted to jump on board. Before he passed away, some people came forward to let me know what was transpiring. After he died, the scope and depths he had gone to shook me to my core. I doubted everything I knew. I got angry all over again.

March 2018

Now, as I come out of the haze and have progressed into different layers of grief, I'm thankful life forced me to take a breath and wait. I need time to heal as well before I can jump in to aid the various projects he worked on before his death.

His solo album sits in the capable hands of Matt Wallace. How, when, why, with who, and where it gets released is anyone's guess. I hope a label who loves Chuck as much as we do hears the music and commits to supporting his last batch of original songs with a proper release. If not, I hope his family allows me or someone else to get it out into the world. The songs are sparse, sprawling, and not made for radio, but the heart of the music and melody and lyrics make for perfect movie scene pairings. Maybe someone can help his music live on through film, much like *Grosse Point Blank*, *Bio Dome*, and *Dirty Jobs* did for "We Care a Lot."

The live album waits on my computer, an unorganized mass of audio and video recordings from 2016 and 2017. When his family greenlights his solo album, I will talk to them and hope to get the go-ahead to finish this as well.

The last two songs we recorded were both covers. Chuck and I wanted to release them on a seven-inch vinyl during a big event, like Record Store Day in April or Black Friday in November. I hope that happens as well.

Update: April 15, 2019

Back in December 2018, Chuck's family gave me the green light to pursue a release of these cover songs. I contacted Blocsonic, who had expressed interest in working with us in the past. We kicked the project into high gear and got a seven-inch record pressed in time for Record Store Day. Traffic Entertainment and BlocGlobal (the new label arm of Blocsonic) internationally released the covers. They pressed 1,000 units of *Joe Haze Session #2*.

Jim Brown, who runs FaithNoMoreFollowers, edited two short teaser videos to help spread the word about our release. His work inspired me to create a video for "Take This Bottle"—the record's B-side. For two weeks, I scoured the internet and my computer for old clips from the road. My hard drive had crashed the previous fall, erasing most of the photos, videos, and audio I had taken during my time with Chuck. Some of the more random bits in the video will make more sense to you now that you've read this book, and it makes me happy to have people to share our inside jokes with.

I posted the video a few days before the record release. It went online around the same time that another Faith No More fan posted a ten-second clip of a dog head-banging to "Surprise, You're Dead"—a song off *The Real Thing*. I checked both videos views tonight. Our video has 5,232 views and the dog has over 21,000. The more things change …

On Record Store Day, April 13, 2019, I woke up early and meandered to My Mind's Eye, a record shop that me and Chuck liked, and found four copies for sale. We had done it. I hung around the shop and waited for someone to notice it, to talk about it, to ask questions, or to grab the thing and buy it.

My phone buzzed constantly with updates of who had found it and where. People posted photos and videos and submitted wonderful feedback about our little release. We had reached stores in Australia, Italy, the Netherlands, Canada, Scotland, England, Germany, and across the United States. Chuck's brother and sister-in-law found it at Amoeba Records in Los Angeles; Rough Trade carried it in NYC, and still my phone buzzed and buzzed until my battery drained. People from all over checked in, some happy to have found it and others disappointed they had left the shop empty-handed. I encouraged people to share news if they saw it in stores or online.

After an hour, no one had come to the shop where I was to buy one single copy. I left the shop. When I turned the corner toward my car, I broke down. I sat on the sidewalk and cried in broad daylight as I wished over and over Chuck had stuck around to see his music spread around the world.

I left to deliver copies to Pip and Erica and spent a couple hours playing with Chuck's grandson, Wolfgang. Sophie had taken her son, Michael (born after I had completed this book), to a birthday party, so I'll deliver their copy later.

A lot went into the making of the record. Without a dozen or more people stepping up, like Joe Haze, Shawn Franklin, Michael Gregoire, Joshua Nelson, and Michele Esper, it wouldn't have happened.

Donn Wobser messaged me from Toledo, where he had tried three different stores with no luck. I swung back to My Mind's Eye and bought him a record. The store owner, Charlie, felt odd selling the record to a guy on the vinyl, but I told him Donn needed a copy, and I had to come through. I waited at the store for another hour, but no one grabbed one.

The short film, *Like an Open Heart It Shines*, which we acted in, has most of the postproduction work done. Writer/director David Collupy says the movie looks great, but incorporating the live audio proved a challenge. His original plan for a theme song was to use one of Chuck's Cement tunes, which has the lyrics of the movie's title. When Chuck passed, David went in a new direction. He has written and recorded his own song to accompany the film. I can't wait to see it.

Chuck shopped his screenplay during his last trip to LA with help from David. Chuck described the premise and gave me a few plot points during our travels but kept the overall story and ending to himself, leery about sharing his idea with a writer. Ironically, David asked me to help him pick up the pieces of the project and to see it through. I offered to help but wonder if I am the right person for the job.

Drew Fortier has taken the helm to captain a documentary about Chuck's life. I've vowed to help anyway I can, though I refuse to take charge or sway its direction. Why? I don't know. Just doesn't seem like something I should be doing, I mean, me of all people ... you know what I mean? This book, if I didn't goof it up, should say what I need to say about my life with Chuck. At some point, I must let him and even my daydreamed future of touring and recording with him go and allow his legacy to grow naturally without my meddling.

That moment scares me more than I can admit.

The realization that Chuck was gone and that I needed to reclaim my life was one of the worst things I've faced up until now. I was swept up in a fairytale, a daydream, a Spielberg movie, and those always have happy endings, right?

So, when it all crashed down, I was no longer a touring conga player, keeper of several social media accounts, and protector of all things Mosley. I was just a man with a failed dream, an empty bank account, and a responsibility to my family to not fuck up things further. But I did.

Sure, I put in long hours in front of the computer to write this book, but, outside of that, everything overwhelmed me. Everything reminded me of Chuck. Everything reminded me that I had failed. Everything reminded me of so many moments he and I shared.

After I had met Chuck in 1997, I wrote my first true screenplay—a horror slasher flick that followed a high-school kid who gets caught up in the fight between dark and light forces. I wrote each part for a specific person in my life, including a homeless man who turns out to be a guardian angel meant for Chuck to play. Even though we had only briefly met and I had no experience or budget, he agreed to get involved.

We planned the climax of the film to take place at Squire's Castle, a small structure about fifteen miles east of Cleveland. I'm sitting at a table in the front lawn of that castle as I type this. I can picture the scene even now, having not read it in over twenty years. Jeffrey Hatrix, now an ex-member of Mushroomhead, Mark Hunter, now an ex-member of Chimaira, and Damien Perry, still a member of Red Giant had agreed to play the main characters along with Chuck. We would've filmed at night, flames glowing from every window. Damien and Mark would fight on the keep's roof while Chuck and Jeffrey waged a different type of battle with each other.

Don't bother telling me the roof isn't intact on the keep of Squire's Castle ... I see that now, but we would've found a way.

Update: April 15, 2019

Drew Fortier wrote a screenplay and asked me to act in it as one of the lead characters. If all goes as planned, by the time you read this, we should have completed filming. Oh, and Jeffrey Hatrix is in it. Talk about things coming full circle. Where are you at Mark Hunter?

Update: October 24, 2019

After filming off and on with Drew through the summer, only taking time off for his wedding, the movie *Dwellers* is nearing completion. It is a found-footage film featuring a cast full of friends of Drew's that I'm proud and excited to be a part of. David Ellefson Films is producing it. Mr. Ellefson, who makes a cameo in the film and has a great improv line about me, and Mr. Fortier are premiering the trailer for the film in two days at a horror convention in Niagara Falls, Canada.

Chuck planned a lot of projects, me included in some of them. I would've loved to hear more VUA music. Would've been first in line to taste the food at another spot run by Chuck. I would've avoided spoilers for the screenplay he pitched in the days before his death. And, after our touring and the Chuck Mosley/Mosleyhead solo experience had ended, I would've enjoyed kicking back and sharing a beer with my friend.

I told him many times that I dreamed of a day when Chuck's band grew too big to bring me along. Instead, he would tour the globe, record a new EP each year, and we would only see each other as he traversed Ohio for a sold-out show. He would give me all access, and I would drink all his free beers before the opening bands even started. I would fill his guest list and push my luck at every turn, because, hell, I had helped jumpstart this jalopy.

Only I didn't.

On May 2, 2018, I opened a CD booklet I found in a bag of trash in my garage. It had belonged to Chuck. How his trash bag had gotten in my garage, I'm not 100% sure. Chuck protected his CDs, so I dunno. Anyway, I had found the bag weeks earlier while cleaning but hadn't gone through it yet. That day, I had received several messages, emails, and texts from people who all missed Chuck. A few had dreamt about him or remembered things from shows or wanted a status update on the book. So, I felt it too. I opened the CD booklet and found a disc labeled, *Chuck Mosley Demos and Live Tracks*.

I put the disc in my computer, and the first song played. I had never heard it before. It sounded like a Cement-era tune—mature, catchy rock.

I instantly teared up. This song (unless I find more hidden stuff from Chuck) will be the last new thing I ever hear from him.

I want you to know Chuck the way I knew him. I want it understood that he always saw himself as a blue-collar musician, like he never wanted the big fame and fortune. He wanted to feed his family and create a better life for them, sure, but he hoped to do it without all the attention and pressure of success. Chuck was a schemer and constantly negotiated whatever he could. He wheeled. He dealed. He entertained. He dreamed. Chuck made it hard to trust him but could charm the pants off anyone.

I keep remembering more and more I want to add to this book, but the story has been told. I need to give him back. We all need to grieve for Chuck Mosley and let his legacy become whatever it's destined to become.

Legacy. In this digital world, when fads come and go, I wonder how his music will remain relevant. When his fans grow old and their kids discover the next hot thing, will what we did these last couple years fade away? It might happen. Hell, most of the world still has no idea what we fought for—the long drives, the arguments, the empty club in Dallas, the glances we shared onstage, the random cover songs, the raising of children on the road for the first time, a debut solo record fifty-seven years in the making, and the comeback, phoenix rising from the ashes style, of one of my favorite singers on the planet. All of it could be for nothing.

But I don't believe that will be his fate. Chuck wrote beautiful songs. He bared his soul and tugged on heartstrings and tapped into something I know has a place. Somewhere down the line, someone will hear one of his songs and realize, as I did, that Chuck needs to be heard.

Even lifted by this knowledge, I still feel so conflicted.

I miss Chuck. I am angry with Chuck. I want to slap Chuck. I want to get onstage and play with Chuck, crack a beer with Chuck, annoy him with a bad joke. I want to get a call from Chuck, to hear him sing, to watch him struggle to find a note, or just to tell me he called for no reason. I miss my friend. I miss my bandmate. I miss my idol, and I miss my Mrs. Bickerson.

I feel guilty for failing him. I feel guilty for possibly accusing him *before* he fell off the wagon. I feel guilty for not being as aggressive as I needed to get him help or to get attention focused on his returning problem. I feel guilty for pushing him out the door, regardless of how noble my intentions felt.

I feel lucky to have heard him sing, to have met him and helped him grow. I feel lucky to have shared the stage with him, to tour and record and experience life with him around. I feel lucky that my wife and children and brother and parents met him after having endured me talking about him for so many years.

I've picked up random pieces of Chuck's puzzle and tried to make sense of them but rarely found they fit together. Chuck led many lives, as his brain never stopped thinking and rethinking and plotting and planning and scheming and writing. I realized I had sections from several puzzles never meant to complete one image. But they do. Underlying themes reverberate through everything Chuck did, not all of them positive or pretty.

One of them was love. Chuck loved his adopted family. His parents and sisters provided a welcoming and understanding home even when boundaries got pushed. He loved his own family. Pip, Erica, Sophie—and Chuck battled together against so many obstacles, but they knew they had each other when things got their darkest. Chuck loved his birth mother and maybe his birth father too, though he never communicated that sentiment. Chuck had been convinced a reunion with his real mother was in his foreseeable future and that it might heal a lot of his self-doubt and fear and insecurities. He felt connected to her, even though they hadn't seen each other since his birth. Chuck loved music and cooking, and he loved all of you too.

He loved swapping stories with you at the shows. He loved hearing about your struggles and triumphs and goals and fears. He loved hearing your music, seeing your art, and observing you operate. Chuck loved getting to know you and for you to know him, even though that prospect terrified him. He loved your warm and generous gestures. He valued your opinions. He appreciated your feedback. Chuck wanted to make you happy. All of you. He wanted, as I've said before, the endless party for everyone … even if he felt overwhelmed in crowds.

Chuck loved his time alone. Chuck hated his time alone. In some ways, battling his self-doubt and his addictions and his nonstop stream of thought, Chuck could never be alone. This weighed on him. As much as I know an overdose of fentanyl killed him, I wonder if he used again because he had forfeited his struggle to fight. I think his exhaustion might've proven too great. He had no Off switch. He had no relief. Hell, if his new album and touring proved successful, it might've made things worse, as he would then have expectations from management and labels and media. Chuck needed blocks of time to sit on a couch with music blaring over the TV streaming constant distractions.

Chuck needed an impossible balance.

Slowly, images took shape as the pieces connected. I got a glimpse of a boy, fifty-seven years old, waiting for his mom to pick him up and comfort him. I saw a twenty-five-year-old grinning and sticking out his shirtless chest onstage, playing air guitar as the energy from the crowd washed away everything but joy. I recognized a father, guilt written all over his face, trying to explain his latest slipup to two daughters who couldn't absorb any more pain. Here, he squeezed Pip tightly; over there, he snuck into the shadows with a needle.

A long line of amps rose from the puzzle, and all it took to decipher how Chuck fit into that section was to listen to his tears as he hid behind the stacks of amplification. He hid from his bandmates, his family, his friends, his boss, his teacher, his manager, and, of course, he hid from himself. His sheepish grin, his cold stare of intimidation, his crooning, his bitching, his bratty cold shoulder, and his tongue bent to the side of his mouth and tucked between his lips as he peered down to find that next fucking note all swirled around as I pieced Chuck's narrative together.

The edges stayed jagged, and the flashes of clarity sometimes overshadowed or straight-out covered up each other. Even when completed, I knew this collage of a puzzle made no sense. Chuck had accomplished so much and affected so many that—

And then it clicked. The image didn't look fractured, because he had so much unfinished business. The pieces weren't random at all. The sections of Chuck could only come together with us to bind them.

I have seen people discuss starting bands to pay tribute to Chuck. Adam Harmless and GAD! Zine are releasing a tribute CD full of Chuck tunes on Halloween of 2019. My wife and Dallas Sheppard recorded a version of one of my favorite songs, "Chip Away." On the day Michele did her vocals, our daughter recorded one background line I had planned on singing, and I couldn't be more thrilled to have her involved.

A Faith No More tribute band in Europe gathered musicians from around the world to collaborate on a recording of "We Care a Lot" to honor him. A book by Adrian Harte, *Small Victories: The True Story of Faith No More*, currently sits at number one on Amazon charts in several countries. Bob Coldicutt has reignited his passion for acting and has already appeared in several indie films. He invited me to Niagara Falls, NY to film a small role in one of them—Anathema. I played a background goon, and I managed to sneak in Faith No More lyrics as my only line of dialogue. He also wrote a unique, scary, holiday-themed screenplay and has plans to film it around Buffalo.

Chuck's eldest daughter, Erica, told me she wants to pursue acting and modeling. Sophie got engaged and gave birth to her first child, Michael Jr. Pip, always a busy artist, has doubled her efforts to get her work into the world. She had her first solo art show open on the one-year anniversary of Chuck's death.

Andy, our UK bassist, started a music promotions company.

I saw Randy, our bassist for part of 2017, drum for his new band, Bar Trash.

Cris Morgan has dived into his guitar work, posting video updates as he learns new theory's and styles. The dude can riff.

Joshua Nelson has rekindled an old band and joined a new one.

Drew is neck-deep in editing his film.

Ian and Ryan, who run Surprise! You're Dead Music and booked many of our UK dates, have expanded and brought some big names across the pond to tour.

William S. Tribell has released a book of poetry that's getting national attention, and a trailer for his upcoming film has international interest. He joined the cast of *Dwellers*, so I spent some time with him on set.

I finished the rough draft of a fantasy/adventure book that had sat idle for a few years. I edited and rewrote a mystery novel this past spring that is surprising me with its deeper meanings. I sang the choruses on a song Chuck's guitarist, Dallas Sheppard, had written. Alex plays bass, and Bobby Gamage, a vocalist we met in Kansas City, handles singing the verses. William Weaver, the guitarist for my old band, the Firmary, and I are teaming up with Joshua Nelson to complete an EP we abandoned ten years ago as weddings and babies forced music into the back seat. Adam and I have kicked around ideas for the next Indoria. Chris Kniker of Primitive Race asked for guidance to write a book about his time working for Ministry, Marilyn Manson, Lords of Acid, and many others. My old high-school bud, Mike Hoban, is also kicking around the idea of us teaming up to tell a fascinating story about the time he won a contest with over six million contestants. Chuck's and my longtime friend, author Brian Paone—who had acted with Chuck in Salem, Massachusetts for one scene in David Collupy's film—edited this book for me, as well as agreed to publish it through the fast-growing music-inspired press he owns, Scout Media.

Numerous fans of Chuck's have been brought together through his music and friendship. I'm inspired every day by us and what risks and creative paths we're emboldened to explore now.

I turned the key in the ignition. I floored the gas. I banged my head and hands on the steering wheel, but, aside from a few sputters, sparks, and high-pitched whining sounds, the jalopy's engine never caught.

I failed. But maybe, when I had set out, it wasn't Chuck who needed the jolt.

www.ingramcontent.com/pod-product-compliance
Lightning Source LLC
Chambersburg PA
CBHW022210090526
44584CB00012BA/375